SHANG-A-LANG

shang-a-lang

life as an international pop idol

LES McKEOWN
with Lynne Elliott

MAINSTREAM
PUBLISHING

EDINBURGH AND LONDON

First published in Great Britain in 2003 by
MAINSTREAM PUBLISHING COMPANY (EDINBURGH) LTD
7 Albany Street
Edinburgh EH1 3UG

Reprinted 2003

ISBN 1 84018 651 8

A catalogue record for this book is available from the British Library

Typeset in Frutiger, Giovanni and Vag
Printed and bound in Great Britain by
Mackays of Chatham plc

WITH THANKS TO THE FOLLOWING FOR PERMISSION TO QUOTE FROM SONG
LYRICS:
Complete Music: 'Money Honey' (Faulkner/Wood); 'You're A Woman'
(Faulkner/Wood); 'Don't Stop The Music' (Faulkner/Wood);
and thanks to the following for their kind permission to quote from their books:
Michael Wale, *The Bay City Rollers* (Tam Paton with Michael Wale)
Johnny Rogan, *Starmakers and Svengalis*

Every effort has been made to trace all rights holders. The publishers will be glad to
make good any omissions brought to their attention.

To Florence Close McKeown (1918–2002) and
Francis Charles Stephen McKeown (1911–2002)

Acknowledgements

Very special thanks to Peko, my beautiful wife, and Jube, my unique son, and Roni and Hari for their love and support. Thanks also to Bubi, Craig, Lynne, Lori, Gail, Teresa and Sandra for lasting friendships; Irvine Welsh for his definitive works on the psychology of Edinburgh and Audrey for scatology; Patrick Callaghan, Jake Duncan, Jef Hanlon, Dick Leahy, Bill Martin, Neil Ross and Phil Wainman for assisting my recollections; Jon Gillam, Alex Valente, John Walker and Alan Wright; Stuart Wood, Alan Longmuir, Derek Longmuir, Eric Faulkner, Ian Mitchell, Pat McGlynn and the Legendaries; Akemi, Hisako, Kiyomi and Mitsuko at RMJ; Sean McLusky, Tony Burt, Neil Peakall, John Mazurka, Scottish Paul, the late Elvis Presley, the late John Lennon, David Bowie, Damien and Mia Hirst, and all the unconditional fans still rollin' around the world.

Contents

Contents

Foreword by Irvine Welsh   11

Foreplay   13

1. The Wee One   17
2. On the Threshold of Fame   35
3. The Bay City Rollers . . . Coming Together   47
4. We Sang 'Shang-A-Lang'   66
5. Rollermania   84
6. The Pleasure and the Pain   103
7. The Scots Invade America   125
8. Clash of the Titan Egos   147
9. Falling Apart   159
10. All Washed Up   178
11. Breakout, Breakdown   187
12. Trauma and a Truce   198

Epilogue – Friends at Last?   209

APPENDICES

1. Band Line-ups   213
2. Timeline   215
3. Websites   219
4. Tartan Memories   221

Foreword
by Irvine Welsh

It's not that long ago that ABBA were considered a laughing stock, 'beyond the irony curtain', something that the cognoscenti just didn't get. Yet the subsequent celebrations of this group in the musical form tell us that success always comes back into vogue at some time. ABBA fans have grown older but they are still consumers and their fans still want a night out at the theatre singing along to the songs of yesterday.

This means that it's probably about time for a Bay City Rollers comeback, as they were a truly massive phenomenon. In fact, it's incredible to think just how big the BCR were back then. In America they had the kind of profile that the likes of Robbie Williams, and anyone else who has been through the British boy band sausage machine, would kill for.

I was never a Bay City Rollers fan. They were everybody's sister's band, with an exclusively female audience. They were the first British boy band, as we now understand the term. Yet over the years I've developed a soft spot for the Rollers because they came from a similar place to me. Specifically, I first became aware of Les McKeown back in the '70s. I was about 14. Although I came from Muirhouse, a housing scheme across the city from Les's Broomhouse, and he was a few years older than me, I had some mates from his part of town. He was to become famous locally for

shang-a-lang

joining the Bay City Rollers, who'd had a Top 10 hit with 'Keep On Dancing'. Obviously, this was a big thing for a kid from a scheme. But Les's other claim to fame, prior to joining the Rollers, was being suspended from Forrester High School for throwing a shit bomb into a lift. I don't know if this is mentioned in the book and if not I apologise to Les for bringing the matter up here.

The thing was that plenty of people did this sort of thing at school, but somehow it was Les who drew the attention. This obviously carried on in later life, and specifically onto the stage, because, let's face it, Les McKeown *was* the Bay City Rollers. Following his departure, the band staggered on with a series of different lead vocalists, enjoying the predictable rapidly diminishing returns.

Les's presence and general behaviour gave the Rollers a PR spice they otherwise lacked. The squeaky-clean propaganda machine that accompanies this type of act could never quite contain him. If, in the punk era, John Lydon had done the things with the Pistols that Les (allegedly) did with the Rollers – shoot a girl in the face for trespassing on his land, batter a photographer's head in with a mike stand, run over an old woman in his sports car at Edinburgh's Western Corner – then his notoriety would have been even greater than it was. In a line-up of synthetic baleful expressions, the more devilishly grinning Les McKeown was the one Roller who always came across as his own man. He behaved exactly how a young guy from an Edinburgh council scheme suddenly confronted with megabucks and superstardom should behave. And it's probably because he did, that today's Les McKeown is a well-adjusted, outgoing, likeable man who is more passionate about music than ever.

Love them or loathe them, the Bay City Rollers were, and are, a pop historical and cultural phenomenon. Much of what kids are served up with the next set of pop idols, the techniques of marketing and promotion, were forged back then in the '70s. As we watch the stars we have made implode under the pressures of fame, the BCR story is an archetypal one for all media and pop watchers. And by far the best person to tell this tale is Les McKeown.

Foreplay

'Oh yeah, the bad boy of the Bay City Rollers. He was the one that ran down an old woman and shot his fans!'

A common response at the mention of Les McKeown.

I would be happier if my life was summarised with 'he fronted the band that sold over three hundred million records around the world' or 'he was the guy who saved a bodyguard's life with a tartan scarf!' – but such is the power of the press.

I've always been expected to uphold an image and very few people know the real me. In the '70s, I was the milk-drinking, clean-living virgin the Bay City Rollers' manager made me. When that illusion was shattered, I was the drug-crazed, hell-raising fallen idol that the press made me. Later, in the '80s and '90s, I was a figure of nostalgia, of neither one former identity nor the other. Finally, in the twenty-first century, I can be myself – whoever that is.

Although generally people that meet me for the first time seem to think I'm 'pretty normal . . . considering', friends suggested I should write this book because they thought it would be cathartic. Having always found it useful to write in order to vent, it has been therapeutic – and the best part is I've saved myself thousands on shrink fees along the way.

You'll not find me droning on about the horrors of megastardom as some of today's stars do. You won't find me complaining about how I had no time to find my inner self, because there were always 25 girls outside the hotel room door screaming for a shag. On the whole, I feel grateful and privileged to have had the experiences I've had. But it's not all been a barrel of laughs. Anyone who thinks they want to be a pop idol will hopefully be more aware of some of the possible pitfalls once they've read this.

I cordially invite you to pour yourself a drink, lie back and let me pleasure you with my story.

Yours,

Leslie Richard McKeown

shang-a-lang
shang-a-lang

14

WARNING
The book you are about to read contains strong
language and material of a sexually explicit and, at
times, violent nature. Enjoy!

The Wee One

Prince Charles had left Scotland's most famous school by the time I started there in 1968.

I loved Gordonstoun and all the tradition and heritage associated with it. Unlike some of my co-students, who took everything for granted, I considered it a real privilege to be able to satisfy my thirst for learning and broaden my mind in this age-old institution of knowledge. Each and every day, I thanked God that I was born into a family of substance with the means to ensure that its children had all they could want or need and more.

What better start in life could I have had? A stable, wealthy family and an education which would set me up for life.

I was studious, but not a bookworm. I had lots of interests outside of school. My family lived in my father's ancestral home in the wooded hills surrounding Carrick Castle in the Argyll Forest Park. At weekends, I would ride my pony, Dick, through the woods, stopping now and then to collect fallen branches. These I would take home and transform into keys for the xylophones I made and sold through a local craft store. The xylophone production exemplified my love of all things musical that I had inherited from my mother's side of the family, and the amazing dexterity I possessed thanks to my father, the Laird Francis.

Not everything in the garden was rosy, though. My parents

were both great lovers of Mozart and Bach. My three brothers and I preferred the more intense and dramatic works of Wagner and Mussorgsky. In the same way that children today vie for possession of the TV remote control, my family would have similar disputes over control of the gramophone. Debates about the relative qualities of composers could sometimes become extremely heated but, ultimately, my father's threats to disinherit us ensured that it was his preference that we listened to. In later life, it has sometimes been difficult for me to deal with such unquestionable authority, but that is the only negative aspect of my upbringing I can think of.

As we sat in the drawing-room listening to music on a Sunday afternoon, I liked to embroider . . . kind of like I'm embroidering this whole scenario.

The McKeown family was not to be found listening to opera on a Sunday afternoon, discussing the intricacies of an aria or overture. We were a typical working-class Edinburgh family, doing what other typical working-class Edinburgh families did. The parents worked hard and the kids played hard – making our own entertainment when there was none to be found, which was often. We were a musical family only in the sense that there was always music to be heard in our house, whether it was my mum's singing or our records.

My earliest memory of any form of music is of my mother's lovely falsetto voice. Mum had sung with the Women's Royal Army Corps and was always singing around the house. If ever I was restless or upset, she would sing traditional Irish folk songs to send me to sleep. My dad was deaf, so he was never able to appreciate his wife's beautiful voice – my first experience of music.

My dear, sweet, beautiful mum, Florence Close, was born in Co. Down, Northern Ireland, in 1918. The daughter of a policeman, she spent the first years of her life in the village of Banbridge, between Belfast and Newry, then moved to the capital when her dad was promoted. Her mother, whom she adored, died as a result of a complicated miscarriage when Mum was just ten. Right up until she died last year, she still cried when she talked about walking home from school that dark day, seeing all the curtains drawn in her house and feeling the darkness come down upon her as she realised something was seriously wrong. Like most kids in Ireland in the first half of the last century, she was no stranger to tragedy. Her little brother George had been fatally burned in a domestic accident that happened before he could walk.

My grandfather, having no way of looking after Mum, her sister and two brothers after his wife died, found himself another Mrs Close six months after the first one died. The woman beat all the children. By the time Mum was 12 she had to leave the school she loved because she had developed chronic asthma, a condition she feels was brought on by the beatings she suffered at the hands of her stepmother. Today, of course, no child would be excluded from school because of an illness, but in rural Ireland back then, if you were away from school more often than you were there, for whatever reason, you lost your right to education. My grandfather taught Mum at home a bit, but it was the knitting and sewing that she had been especially good at in school that provided her first job.

When my grandfather died at 52, my mum was thrown out of the family home. By now she was working as a skilled seamstress and the aunt of a friend she worked with took her in. After a short while, the wicked stepmother was begging Mum to come home, but only because she needed someone to clean the house and cook for her. Once she'd got her way, the abuse started up again. One by one the four children escaped, by whatever means was available. One sister married to get away, only to find violence was to be a major part of her new life, too.

It all sounds a bit too dark and dismal to be true, but when you see a film like *Ryan's Daughter* or *The Magdalene Sisters*, where we're shown in graphic detail how harsh life in Ireland was for some people, it makes it all the more painful and real.

At work Mum had met the man who would become her husband: Francis Charles Stephen McKeown. He was a tailor, the son of a publican, born in Ballymena, Co. Antrim, in 1911. When he was a little boy, he'd got off his head on stout in the pub and was violently sick. As a result, he developed an understandably serious dislike of alcohol. After that, he never touched a drop.

My dad's loss of hearing was caused by an accident he'd had on his bicycle when he was four years old that severed the nerves in

shang-a-lang

the back of his neck. Because he couldnae hear from that point on, he didnae learn any more speech and soon stopped talking. My mum, my brothers and I therefore had to develop other means of communicating with him – our own form of sign language. Being the youngest, the structure of this communication was already in place by the time I came along. It seemed completely natural to me because I never knew any different. My dad could communicate anything to us – whether it was a request to go and buy some milk, or to shut the fuck up – just with gestures and a whole range of often comical expressions.

Eventually, we all learned basic manual sign language, but not until I'd started secondary school. One day, somebody from the RNID came to talk to us all there and afterwards we were given a card, showing how to make the sign for each letter of the alphabet. I learned how to do it and so did my brothers, which was great. The only problem was, once we'd learned how to sign, it was harder to communicate. It just wasnae as effective as our own way of doing it. That sounds strange but with signing, the process became theoretical and mechanical. You cannae express emotions and feelings so well with sign language, at least not when you're just starting to learn it. It was useful though, for specific words and names, and later my wife and son, with the benefit of being able to sign properly and use some of the communication methods we'd developed, could talk with my dad as effectively as the rest of us.

When I was growing up, I developed a wee bit of a sixth sense, or at least the ability to know things about people based on feelings alone. This may or may not be a result of my dad's disability. It doesnae work with everyone, but sometimes I instinctively know the true characters of people I meet. I'm also able to detect moods and stuff in a way that other people cannae. It might be more a case of intuition than an extrasensory skill – if the two are different – but throughout my life my first impressions have more often than not been spot on.

Some time after meeting and falling in love with my dad, my mum spotted an advert in the newspaper placed by the Edinburgh textile firm, Manclarks. They were desperate for skilled tailors and seamstresses. They decided to up and leave as soon as possible (by this time, it wasnae just Mum on the receiving end of the stepmother's fist – she'd smacked my dad once or twice, too).

At the end of their first-ever journey outside of Ireland, and at the start of their biggest adventure, Florence and Frank were met at Edinburgh's Waverley Station and taken to digs. Dad was put in comparatively smart accommodation while Mum settled in at the YWCA on George Street. She later moved into digs run by Nellie Porteous, who became a friend for life. It was Nellie who suggested that Mum and Dad should get married, as in the true Scots manner she considered it a waste of money for them to be paying two lots of rent and travelling backwards and forwards from one to the other all the time. They were married in 1949, with Nellie and her brother-in-law Reggie as witnesses. It wasnae long before their first son, Ronald, was born, soon followed by Harold, then Brian (latterly known as Brian the Treacherous) and, finally, me. It was 12 November 1955, and Carl Orff's *Carmina Burana* (*The Omen* music), was heard throughout the land. Two weeks later, a lady called Rosa Parks – a seamstress like my mum – refused to give up her seat to a white man on an Alabama bus and was arrested, so sparking the Civil Rights movement in the USA.

Mum and Dad moved to the Broomhouse area of Edinburgh, aka the Irish Ghetto, soon after they were married. The estate was on the outskirts of the town, at the end of the number 12 bus route. When they moved there it was fairly new. There were estates and 'schemes' springing up all over the place to house what we now call low-income families, but in those days they were still called 'the poor'.

The estate where we lived was brilliant, though, compared to the high-rise blocks in the schemes where the slum-dwellers were relocated. Our bit consisted of three tenement blocks, bordered on one side by the government buildings and on the other side by an industrial estate. Beyond that there were just miles and miles of hayfields, which eventually became Glasgow.

In the middle of the three tenement buildings was a big grassy area where the wee kids from the flats spent most of their time, watched over by their mothers in their kitchens. While I was in primary school, rounders was the preferred sport, and I spent a lot of time and energy playing it, convinced I was to become the next Babe Ruth.

Other sport was provided by the government buildings and the factory estate. We used to climb over the wall that separated us from the government buildings to taunt the security guards. Golden Wonder and Schweppes had factories on the industrial estate on the other side, and there was big money to be made there. We would acquire crisps by the box load but by far the best booty was the empty soda bottles we could get from the Schweppes factory. If you bought a bottle of Schweppes, like most other soft drinks, you could take the bottle back to the shop when it was empty and get some money back. Getting hold of a crate of them would keep us rich for weeks.

So fuck all you pigs! NOW I can admit it was ME that was the brains behind The Great Crisp Robbery of '65! Come on, if you think you're hard enough – PIGS!

Cough.

The railway and its embankment that ran past our estate provided another play area for the local kids. There was a big old oak tree there that someone had tied a rope to years before. Swinging on this was far more fun than the purpose-built playground at the end of our road, as was the old derelict farmhouse nearby that we were convinced was haunted.

Another of our favourite estate duties was building bonfires. This was a local tradition. My brothers and their friends had spent their younger years doing it, and as they grew up and out of it, the younger ones were handed the chalice and continued the ritual. Collecting wood for the bonfires was a massive task. We'd knock on every door on every street in the neighbourhood, asking for anything that could be burned, and then build an enormous pyre back home by the rounders pitch. When we had enough to make a spectacular fire, everyone on the estate would come out to watch. There was a real close-knit community spirit and we revelled in the warmth of both the bonfire and the love . . . but then someone would annoy somebody else and there'd be an almighty fight and somebody's 'mooth' would get 'broken'.

Mum enrolled me in the Boys' Brigade, and bonfires were one of the best bits about that, too, but there they were made for cooking sausages and beans. The Edinburgh 12th Company was a good 30-minute bus ride away, at Fountainbridge, but it was worth the trek. I would use up loads of energy running and climbing and swinging on ropes, but there was also the practical side to proceedings and I learned how to tie a lot of knots. I also learned how to make sugar bombs (not from the Brigade leaders!) and we had great fun with those back at Broomhouse as well.

When I wasnae engaged in fire- or bomb-making activities, I'd spend hours on end watching my dad making things. He could turn his hand to anything that needed to be constructed or made. He built a tool shed in the garden in no time at all. I couldnae believe how it was that when all the parts were ready they all fitted together perfectly, without any gaps or rough edges. I was in awe of his abilities; oblivious to his disability.

It seemed to me that my dad could come up with a practical solution to anything. When I started to go ice skating, he made me a pair of PVC trousers so that I wouldnae get a wet arse when I fell over on the ice. Later, when I went camping in France, he made me a waterproof drawstring sack to keep my sleeping bag clean and dry.

Family life was rich, much as you would expect it to be when there are four young boys living in one small house. As the baby of the family, I got special attention from my mum – at least that's what my brothers seemed to think – and they reacted to that as you'd expect. Of course, Dad's special efforts on my behalf, like the skating trousers, were further undeserved benefits that I received. My brothers were always teasing me and picking on me and to get back at them for having a go at me for something that wasnae my fault, I would wind them up at any given opportunity. Then I'd hide in a cupboard to escape their shouting and swearing. One time I fell asleep in a box in the cupboard. When I eventually woke up and came out, I discovered the whole family and half the neighbourhood had been frantically searching for me, thinking I'd had enough and run away, or worse. This only made the brothers more unpopular as they were accused of having driven me away, only to realise later it was one of my pranks that had found them out of favour yet again. After the initial relief came the ranting and the raving, so back I went into the cupboard. And so it went on.

Like all of my brothers, I went to Broomhouse Primary School. I never missed a day in the three years I was there. I loved going to Broomhouse and I had a fantastic teacher called Mrs Simmons. She was warm and kind and encouraging. Even when I fell over in the playground when they were resurfacing it, filling my knee with stones and gravel causing it to swell up to the size of a football, I still hobbled in the next day.

A far more serious health issue occurred when I was nine, but luckily it was during the summer holidays so I'd not have to be away from school. I contracted meningococcal meningitis, probably from drinking dirty water while I'd been away at Broomhouse summer camp. A few days after I came home from the camp, I didnae feel right.

'Mum! Mum! I'm burning up!' I shouted, followed a few minutes later by 'Mum! I'm freezing!' Mum wasnae taking any chances and called our GP, Dr Stewart, straightaway, and I was rushed to hospital. They said that if I'd arrived there half an hour later, I would have been deid. I was held down by four doctors so that they could stick a needle in my spine. The slightest movement while they were doing the lumbar puncture could have paralysed me. I had never been so scared in my life and I have never been so scared since.

Because of the seriousness of the illness, I had to be isolated in the hospital for a few weeks while I recovered. I slept in a glass cubicle next to another kid from school in another cubicle, and had to lie on my stomach all the time because of the lumbar puncture. The hospital food, as always, was rank, so Mum brought food in for me every day, and I'll never forget how much I looked forward to my mum walking through that hospital door. It helped me to make a speedy recovery and soon I was back on a normal ward, eyeing up the nurses and the wee girlie in the bed at the end. Clearly I was better and I was sent home again to enjoy the rest of the holidays. I think it was during those holidays that I became more aware of, and a lot more inquisitive about, the opposite sex.

Mum said that I was never the same again after the meningitis. She said I became 'high strung' and tense, and stayed that way until quite recently, when I became a bit less *tangentum infinitum*.

The next year's summer holidays were different. I spent most of them worrying about moving from Broomhouse Primary to 'big' school. I'd loved my first school so much and bad things seemed to happen to everyone I knew who left its warmth and familiarity for Forrester High School . . .

Roni was OK there for the most part but got into some kind of trouble at one point and ended up in a horrible special school for a wee while. It wasnae unusual for kids from the estates and schemes. Doing something that today would get you a smacked wrist could get you taken from your family and whisked off to some kind of institution in no time at all back then.

I remember Roni crying one night in his bedroom with my mum and then he was gone. Mum and I went to see him one day and the place scared me shitless. He was soon home again, though – it was, thank God, a short stay for him.

Dad hadnae reacted too well to Roni's misdemeanour, whatever it had been. Having no means of voicing his anger, he resorted to the only other means of communication available to him. When Hari was the next one to find himself on the wrong side of the law, Dad was the same with him. However, the things that Hari was getting punished for were trivial, meaningless offences that weren't his fault and this made it much harder for him to come to terms with the situation.

Hari had been at Forrester's only a few weeks when he caught up with two schoolmates on the way home to discover their coats were stuffed full of crisps and chocolate. They told Hari they'd broken into the school tuck shop, and where the remaining loot was. At 11 years of age, the idea of shed loads of free tuck was too much for wee Hari, so off he went to claim his share. Taking inspiration from the perpetrators of the crime, he concealed his stash in his coat. On the way home, he was stopped by the police, who had noticed his body was way too big for his wee legs. Not wanting to split on his mates – which you never, ever do in Scotland – he was obliged to say that it was he who had broken into the tuck shop and off he went to the police station. A few days later, he was walking to school along the railway embankment, a route that most of the local kids usually took, unaware that the embankment was in fact private property and that they were trespassing. The police caught Hari there and off he went to the station again. After that, he was mucking around outside our house one night on a friend's scooter, pushing it up a slope and freewheeling it down again. There were the police again, who obviously thought they had a serial killer on their hands rather than a kid who was caught in possession of stolen crisps with a tendency to trespass. He was nicked again and banned from driving for 25 years.

At the age of 11 and a half.

Things got progressively worse for Hari from then on. Because he'd been nicked three times in the space of a few months, the social services were notified by the police. The social workers went to see my mum and dad and seemed to be full of concern and eager to help. They told Mum it was understandable that she was finding it hard to cope with four sons – although she wasnae at all – and convinced her that it would be best for Hari if she was to hand him over to them. Dad, who had probably never got the full story about the stolen tuck, the trespassing or the driving offence, was convinced that his second son was just bad. Hari was taken off to some kind of home for young offenders while the social services decided where he was to go.

On his first night away from home, at the Gilmerton remand home, he was raped by the night-duty officer.

He was then moved to the Mossbank Approved School in Glasgow where he was to stay for the next three years. Instead of the dormitory for new internees that he was supposed to be in for his own safety (because he was one of only a handful of kids from Edinburgh there) he was placed in a dormitory with 36 Glaswegian gang members, all serving their apprenticeship for Barlinnie. I cannae write about what they did to him there, but if you delve into the most sordid and revolting realms of your imagination and multiply it a hundred times, you'll start to get the picture.

On the second day, Hari told someone what had been done to him. From then on his life was worse than hell. There was no one to help this frightened 12-year-old boy and there was no escape. He sank into a helpless despair and a downward spiral that reached an all-time low when a contract was put out on him in the late '90s. He suffered a broken jaw, fractured skull, permanent damage to the spinal chord and loss of feeling in his face, three broken ribs, a broken collar bone and four lost pints of blood. I wish I could have done something and I still wish I could do something, but I dinnae know what it is. All I do know is that Hari needs to get it all out.

Having seen two brothers sent away from the school that I was about to enter, it was no wonder that I was more than a little bit nervous as I walked through those gates for the first time.

I remember my first day at secondary school very clearly.

Forrester's was unusual, to say the least. It was a special school, hand-picked by the government (because of its deprived location) to try out a new way of stimulating the kids' learning abilities. This was to be achieved by attempting to submerse them in a more natural environment where they would, it was hoped, find it easier to absorb information.

On my first day, everyone had to have a full physical examination, complete with the embarrassing coughing exercise and a check for fleas. Even more embarrassing, we had to leave all our clothes in a little locker by the school entrance. Next we went out into a kind of courtyard where the whole school, teachers and pupils, were walking around naked. It was just so bizarre.

Obviously, classes such as metalwork or joinery could prove hazardous, so in those classes compromises had to be made and we could wear protective aprons, but in art and English and stuff, there were no restrictions. The scheme worked really well for a while, but it was brought to an untimely end by the escalating fuel costs, shortages and the cuts of '71. They couldnae justify the cost of running the project with such astronomical heating bills. After that, you could wear anything you wanted.

If only that were true. The reality was this:

When I started at Forrester's, I was very small for 11, as my brothers had been. None of us showed any signs of growing up till we were well into our teens. So we all got picked on for being small, and for having a deaf and dumb dad. We were terrorised by the prefects, who were worse than Flashman in *Tom Brown's Schooldays*. They literally terrified people and I began to dread going to school each day.

After a year or two, I eventually found a way to make friends and discourage this unwanted attention from the bigger boys and prefects, by misbehaving, fooling around and gaining respect – at least in the playground sense. My wee gang began to take shape, consisting of kids not just in my year but in the higher years as well. There was one guy a couple of years older than me, who I'll call Donald McDonald, who was a bit slow but built like a gorilla. He didnae have many friends on account of his parents having given

shang-a-lang

27

him a stupid name and his lower-than-average intelligence. Donald was happy to act as my personal bodyguard in return for having a pal. Having a protector was a big plus for me, as it meant that I was a wee bit less likely to get picked on.

Even the dreaded prefects lost interest and found other targets, especially after one of them caught me smoking in the toilets and said he would hand me over to the headmaster unless I surrendered my fag. This I did, but not as he'd expected – I stubbed the thing out on the radge's hand, which, needless to say, resulted in a bit of a tussle.

As far as lessons went, I wasnae particularly interested. Initially I spent too much time worrying about what the prefects' next torture would be to be able to concentrate on school work. Plus, none of the teachers were anything like my beloved Mrs Simmons, they were more like army sergeants. Whereas Mrs Simmons would have been calm, encouraging and warm, the Forrester's staff would shout, 'McKeown, open your book!' to which I would take offence and respond 'Fuck off!' and get belted.

From then on, I developed a healthy dislike of all teachers and anyone in a position of authority, with one exception – Mr Cunningham. He cut me some slack and we got on well. As a result, I enjoyed my art lessons.

He was the only teacher I had at that school who took an interest in me and made me feel I could achieve something. He encouraged me to develop my artistic side and the creativity I didnae know I had, and saw to it that effort and results were rewarded. In his classes, I made a 24-foot square mural of as many clay tiles, which was put in the main entrance of the school. I also made a head of clay that was displayed at the Scottish Academy. As far as I know, both examples of early McKeownite art are still on show today.

Mr Cunningham was by far the scariest teacher at the school. In those days, it was completely acceptable, and expected, to discipline a child who misbehaved in any way, usually with the aid of a leather belt. The belt would be about eight millimetres thick and about a metre long, with two tongues. Once my pals and me were fooling around with the girls in a cookery class and we ended up pelting the blackboard with flour and eggs. On that occasion most of the class were involved and we couldnae all get belted, so me and one of my friends took the rap for everyone.

Being on the receiving end of Mr Cunningham's belt was another story. The other teachers' belts were soft, but his was stiff – like a lump of wood. It was a lot sorer when you got hit with Cunningham's belt. You knew that if you got belted by one of the other teachers it would hurt, but an imminent thrashing from him would scare you shitless. I was often in trouble and finding myself subjected to his heinous punishment, but nevertheless we developed what I guess you could call a mutual respect. I got the very distinct feeling when he belted me that he'd not really wanted to have to do it, a bit like when a kid's disciplined by the parent other than the one that usually does the punishing.

I also developed what became known as 'the Cunningham technique', which was a way of minimising the pain inflicted by his belt. If you pulled your hand away suddenly as the belt came down it would hurt more, but if you really concentrated and moved your hand with the motion of the belt, it wasnae so bad. I took pleasure in teaching this technique to other kids who'd been found guilty and were awaiting sentence, and acquired more friends.

In my last year at Forrester's, when I was 15, things got a bit out of hand.

There was one kid in my year who was a bit posh. That would have been OK in itself, but he had a superiority complex that wound people up, so he got picked on. While I wasnae the worst offender, I did more than my fair share of hassling the lad. Of course, what I should've done was stand up for him, but this was a rough school and unless you relished the thought of a very severe kicking, you went with the flow. The one law we all lived by was to never show any weaknesses, and I've lived by that law most my life.

One spring afternoon we were all coming out of school, in high spirits. The posh lad was sitting in an open-top car with his brother, pointing me out. Suddenly, big brother jumped out of the car, grabbed me, spat in my face and told me in no uncertain terms what he would do to me if I didnae leave little brother alone. There followed a bit of a case of bad timing. For some reason, the frustration and anger that had been festering in me since my cupboard-dwelling days and sleepless nights on account of the prefects, chose that moment to come to the surface.

With an icy stare, I turned and walked away.

I found some bricks and other missiles, went back, and

proceeded to smash the car to pieces. Its owner blew a fuse and came at me again, but by now Donald McDonald was on the scene, so he backed off, and called the police instead.

Unfortunately, I wasnae unknown to the Corstorphine Police, and with them, any degree of previous meant guilty until proven innocent next time. The year before I'd been on my way home with some pals and we were thirsty. As we walked past a pub with a small window left open, it was decided that because of my size I should be the one to shimmy in through the window and nick a can of Coke or two. A police car drove past as I was halfway through, and off I went to the nick for the first time. I had to go to court with my mum and she was fined five pounds, which made me feel terrible.

Given this previous form, and their dealings with my brothers not so long before, I couldnae see the police being about to let another McKeown delinquent off lightly. With my head full of memories of visiting Roni in that awful remand place and Hari having been taken away, logic deserted me. I decided that life was unfair and set about seeking my revenge – not just against this latest situation, but against everything.

I was a bit overzealous with the posh kid and he ended up in hospital.

The next day, Mr Cunningham and one of the other teachers got me and beat the living shite out of me in a classroom.

You might find that hard to believe. The same thing would be unlikely to happen today, what with Social Services and everything, but this was a tough school in a tough neighbourhood and different rules applied then. Where discipline was concerned, there weren't many rules. By now I was angrier than ever.

Blinded by rage and frustration, I decided I would get back at them by vandalising the teachers' lift in a particularly offensive manner. It was easy to recruit co-conspirators as most kids thought the car-trashing incident was justifiable and provoked, and they were happy to contribute the requisite ammunition. The fact that I'd been beaten up by Cunningham and remained unbroken had earned me a kind of heroic status. Add to that the sheer audacity of my plan and I had an army the like of which had not been seen in Scotland since William Wallace's day.

My scheme was carried out like a military exercise, planned to the nth degree and timed to perfection. Seven years later, the IRA inhabitants of Northern Ireland's Maze Prison used similar 'dirty protests' to demonstrate their anger. It didnae do them any good and it didnae do me any good either. I was expelled, but it was worth it because operation 'make the fuckers walk up the stairs' was successful; the jobby was done.

I would like to say something here in defence of what many people will think was a revolting and extreme thing to do. In Scotland, many people – particularly of my gender and social background – have some kind of fascination with, and get a lot of amusement from, scatological matters. I'll save you going to look up 'scatological' – it means, according to *Merriam-Webster's Collegiate Dictionary*, 'an interest in, or treatment of, obscene matters, especially in literature', or 'the biologically oriented study of excrement'. I've discussed this with many people from all walks of life recently, and most have agreed with me about this national trait. In many cases, those people have contributed tales involving shite of their own, so it really wasnae such a bad thing to do.

Not so long after I was expelled, I was back in court. I was done for malicious damage to the convertible and grievous bodily harm to the boy. Mum paid out another ten pounds or so in fines.

If I had to pick the time in my life when the boy became a man, that couple of weeks was it. The childish innocence that had been slowly disappearing until that point was extinguished like a flame. Now I saw the world through new, cynical, resentful eyes.

Looking back, when I think about what happened to Hari and how minimally, in comparison, I was punished for far more serious offences than he'd committed, I was lucky. But it wasnae really just a matter of luck. There'd been amendments to the law around that time which changed the way that young offenders were dealt with, possibly in response to the growing awareness of cases like my brother's.

To protect me, or to protect herself from the fear of losing another son, my mum declined to share details of my activities with my dad. As a result, I escaped the violence with which he tried to tame Roni, and the 'tough love' approach he used with Hari. I experienced nothing but love and support from him throughout my childhood and teenage years. For that I'm extremely grateful and humbled and I won't feel guilty about it.

My social life during my early teens was as enjoyable as my school life had been nightmarish. I had a really fantastic time out of school. I still spent most of my time with my brother Roni, who was five years older than me and by now all grown up, good looking and popular – a babe magnet.

Our outings to Cowdenbeath for the stockcar and speedway meets fuelled my desire to know all there was to know about cars and bikes. Sometimes I had to be transported there in the boot of the car, either because there wasnae a seat for me, or because Roni and his mates didnae want me to see what was happening in the back seat. Uncomfortable and dark though it was, I didnae mind. I was used to being in dark confined spaces and I would have allowed myself to be strapped to the roof if I'd needed to be.

When Roni got his first Lambretta, I was smitten. Every spare moment my brothers and I had would be spent working on his new bike, taking it apart, cleaning it, and putting it all back together again. As the rest of us each reached the magical age of 16, we acquired our own scooters and immediately set about metamorphosing our machines. The priority was to make the bikes louder and faster, so we rebored the pistons and added expansion chambers, otherwise known as 'bell enders'. Next, all the fairings and panels came off for painting, with artwork inspired by the movie *Easy Rider*. The finishing touch to mine was the addition of a load of steel tube provided by a mate who was a plumber. This was bent and polished and attached to ensure that my scooter was by far the best looking for miles. It was a great-looking convoy of McKeown brothers that followed their mum and dad to the port when they eventually went back to Ireland for a visit once the stepmonster was deid.

Having whiled away the weekend daylight hours working on my scooter, at night I used to follow Roni and his cool mates to discos. On the way, they would buy wine and when they got there, if there was any left over, they'd give it to me and my pals before disappearing into the disco. After a while, it got to a point where they'd let us go inside with them.

Going to discos with Roni was brilliant. The girls wanted to look after the wee brother as a means of finding favour with the big one, and there were lots of slow dances to be had. Because I was small,

I usually found my head nestled in their chests – or better, if they were tall – which was the best thing ever at that age.

Being part of the disco scene at an early age brought many other temptations. The wide range of beverages on offer was intoxicating by sight alone. An early experiment with rum had the same effect on me as my dad's one and only experience with alcohol – I was completely wrecked, threw up for 24 hours and got jaundice into the bargain. I was 13 at the time and applying the logic that it was best to get straight back on a bike you'd fallen off, I waited a few days and then tried something else. McEwans lager, perfectly named though misspelled, was far nicer and didnae make me sick. That particular love affair continues to this day, although sometimes, especially late at night, my old mate Jack Daniels is the friend whose company I prefer.

All of a sudden, Roni was 17 and I realised that scooters were boys' toys – real men had cars!

On the day that Roni got his first car, we were all at home anxiously waiting to see the first family vehicle. It was a momentous day not only because son number one was about to be let out on the road alone, but also because we'd had a brand-new twin-tub washing machine installed that morning. Finding even domestic appliances fascinating, I'd seized control of the new machine and set it in motion. Suddenly, Roni pulled up outside with the car windows wound down and the radio blaring, shouting, 'Right, everybody out! We're going for a drive!' Into the car we piled, all of us forgetting that Mum's non-automatic washing machine was doing its stuff in the kitchen. When we came home an hour or so later, the thing had boiled itself dry and incinerated its contents, filling the house with smoke. Luckily we were home before the fire brigade was called.

Another close brush with one of the other emergency services happened when Hari was back home again – all of us blissfully ignorant of what he'd been through. He'd gone out with some of his new friends in a Mini and had come back to get something he'd forgotten. While he was in the house, one of his friends tried to drive the Mini up the lamppost opposite. We heard the crash and ran to the window, all shouting something along the lines of 'Fuck, Hari! What the . . . ?!' We then learned that the Mini in question belonged to none of Hari's friends. A neighbourhood spy called the dreaded Corstorphine Police who, thankfully, didnae show up before we'd all run out to clean any incriminating prints off the car.

It might seem as though there was always something going down *chez* McKeown, but for the most part we'd all four of us just sit in one of our two bedrooms playing records when we weren't tinkering around with our scooters. We'd whack up the volume and argue about whose turn it was to pick the track. I'd always choose Bowie, Roxy Music (the *real* Roxy Music, before Brian Eno left) and Deep Purple or Led Zeppelin. Roni always went for blues and Motown numbers, which I didnae object to. There wasnae much played that I did object to – I loved all kinds of music. Mum used to bring us our tea and never complained about 'that awful racket' like other parents did. As far as she and Dad were concerned, they were happy because they could keep an eye on us. They knew where we were and what we were up to most of the time. We weren't hanging around the streets like lots of the other kids, getting into far more trouble than we did.

One time they couldnae keep watch over me was when I went hitchhiking to France with a wee pal. We were about 14 at the time, and I'd never been on holiday before, let alone out of the country. The trip was a great adventure. We travelled as far as Avignon and went grape picking to earn some cash to pay for the rest of the trip. All in all I was impressed with this new land and the people seemed kind and friendly, especially the wee French lassies! Thanks to them I learned masses of new French words, but unfortunately I was belted for using them when I got back to school.

On the Threshold of Fame

In 1971, aged 15, I had to decide what I wanted to do with my life. I had to think about finding a job, and having been cast out of the education system before my time, the prospects were even worse than they were for the kids that stayed the course.

I loved Broomhouse when I was a kid, but as I grew older, childish perceptions dissolved into grim, ugly realisations and I saw people's lives as they really were. I didnae like what I could see coming my way. I didnae want a futureless existence. Edinburgh was not an inspiring place and I needed to escape. When I go back there today, it feels good to start with because the earliest memories come first. But after a wee while, the latter feelings come flooding back and I get that same intense need to get the hell out.

I'll try and describe what it was about living in Edinburgh that I found depressing. First, there's the grey stone. Ninety per cent of buildings are built of it; big blocks of battleship-coloured rock hewn from the hills, each one soaked with the sweat of the poor bastards who broke their backs to get them out and to the town. Put a backdrop of cloud and drizzle behind those grey buildings and you begin to get a feel for the place. The Castle, which can look majestic and spectacular to tourists on a sunny day, just emphasises the feeling of being imprisoned for many of the residents.

A lot of people who've visited the town, and some of the better-off who live there, are going to disagree and say how fantastic it is. Remember, I'm talking from a very different viewpoint. Life in the schemes, riddled with crime, drugs and prostitution, is not something you're going to read about in a *Rough Guide* or the Edinburgh and Lothians Tourist Board's pamphlets. If you want to know the real Edinburgh, read Irvine Welsh's literature. After a few chapters you'll maybe start to see the way that social conditions like we had up there make people think. In the absence of ambition, it's too easy for causing aggro at a footie match at the weekend to become the highlight of your life. It wasnae *that* bad for me, though – I was too busy with my scooters and songs to give a toss about football and I had more ambition than you could shake a stick at.

When Irvine's books became successful and he moved to London, he noticed one major difference between behaviour in the two capitals which it's worth sharing: 'In London, when you get mugged, it's for money. In Edinburgh, you can get beaten to a pulp for fuck all and they'll not take your money. It's a matter of protocol.'

It's true. I once went to a mate's flat up at Sighthill with another mate, and when the lift came, two middle-aged geezers got out, asked us what we were looking at and smacked us in the mouth. This is normal behaviour in Edinburgh. Having recovered, we got into the lift, relieved that it was working for once. We still had to hold our noses, though, so as not to inhale the stench of junky piss.

As a wee kid you dinnae see all this. As you grow up, it all comes into focus and the picture ain't pretty.

My friend Jimmy Redpath's dad was a captain in the Merchant Navy. To a forlorn, puberty-ridden 15 year old, the idea of sailing the high seas, far and away from Edinburgh, was very, very attractive. Here was my chance to cut loose.

Jimmy's dad's ship was moored at Leith Docks, so it was arranged for me to go and have a look around. In the meantime I revised all the rope tricks I'd learned at Boys' Brigade, hoping that when they saw how enthusiastic I was they'd let me in there and then. The tour of the ship and the people I met that day were brilliant and I couldnae wait to join up. I filled in the forms and fell asleep each night imagining the exotic places I would go to, the interesting people I would meet and the beautiful women I would

shang-a-lang

seduce. I was absolutely devastated when my application was rejected because I'd been expelled from school. I cried and carried on crying for ages. It seemed I was doomed to doss around Edinburgh for the rest of my life, a life that would be just as uneventful and unrewarding as everyone else's. I didnae want to be a brickie or a plumber or a gas fitter or on the dole. I wanted to see the world and experience the planet. I wanted a job that would let me do that and now I couldnae have that job.

Eventually, when the disappointment of not being able to join the Merchant Navy died down, I began to work on another escape plan . . .

For as long as I can remember, I've loved music, not just listening to it, but singing it especially. I always had the radio on and would sing along all the time whether I was at home in my room, in Roni's car, wherever. People used to say I had a good voice.

My first public performances were at the local community centre. There'd be bingo and chat and sometimes there would be a band playing. When they'd finished their set they would sometimes invite members of the audience up on stage to sing. I was always the first to volunteer and when I'd finished, everyone would stand up and applaud the wee gadgie with the brass neck to get up and have a go.

One day it dawned on me that this was something that could possibly be developed and provide me with another means of getting away. I began to take a more serious interest in music and the industry as a whole. If I couldnae be a sailor, I'd be a pop star. Getting into music was definitely the only exit route left open to me and I went full steam ahead towards that door. It was my last chance.

At weekends, I began visiting the Radio Edinburgh Studios, just to find out what went on there and how things worked. Despite its name, Radio Edinburgh was nothing to do with radio. It contained recording studios much like any others and was run by a guy called Neil Ross.

I used to hang out there, just to be in the thick of it and soak up the atmosphere. I made cups of tea for Neil and the technicians and constantly bombarded them with questions about how everything worked. Neil says that whenever he looked over his shoulder, there I would be, watching every button he pushed and every dial he twiddled. I was in awe of the bands that recorded there and wanted more than anything else in the world to have one of my own. That would, of course, require money and as I didnae earn any money at the studios there was no alternative but to get a job to finance my dream.

I had a girlfriend at the time whose dad was a foreman at the Scottish & Newcastle Breweries. They were looking for a lab assistant and the prospects were good because the person they employed would learn the ropes then work his or her way up through the ranks. The interview was a formality. I got the job and started on my 16th birthday, in the winter of 1971. I was given a proper lab assistant's white coat and an access-all-areas pass – something that very few of the other workers had. It didnae take long for me to catch on that these special access rights were a highly exploitable perk. For instance, I could go to where the beer was brewed and siphon off the unpasteurised beer, which was an elixir to my fellow workers. This made me very popular and to capitalise on that and to ensure that our enjoyment was undisturbed, I set about building a pile of wooden pallets with my forklift truck, leaving a hole in the middle big enough for several people to hide in. There we would secretly sup my bacterially superior pilfered brew. Also on the drinks menu were 'wee heavies', available to all employees but made only for export on account of the fact that the brew was considered too strong for the average man on the street. I never understood the theory that the inhabitants of the alcohol capital of the world couldnae handle this stuff, but foreigners could.

I was more than happy to acquire these treasures on behalf of my new pals and revel in the acclaim that brought me. I remember often cycling home, off my wee head, which seriously worried my poor mum. Sadly, our pallet party piss-ups didnae last too long. One day we were discovered and I got fired.

Having worked out that it was probably not a good idea to combine work and alcohol, I used my pallet-truck-driving experience to get a new job at a soft drinks factory. My new truck was a nifty little number, different from the one at the brewery only in the sense that I had to sit on it to drive whereas I'd stood up on the other one. Having soon mastered it, I whizzed out of the warehouse into the car park one day and for some reason I turned the steering wheel the wrong way. Before I'd realised what I'd done, I'd driven straight through the MD's Merc. Red as a beetroot and shaking like a leaf, I got off the truck and went home. I didnae see any point in hanging around, waiting to get fired!

I had God knows how many different jobs after that – you name it, I did it. Delivering bread for the local bakery was one, but one day I had to deliver to a Salvation Army home for the aged on the Grassmarket and the smell that hit me as soon as the door was opened nearly made me throw up. In search of more pleasant aromas in the workplace, I worked in a laundry next and then a chemical factory. There was also a stint as an electrician's apprentice at some point.

All the time I was flitting from job to job, I was dreaming of the day when I would have my own band, become successful and travel the world. I knew that a band was not going to appear on my doorstep begging me to sing with them, so I decided to seize the initiative. I set about finding other members for my new band by advertising in the *Edinburgh Evening News* and Bruce's Records, a music store on Rose Street in the town. Bruce's Records was the hub of the music world in Edinburgh, because its owner, Bruce Findlay, had his own music charts which all the radio stations in Scotland used. He went on to manage Simple Minds, helping to take them to the top of the charts between 1978 and 1990.

Once I'd started taking positive steps towards finding myself a band, Hari was on the case – supportive and encouraging. He put me in touch with a guitarist who lived near us who said he'd let me know if he came across any bands in need of a singer. Hari also knew a lassie called Pamela Cormack, who ran the fan club for a well-known Scottish band, the Bay City Rollers. The club was run from the Prestonpans home of their manager, Tam Paton. As Tam was an important, if not the only, music industry figure in Edinburgh, Hari felt I should meet Pamela, so off we went.

While we were at Tam's house visiting Pamela, a phone call came through from a guy called Alan Wright. He was putting together a band called Threshold with his friend, Alex Valente, and told Tam they were looking for a lead singer. Within seconds I was on the line. The conversation went something like this:

Alan: 'Hi, Les . . . are you a singer?'

Me: 'Aye.'
Alan: 'Have you sung in a band before?'
Me: 'Aye!'
Alan: 'Oh, aye, and what were they called?'
Me: '. . . Teabags.'

Despite lying my way through my first music-world interview, my 'brass neck' got me the job with Threshold. I went along to meet Alan, who was the bass player, and Alex, the lead guitarist. I nicknamed him 'Thatch', because he did his hair in a way that reminded me of a thatched roof. He looked like a smaller, skinnier version of Lenny Kravitz. Alan was a good-looking guy and laughed a lot. Also in the band were the equally hunky John Walker on rhythm guitar and Jon Gillam on drums.

We began rehearsing together at each other's houses and at a church hall down the road from my house, where we later got our first gig. Sometimes we rehearsed in my back garden, but never for very long. Usually at least one stick-in-the-mud neighbour called the police to put a stop to it, claiming that we were creating a disturbance. As there was a lot of drum and bass involved in our favourite numbers – Deep Purple's 'Smoke On The Water' and 'Alright Now' by Free – maybe they had a point. What was possibly more annoying was the never-ending repetition as we tried to get to grips with whatever latest Top 30 hit the kids wanted. More often than not we practised at Alan's mum's house in Abbeyhill, mainly because she was the only one with a telephone. This meant we could call clubs, do our promotion and administrate our bookings from there.

By the time we started to get gigs, Roni was a DJ of note in Edinburgh, as much for his way with the ladies as with the discs. We hit on the idea of selling Threshold and Roni as a package deal. The format was a three-hour set – Threshold for the first hour, Roni for the second and then back to Threshold for the third. It worked really well and saved club owners the hassle of having to book their DJs and bands separately. The combination of records and a live band was a novel concept that hadnae been done before – when you went out on a Saturday night, you either went to a disco where DJs played records or to a club to see a band or two. By offering the best of both, the clubs where we played quickly increased their audiences and we were invited back again and again. At the

Americana on Fountainbridge, for example, we soon had a firm three-nights-a-week booking alongside Hari, who was also DJ-ing by now and worked there from time to time.

One club we occasionally worked in was not too salubrious a joint. It was owned and run by a local hard man who we all tried to steer clear of as much as we could. He must have known this because he got a kick out of making one of us go up to his horrible 'office' after the gig to ask for our money. There were always arguments about whose turn it was to go upstairs and request our payment, and on one particularly unlucky occasion, John Walker drew the short straw. He came back looking like he was about to throw up. He told us how he'd knocked on the office door and was commanded to enter, where he was confronted with the sight of the not-very-attractive owner with a young, relatively attractive girl bouncing up and down on his lap . . . and not because she was jigging around in time to the rhythm of the music downstairs booming through the floorboards. Poor John managed to stutter out a request for our money, trying to avoid eye contact with either the man or the girl. He had to leave after a fraction of what was owed to us was hurled across the room at him so that he had to scrabble around in the layers of ash and God knows what else to gather it up. We gave him some stick for not getting all of our money but as none of the rest of us was volunteering to ask for the balance, we cut our losses and left.

Not all our venues were as bad. At the Irish Club in Glasgow's notorious Gorbals district, the club management dealt with an unpleasant situation quickly and professionally. When a guy near the front of the audience slowly started to tilt sideways in his seat, with his eyes rolling back and foam coming from his mouth, he was very considerately dragged away from the stage and thrown into a cupboard, from where he could no longer distract the entertainers. At another high-class venue, the stage wasnae level and John and Alex had to perform the whole set rooted to the spot, with one foot each holding Jon's drum-kit in place to stop it sliding off the stage. Jon was an absolutely brilliant but unconventional drummer – he had his drums set up in his own peculiar way and played them seated almost on the floor, leaning back so that he was nearly horizontal. This was fine normally, but on a sloping stage it could've been lethal.

Threshold were your typical long-haired rockers – we wore mainly jeans and T-shirts to start with, but I did invest in a black crushed velvet jacket that I was particularly fond of.

Then my dad started to make some stage gear for us. Having watched *Top Of The Pops* in forced silence, he concentrated on how the bands looked and decided he could make us stand out from our contemporaries. He gave us a visual edge and, with the music and the look established, we started to attract quite a substantial following of young lassies. Within a matter of weeks, they were coming from as far away as Aberdeen to camp outside Alan's mum's house in sleeping bags.

I was in my element – part of the Edinburgh 'scene' and on the receiving end of a lot of very attractive offers from those lassies that it would have been rude to decline. At the same time, my musical education was benefiting as Alan introduced me to the pleasures of Yes and other rock bands I'd hardly heard of because they'd not get played much on mainstream radio. Alan also increased my appreciation of music with marijuana. I'd only ever smoked tobacco up to that point and remember thinking the first time I tried a spliff that it wasnae having any effect at all. Then I started to laugh a lot and it seemed like I was thinking on another dimension. It helped me appreciate music more because after half a spliff, even a mediocre tune sounded fantastic. Anyone who's tried it will know what I'm talking about. Every note is cleaner and sweeter, every chord more atmospheric. I loved it. I loved all the benefits of being in this band.

As our reputation spread, we started to get booked for gigs farther afield. We started to travel all over Scotland to perform, which was great, because it got me out of Edinburgh. But although we were getting more and more gigs, we never really made any money. In fact, by the time we'd paid for van and PA hire, fuel and other stuff, we usually *lost* money. And it was really hard work. After we'd finished a gig we'd have to load up all the gear, drive for maybe two or three hours to get home again, unload the gear at the other end and sometimes even return the van the same night. If we were lucky we'd have enough cash left over to stop off for something to eat on the way back because we always had the serious munchies after a gig. The long journeys home were definitely the worst bit about band life. We always felt a bit deflated after the adrenaline fix we got before a gig and during a performance. When faced with the choice of a bit of post-gig fun or a miserable journey back home, it was impossible to resist. A few bevvies, a wee bit of puff and the eager-to-please attentions of the less-virtuous girls in the audience made the unavoidable journey back more bearable.

Maybe it was because our minds were distracted by the pleasures ahead that we lost Roni on the way to a gig one night. We had set off for a new venue at Ardrishaig, right over on the west coast of Scotland. As usual we hired a Ford Transit Luton van from Hunts, telling them we needed it to shift furniture because they didnae like to rent to bands. The first thing we did was disconnect the speedometer cable so that they couldnae tell how far we'd travelled when we took it back. At an extra ten pence per mile, we just couldnae afford the mileage charge. That done, we set off. When we reached the port of Helensburgh, on the other side of Glasgow, we stopped to buy snacks and smokes. We all waited in and around the van while Roni jumped out of the back to get the supplies. Caught up in conversation and camaraderie, we all got back in, not realising till we arrived at the venue that Roni wasnae with us. The Luton van had a driver's compartment completely separated from the back, so when we'd resumed our journey, the guys in the front of the van thought Roni had got in the back and those in the back thought he'd got back in up front. After hanging around for a while waiting for us to go back for him, Roni decided we weren't coming back. Luckily he managed to hitch two lifts to Ardrishaig and arrived with just half an hour spare to set up.

They liked us in the small village so we went back another time. Again, the trip was not to pass without incident. After the Saturday-night gig we indulged ourselves a bit and eventually hit the winding, coastal road in the early hours of Sunday morning. Our driver that night fell asleep at the wheel and drove into a stone wall, which was lucky because if he'd swerved the other way he'd have driven us all off the road and into the sea. Not knowing how far we were from civilisation, there was nothing for us to do but wait in the van until the morning. We consoled ourselves with a couple of leftover joints, chatted, dozed and waited for the sun to come up.

In the morning, we set off in the rain to Inveraray, which we guessed was about two miles ahead. We arrived at about ten o'clock. Back then the pubs didnae open on a Sunday (even in Scotland), so we had to wait for the local hotel bar to open up. To pass the time, and in true decadent rock 'n' roll style, we took to cruising the streets chanting 'Sex! Drugs! Booze!' over and over again. As we cruised, we found a garage and arranged to get the van fixed. Then all we could do was wait in the bar and, with the exception of the driver, get pissed again.

We embraced the rock 'n' roll lifestyle for all it was worth. The sex, drugs and booze we sang of in Inveraray were on tap.

At a gig at Rosyth naval base, we were given a table in the audience and a bottle of rum, which was emptied before we staggered on stage. There was always free booze after a gig, too.

In July '73, we were booked to play two nights at a swimming pool in Dunbar, east of Edinburgh, on the coast. At the second gig, after the show, we decided to take advantage of the facility. Because I hadnae been wearing any pants under my tight stage trews, I had nothing to wear in the pool, but figured that no one would be able to see anything under the water. After a wee while, this cute girlie came into the pool and we got chatting. She had been completely unaware that I was naked, and I had forgotten, until I moved in for a snog . . . at which point she swore, dragged herself out of the pool and ran for her life. I decided to pursue, shouting, 'Come back! I only want to talk to you!' It wasnae until I'd run a good few yards after her that the other guys pointed out that my prominent arousal clearly went against what I was saying!

Another time, after a gig, we'd escorted several young ladies back to the van. We were very virile, but not insatiable, and once they'd let us have our wicked way we basically just lay back and let them get on with whatever they wanted to do. Alan, presented with another bare arse but bored with the proceedings by now, took out a pen and drew a big smiley face on the girl's cheeks instead. The rest of us couldnae stop laughing for ages.

Experimentation was rife. We tried anything and everything – because we could. One time there were the five band members, a snake, a dozen or so rats and masks involved . . .

No, hold on . . . that wasnae with Threshold, that was later, when I was with another band. The snake was a particularly venomous, constricting species and there were far more rats than that. And the buggers in masks are still concealed.

While Threshold was going from strength to strength and shagging for Scotland, I was being fired from countless jobs for being too tired to show up because of our gig and après-gig activities. Eventually, I landed a job at a paper mill for the princely sum of £70 a week – a hell of a wage in 1972. Sixty-nine quid of it was danger money. My job was to stand next to the production line watching for breaks in the stream of paper as it was pressed through massive high-speed rollers like washing mangles. If there was a tear in the paper, I had to dive in there with a knife and slice it all the way across, then dive out again, being careful not to get sucked in and crushed by the rollers . . .

My big salary meant that I could help to buy more stuff for Threshold, like a PA and our own van. That meant our overheads went down and we actually started to realise a bit of a profit. Our bookings were still increasing, and agents and managers were starting to enquire about signing us up. We had never had a manager because there didnae appear to be any need for one – we were getting plenty of gigs on our own and we didnae want to have to spread the little bit of money we were making any further.

We did consider it once or twice, though. One of my brothers' mates, Rab, was a candidate, but only because he had his own van and would've saved us van-hire costs. Although personally I dinnae recall the event, some of the other guys reckon we approached Tam Paton.

Jon Gillam says he remembers going to see him. Apparently Threshold were told that they would have to change their image, cut their hair and be generally more clean-cut to make any serious progress. Worse than that, he wanted us to stop playing rock and move to pop. Obviously no one liked the idea because we carried on as we were, manager-less, randy and free, while our profits got bigger and bigger. A lot of my share was spent on going to see concerts by Bowie, Pink Floyd, Led Zep and anyone else who I might learn something from. If there was a big name playing in Edinburgh and I had enough cash, I was there.

Those were great times. Threshold was a surreal, enjoyable apprenticeship and I was living the dream. And for the benefit of the disbelievers out there who feel the need to question the success of my first band, Alex has documentation which shows that over 7 months in 1973, we played 54 gigs and earned nearly £1,200 – so there!

In November of 1973, we had another gig in Dunbar. As usual I was wearing really cool gear that my dad had made for me – on this occasion, a pair of bright-yellow flares, made of stretch nylon fabric and measuring 36 inches at the hem. My waist only measured 24 inches, so I probably could have put them on over my head!

Once again I was following the Scottish tradition of not wearing underwear. Yellow stretch flares looked much better without a visible panty line.

At the time, I thought I looked the dog's bollocks. I didnae much care that most people were finding it hard not to look at mine. I didnae know, on stage that night, that one member of the audience in particular was especially drawn to those tight trousers. After the show, Tam Paton and Eric Faulkner came to see me backstage.

shang-a-lang
shang-a-lang

46

The Bay City Rollers . . .
Coming Together

This would seem like a good place to tell the story of the Bay City Rollers before I joined them.

Alan and Derek Longmuir, born in 1948 and 1951 respectively, formed a band while they were still at school and called it The Saxons. Later they changed the name to the Bay City Rollers. Legend has it that the new name came about by sticking a pin in a map of the USA. Alan said the first few attempts didnae sound right (Arkansas was one of the unlucky recipients of their little pricks), and it took a few more tries to land on Bay City, Michigan, or Bay City, Utah, depending on whose version of events you subscribe to.

Meanwhile, the aforementioned Mr Thomas Paton of Prestonpans, the son of a potato merchant, was playing with what he called an orchestra but was really a big band at the Edinburgh Palais de Danse. Before his foray into show business, he'd been in the army and had then worked for his dad's firm, where his main responsibilities were driving the lorry and transporting tubers – not just shovelling a few from here to there, but carrying a hundredweight sack on each shoulder. If you've ever tried lifting a hundredweight of anything, you'll have an idea just how heavy that is and what sort of strength 'Tattie Tam', as they called him, needed to shift it. He's never lost the potato connection, which proves that you can take a Tam out of a potato field, but you can never take the potato field out of a Tam.

He'd once been in a seven-piece band called The Crusaders, which if nothing else gave him the chance to have a chat one day with the legendary Brian Epstein, manager of The Beatles. At least that's his story – although coming from a guy who can embellish to the extent that he does, it's possible the meeting never happened.

He says The Crusaders had entered some sort of talent contest and got through to the finals, where Epstein was on the panel of judges. Having come almost last in the contest, Tam cornered Epstein after the event and asked what the band was doing wrong. Epstein allegedly replied that their music was all right, but that they lacked image. It's this short interchange that Tam says set him on the road to creating a supergroup.

Whatever, if Tam *did* meet him and *did* use his advice with The Crusaders in an attempt to make them successful, it didnae work. The band sank without trace and Tam found solace at the Palais, where his days with the orchestra were also numbered. Dance bands were dying out and lively young rock 'n' roll bands were coming in. At other venues, dancing to records instead of bands became the preference. For Tam it was decision time; his career path had reached a dead-end and he needed a new occupation. Luckily, the Palais management asked him to take responsibility for booking the bands that would appear at the venue. Given the chance of retaining his place in the showbiz world, and not wanting to return to humping tatties, Tam gratefully accepted the position. He'd already been dabbling a bit with young bands and relished the new role.

In 1975, Tam Paton published his story, entitled *The Bay City Rollers*, in collaboration with Michael Wale, a respected music journalist. In that classic tale, he recalls that in the late '60s, 14-year-old Alan Longmuir would go and see him at the Palais, and that they would chat occasionally. During these chats, Alan was always trying to persuade Tam to go and listen to his group. In other accounts, Tam says he was constantly pestered by both Longmuir brothers and that he turned down their requests for him to be their manager because he was too busy.

Alan was not 14 when Tam first met him, but if Tam had given

Al's real age in his story, there was a risk that someone would spot that between those first meetings and publication of his book, he had unceremoniously hacked five years off both Alan and Derek's ages. This he did because he thought they were too old for the band by then and that their fans wouldnae love them any more if they knew their true ages. This is just one example of Tam Paton's tendency to flirt with fiction, justified later – like so many other 'facts' – in the name of PR and 'in the interest of [. . .] careers'. Having finally given in to Alan and Derek's constant demands to hear their band, which at the time was fronted by a guy called Nobby Clark, Tam hired them to play at the Palais. He decided they had potential and started to go with them to gigs. He appears to contradict himself in his book on this issue as well. On one page, he refers to the Rollers' first gig 'under his management', just one week after 'taking over'. Two paragraphs further on, he imparts that after the gig, the band asked him if he would like to be their manager . . .

The Rollers' big break came in 1971, when the boss of Bell Records, Dick Leahy, happened to be in Edinburgh one night having missed his plane back to London. At least, that's the story Tam always tells. The reason was that a guy called Chas Peate had seen the Rollers and suggested to Dick that he might be interested in them. Bell Records, owned by Columbia Pictures in America, was an important and successful label who'd recently signed Gary Glitter. 'Rock 'n' Roll Part I' and 'Rock 'n' Roll Part II' had catapulted Glitter to the top of the charts and in their blissful ignorance, everyone thought he was wonderful. No one knew that Glitter/Gadd was in fact a sad tosser who liked little girls, and whose name would later be used as Cockney rhyming slang for the rectum. Later, Bell got David Cassidy, and also Showaddywaddy.

As Dick was on his way up to Edinburgh, Tam was signing the band to a production company run by two guys called Tony Calder and David Apps. All was not lost for Bell Records – Dick saw the band, liked them, and did a deal with the production company instead. Calder and Apps were paid a £5,000 advance. At the same time, an inducement letter was signed by all parties that stated that if for any reason the production company ceased to exist, the contract would continue between the band and the record company. This was standard procedure in deals of that nature and was actually designed to protect the band. It did just that in this case because within a matter of weeks, Calder and Apps's firm had gone into liquidation. The Rollers still had a contract, now directly with Bell, but the £5,000 advance had gone down the tubes along with the production company.

Bell Records assigned the Rollers to one of the hottest record producers of the day – Jonathan King, who'd had a hit or two in the '60s, including 'Everyone's Gone To The Moon'. King recorded the Rollers' first single, a cover of The Gentrys' 1965 US Top 10 hit 'Keep On Dancing'. The song had originally been recorded by The Avantis in 1963. It took six months to make the charts, but make the charts it did, ending up at No. 9.

Tam Paton, overcome with the success, hired a London agent – Barry Perkins – who would later become his partner (in the business sense of the word). As was often the case with Tam, this was premature, because the Rollers' next single, 'We Can Make Music' – recorded at the same sessions as 'Keep On Dancing' – failed to make an impact. Jonathan King lost interest, saying that he wasnae the man to continue the band's success. What he probably meant was he'd not wanted to waste any more of his songs on the Rollers' B-sides (he'd had 'Alright' on 'Keep On Dancing' and 'Jenny' on 'Music') if they weren't going to make him any money. Bell Records didnae care anyway because they didnae like any of the other material he was putting forward for the group. King, of course, went on to enjoy a hugely successful career, notching up a few more hits for himself such as the horrendous 'Una Paloma Blanca', and lopsidedly presenting his own TV series on US entertainment.

King and the Rollers sometimes crossed paths later, usually at his celeb-ridden parties, if that's what you'd call them. The first time we went to a party, I thought it was funny that there seemed to be lots of young lads but not many lassies around and it didnae take too long to work out why. I used to stand firmly with my back against the wall and observe, and assumed that that sort of thing was normal in the music biz.

Mr King was found guilty in November 2001 of various acts of indecency and attempted buggery against under-age boys dating back over 20 years. None of us were surprised. It was only ever a matter of time before one of his conquests summoned up the courage to say something. Jonathan's pal, Chris Denning, a former Radio One DJ, had been jailed in the Czech Republic for four and a half years a few months earlier for having had sexual contact with under-age boys. Somehow, he managed to remain anonymous in the papers initially, but we all knew who he was.

When the first King victim went to the police, it didnae take long for the press to rediscover his Bay City Rollers connections and my office was inundated with calls. After the first few, we recorded a message on the answering machine stating that the Rollers had worked with King before I had joined them and I therefore had no comment to make. We left it switched on till it all died down. Then, some dick called Deniz Corday, who used to run a kids' disco called the Hop in Walton-on-Thames, Surrey, where King used to prowl, pissed me *right* off. Interviewed in his local newspaper, he stated that the Rollers were frequent guests at his disco, and that our first No. 1, 'Bye Bye Baby', had been released only because the kids there had picked it from a series of songs we'd done live there one night. Horseshit. What was so annoying was that I would never have known about that article, associating me (however loosely) with that slimeball King, had I not had a mate who lived near Walton who happened to see the paper.

In the space of a few pages, we've come across three convicted paedophiles – Gary Glitter, Jonathan King and Chris Denning. That's three I can talk about. What about the others? One of my pals from the '70s who worked closely with various important figures in the industry, says that although it was generally suspected that whatever King was into wasnae quite kosher, there were others of equally high profile, and higher, who were less than discreet about their perverted activities. Just after King was sentenced to seven years, the *News Of The World* (it *must* be true!) reported that they'd had access to a police dossier which contained details of another load of them. The newspaper wasnae allowed to give names but described some of the more significant ones. One was 'a member of [a] world-famous pop band whose bizarre clothes have been copied by die-hard young fans . . . [who] figured on thousands of posters on teenagers' bedroom walls'. How many people read that and automatically assumed it was a Bay City Roller? At least it says 'have been copied', instead of 'were copied', which makes it sound like this is a member of a more recent band than the Rollers.

The thing is, as long as it's one person's word against another's, and you might end up losing your hoose if the other guy's got a load of wedge and a great libel lawyer, these buggers will keep getting away with it. As people move on and get themselves new lives, they bury what happened, and they're less and less likely to dredge up the shit from years ago – so again, the nonces stay safe and pontificate about laws needing to change so that victims who finally find the courage to act, years later, have no case. Respect to the guy who was the first to report King, so far down the line.

Back to those squeaky-clean Rollers.

Despite their hit single, they were still massively in debt. Tam wrote that after 'Keep On Dancing', they actually still owed the record company money as a result of losing their advance in the transfer deal. The band were now desperate for cash and forced to take any gigs they could get, mostly at cabarets and working men's clubs throughout Scotland and the north of England.

It must have been around this time that Tam remembered Brian Epstein's words of wisdom. In an interview with Tam, published on the Internet in 2000, he describes the moment he saw what Epstein had meant about image. Having watched the young Rollers in action at the Palais de Danse, before he got involved with them, he'd 'realised the popularity was due to how they looked and how tight they wore their trousers'. He'd probably had a lot of fun researching the theory, studying the cut of the fabric around the groin area, the effects of light and vibration and other techniques that could be used to exaggerate the natural contours of the male form, and how that might result in increased record sales. He was obviously still hung up on that theory when he and Eric came to see Threshold in Dunbar. In fact, I've often wondered whether he would have offered me the job if I'd just been wearing the jeans and T-shirts we used to wear before my dad had gone to work on the stage gear . . .

Tam set about establishing the all-important image for his boys – to capitalise on their chart success and bring them more. He decked them out in satin suits, bow ties and frilly shirts, fetchingly teamed now and again with *see-through* trousers – the obvious conclusion to his research!

Maybe if the Rollers had been playing to hen-night audiences and in gay bars, Tam's choice of look for the Rollers might have got better results, but as it was, the effect was catastrophic. For some reason, the satin and frills didnae do much to win over the clientele of the down-to-earth clubs they were then performing in. Sometimes the guys were even physically attacked because of their 'pretty boy' looks. That in itself was bad enough, but Tam's first attempts at establishing an image actually wiped out the positive effect of their Top 10 hit. Around the time of 'Keep On Dancing', they'd had a certain amount of kudos. There were very few real bands in Scotland at the time and even fewer that had been in the charts. The Rollers had civic pride. They were looked up to by Scottish kids who badly needed something, anything, to aspire to. Tam's frilly shirts took that respect and squashed it. For the first time, people began to question the band's sexuality.

Tam put together other plans to move the band forward. Despite being so badly in the red, he decided to add to the debts by having hundreds of photographs printed. With these he bombarded the *New Musical Express* (*NME*), other magazines and DJs. He also sent more photographs and newsletters to fan club members, most of whom had lost interest because the band weren't playing the venues where they could see them any more. Then he asked Bell Records to pay the bills and was surprised that they wouldnae, saying that having had no part in the decision to carry out the promotional activity concerned, they couldnae be expected to fund it afterwards. Tam minced off and moaned that he wasnae treated like a real manager by Dick Leahy and that he was resented in London – a place he despised – because he was the manager of a group from Scotland. Dick doesnae know why Tam felt that way, and had nothing against him at all. 'He was a bit eccentric, but he was all right.'

More than any publicity gimmick, the Rollers needed songs to sing. With Jonathan King gone AWOL (probably cruising South London in his Rolls), former BBC employees Ken Howard and Alan Blaikley were brought in to try and save the Rollers. Howard and Blaikley had hit the big time with a band called the Honeycombs in 1964. They'd a hit with a song called 'Have I The

Right', which was later covered by a glam-type one-hit-wonder band called the Dead End Kids, also from Edinburgh, in the '70s. They also managed and wrote for Dave Dee, Dozy, Beaky, Mick and Tich, who were much more successful with 13 consecutive chart hits in four years including 'Bend It', probably the band's most remembered hit. After that, they took over and rearranged the Herd, promoting a certain Peter Frampton from guitar to lead vocals.

For the Rollers they wrote 'Mañana', which won a song contest in Luxembourg but failed to chart at home. By the time 'Mañana' was released, Eric Faulkner and John Devine had been brought into the band, to replace Neil Henderson and Archie Marr. Eric came to the Rollers from a band called Kip, and before that he'd been in one called Sugar. Also a Sugar member was my former Threshold bandmate, Alan Wright, who recalls the small bubbles that used to accumulate at the sides of Eric's mouth more clearly than any musical talent Eric may have had.

It was this continuing high turnover of band members that was the most important factor in the establishment of a dictatorial regime, the like of which had never before been seen in the music industry.

Countless Rollers had been and gone, usually, according to Tam, because they wanted to concentrate on their school-work or, more often, because they wanted to spend more time with 'some female'. Realising that it couldnae go on, Tam made a set of rules which the band had to obey – 'Special rules designed to govern their conduct and prevent the mass exodus that had plagued previous line-ups', it says in Johnny Rogan's *Starmakers and Svengalis* (Futura, London, 1988).

The effectiveness of those rules is well documented. In the same book, songwriter Ken Howard remembers that the Rollers never swore or drank in Paton's presence, and describes an incident which demonstrates how he, Paton, dealt with the band. The guys were mucking about in a swimming-pool when Tam appeared and told them to go straight to bed:

> They immediately stopped and went off to bed as meek as
> lambs. I have seen many groups over the years but never
> anything like that. Tam was a Svengali, a Scottish patriarchal

figure. The Rollers were zombie-like. It was almost as if they had a switch in their brain. Whenever you'd ask them to do something they'd come to a halt and direct you to Tam.

When Ellis Allen wrote *The Bay City Rollers* (Granada Publishing/Panther Books, London, 1975), an early account of the Rollers' rise to superstardom, he quoted an early band member, Dave Paton, as having said a few years later that he had left the group because he 'couldnae take any more', and that he had learnt a lot from the Rollers, but that it was 'nothing musical'. Allen took this to mean that he had discovered more about the pop business itself than music, but I suspect something different.

Here's another quote from Dave, worth a moment of analysis: 'We know the Rollers fairly well and they're OK . . . tell them we've written a song they could use. It's called "Boys Will Be Boys"'.

Looking at this and Dave's previous comment together, maybe there were things he might have wanted to share about his time in the Rollers but didnae feel able to at that time. What could he have meant? Why did so many other early Rollers leave the band with such alarming regularity? Finding out what Dave Paton was trying to say and the meaning of the 'Boys' song might help. I tried contacting him to ask these questions, but he didnae want to talk.

You'd need to track down other early Rollers such as Neil Henderson, Archie Marr, Dave Pettigrew, Eric Manclark, Greg and Mike Ellison, Keith Norman and many others to verify the real reasons why they left the band. This should be easy to do, because almost anyone you speak to in Edinburgh will know someone who was once a Bay City Roller, or has at least slept with one. I think it's pretty unlikely, though, that any of them would really open up even if they wanted to after all this time. Maybe a *Trisha* special – 'I was a teenage Bay City Roller' – would help!

To the best of my knowledge, only three former Rollers stayed in the music industry – Billy Lyall and Dave Paton went on to form the band Pilot and had hits with catchy little numbers called 'January' and 'Magic', among others. Sadly, Billy Lyall died of an Aids-related illness in 1989. Dave reinvented himself as serious musician David Paton and played on the hugely successful Alan Parsons Project albums before joining Elton John's band. Archie

Marr left the Rollers to join Middle Of The Road (one big hit – 'Chirpy Chirpy Cheep Cheep').

With the rules and rod of iron in place, the Rollers continued trudging the weary road to real fame and fortune.

Ever the financial wizard, Tam decided that the band's third flop with 'Mañana' provided a good excuse to blow a few hundred quid on a holiday for him and the boys in Europe, so off they went to Spain. When they came back, they found out that Dick Leahy had appointed two new writer/producers to work with the Bay City Rollers. They were his old friends Bill Martin and Phil Coulter, who had written numerous Eurovision Song Contest hits, including Sandi Shaw's 'Puppet On A String', Cliff Richard's 'Congratulations', and Dana's 'All Kinds Of Everything' – a very impressive catalogue. By this time, Bell Records had moved to Mayfair, next door to Mickie Most's RAK Records. RAK had signed loads of big names – Sweet, Mud and Suzi Quatro to name a few. Most of their material was written by the massively successful partnership of Nicky Chinn and Mike Chapman, and Bill Martin and Phil Coulter told Dick they too could do what Chinnichap were doing. Dick's response was, 'I have just the band for you . . .'

Bill 'n' Phil clearly had what it takes to pen a catchy little number. Dick Leahy had it sussed when he put the duo onto the Rollers. The combination was a sure-fire winner. How soul-destroying it must have been for the guys when their fourth single, Martin and Coulter's 'Saturday Night', failed miserably. How ironic that the very same single later went to No. 1 in the US and is probably the most well-remembered Bay City Rollers hit there today.

By now it was June 1973, two years since 'Keep On Dancing' had charted. Bell Records were on the verge of giving up, as were several members of the Rollers. Martin and Coulter's next attempt was called 'Remember (Sha-La-La)'. Nobby Clark, still the lead singer, recorded the song, saw it released and promptly decided it was time to quit. He agreed to stick around, though, until a replacement lead vocalist could be found.

The reasons given as to why Nobby left at such a crucial time are varied. One theory says that he was pissed off about not being allowed to have his own material on the flip side of any of the singles, let alone on the A-side. It was Eric who later used to fight with Tam over B-sides and as far as I know Nobby never penned a line. Others will say that it was Nobby's frustration at Bell Records' insistence that session musicians were used on the Rollers' recordings, instead of the band members, that drove him to quit. Given that it would still have been *his* voice that was heard, I think that one's unlikely. The reason with most weight behind it is that, as Tam might say, 'he wanted to spend more time with some female'. Eric has since said that Nobby left to get married, and that he, Eric, did not think this was a wise or well-timed move. Apparently, the young lady in receipt of Nobby's attentions was 'an out-and-out groupie' and that there was 'no way . . . their relationship [would] last after he left the group'.

Anyway, he quit.

Nobby's departure badly affected poor Derek, who by now was also about to call it a day, primarily because he could see no way of ever being able to repay the band's mounting debt, which now stood at over £7,000. Meanwhile, Tam and Eric went out to look for a new lead singer with the right kind of bulge in his trousers, a perfectly proportioned god of a boy . . .

When Tam appeared backstage on that fateful night and introduced himself and Eric, I remember thinking first of all how big he was. Built like the proverbial brick shitehoose, he was strong and scary – nobody in their right mind would mess with him. Eric's presence was very much overshadowed by this man-mountain, but I remember thinking he was a good-looking geezer who looked after his hair, and he seemed friendly enough.

The conversation that took place between us wasnae a lengthy one. They congratulated me on my performance and Tam asked me if I'd like to join the Bay City Rollers. I said I'd think about it and get back to him.

You might imagine that I would have been whacking one off about the chance to join the Rollers. Not quite. I was pleased to have been asked – dinnae get me wrong – but remember that at this point the group owed large sums of money and was on the verge of splitting up. The Rollers wouldnae have been high on the list of bands I'd have wanted to join. They'd had their hit, done nothing since, and they dressed funny. In Tam's book, though, you can read about how I used to constantly pester him for a job with the Rollers and how, like the Longmuirs, he finally made my dream come true.

The day after the meeting with Tam and Eric, I went to the Radio Edinburgh studios and discussed Tam's offer with Neil Ross. Taking the job would mean slashing my income from £70 to £10 a week, but, as Neil pointed out, I would have no expenses to pay with that £10. Neil's main concern was the frequency with which the Rollers' band members came and went and the reasons why that was the case. He didnae want to see me abandon the promising future I had with Threshold only to be cast off by Tam Paton a few weeks down the line if I didnae do as I was told. I decided I would need a contract, and a chastity belt, to cover myself.

I also talked to my family, especially Roni. Roni felt this was an opportunity not to be missed: whereas Threshold was definitely an up-and-coming band, the Rollers were already there – if only in the sense that they still had a recording contract. However good Threshold were, there was just no guarantee that they would one day have a hit record. Roni said it would be daft to wait around maybe for years for something major to happen and miss other opportunities in the meantime.

All things considered, I decided that I had to join the Bay City Rollers. It would make me a professional artist. Whether the Rollers went on to have more hits or not, it didnae matter. Even if they folded six weeks or six months down the line, I'd still be a professional, and a professional singer was what I wanted to be more than anything else in the world.

Before I told Tam I would accept his offer, he asked me to step in at the last minute for Nobby at a gig at an American air base in Perth – a venue where the band had played many times. Tam picked me up from my house and we drove to the gig, where I met the Longmuir brothers, John Devine, and the roadie, Jake Duncan, for the first time. I was relieved to find that they were just a normal bunch of Edinburgh kids, just like me.

I'll never forget that first gig. Talk about in at the deep end – I didnae know any of the words of a lot of the songs we were to play, and there was no time to learn them, so Jake had to stick bits of paper with the lyrics on all over the stage. The improvisation worked well. Tam was pleased, and no one in the audience realised

I was inventing karaoke. Another challenge I had to deal with on that first night were the Nobby fans, the girls who hated me in the same way that Alan Longmuir's followers would detest his replacement several years later. I think they would have been nicer to someone who'd killed their pet dog. They showed their disgust at Nobby's sudden departure and this skinny wee kid who'd been brought in to fill his shoes by spitting at me throughout the set. You'll remember I have some previous for fighting back when I'm spat at, but with the culprits in this case being 'ladies' (with extreme facial disfigurements), I managed to control myself.

The set that night was quite similar to the kind of thing I had been doing with Threshold – covers of rocky chart hits. One exception was Marvin Gaye's 'I Heard It Through The Grapevine'. This was a song I hadnae performed before, so the lyrics were stuck on one of the pillars on the stage. I was able to take a rest while Eric played his 'jig' on the violin – the very same jig that he would perform at the Edinburgh Millennium Festival more than 25 years later – and swot up on the lyrics for the next number. 'Keep On Dancing' and 'Mañana' were in there, too. The audience knew all the songs we played and, with the exception of the Nobbettes, they seemed to enjoy themselves.

On the way home after the gig, I was pleased with myself for having coped with knowing hardly any lyrics and for being the consummate professional when spat on. I decided to formally accept the position of lead vocalist with the Bay City Rollers.

Within minutes I had my first-ever altercation with Eric Faulkner. He told me that, as a member of the group, I must not have a girlfriend.

I was mad as hell.

'Who the fuck do you think you're talking to, ya wee fucking Grangemouth poof? Step out of the car and I'll slap your arse! No fucker who puts on that amount of make-up and eyeliner is going to tell me what to do!'

Actually I wasnae quite *that* mad. I simply pointed out that I didnae see it was important whether I'd a girlfriend, boyfriend or dogfriend. I told Eric that in any case he had no right to tell me what I could or couldnae do as he wasnae the manager of the band.

The next morning Tam came to see me at home and clarified the girlfriend issue. He explained that if I were to have a girlfriend she should preferably not be seen out with me and should certainly never be mentioned to the press, as it might make me seem less accessible to potential fans. Put across in this way, with reasoning, it was more acceptable, though I still thought they were all living in a dream world if they thought the press or anyone else would be interested in who I was seeing. But as far as Tam was concerned, we had to eat, drink and think like the pop stars he was convinced we were destined to become.

With that first confrontation sorted, I felt positive. I found myself walking around with a sly grin and a smug feeling. I took pride in the thought that I was now a professional singer. The light at the end of that tunnel out of Edinburgh wasnae a car's headlights coming to run me down, but a real escape route.

With hindsight, standing up for myself so early on was the smartest thing I could have done (well, I could have run like fuck and never looked back, which would probably have been even smarter). I think my reaction to Eric showed Tam Paton that for me being a Bay City Roller meant a lot, but it wasnae the be-all and end-all. Right from the start, I was the gobby one who had the balls to defend himself.

Alan and Derek (and to a lesser extent Eric and John) had been through long, hard times with the band and would do anything to keep it together and make it successful. I think this is what gave Tam the upper hand with the four of them and made them accept the rules and conditions he placed on them. I cannae think of any other reason why they all just did as they were told without question, apart from the possibility that there was some real physical deficiency in their vertebral structure.

I still sometimes wonder why Tam didnae just tell me to fuck off when I told him I didnae want to be in the Rollers. Maybe he realised that he finally had a near perfect line-up of bulges and, under pressure from Bell Records, he didnae want to delay any longer by having to find yet another vocalist. Maybe he thought that he would deal with me and my attitude later on, but as things progressed I dinnae think there was ever a right time to do that – not until a lot further down the road.

The next thing I had to do was tell the Threshold guys I was leaving the band. This was going to be hard because we were starting to earn £30 a night, versus the £4 or £5 we'd got in the beginning.

The fact that Alan Wright had just left to fill a space in another of Tam's bands, Bilbo Baggins, should have made it easier for me. After all, I wasnae the first deserter. But it felt like I was driving the final nail into the coffin. Also, my behaviour towards Alan when he told us he was off was less than honourable, so I had hypocrisy to deal with too. Bilbo Baggins already had a record deal and I know any of us would have done the same given that opportunity, but when Alan told us he was leaving, I was mortified. The two of us had become really good mates and I'd felt let down and miserable. We'd had so many great times together and I reckon I felt as bad when he left the band as most people do when a relationship ends against their will. Even if we'd got a replacement for Alan, it wasnae ever going to be the same again. If I'd known that a couple of weeks later I'd be in the same position myself, those few days would probably have been a lot more bearable, but at the time I was so pissed off with Alan I just didnae speak to him again.

When I started writing notes for this book, I realised I'd forgotten a shit load more than I thought I had, so I took myself back home to do some research. Roni and Hari could remember bits and pieces but not enough, so I asked the *Edinburgh Evening News* to help me track down the former Threshold members. It took less than a week to find them all, and a month later we all met up again at the trendy Point Hotel on Bread Street, a stone's throw from the Americana, where we had played so often. Before meeting the guys, I'd been apprehensive. It was 28 years since we'd been a band, and I didnae know what to expect. Maybe they resented the success I'd had (a weird trait of lots of Scots, if not all Britons). We met at six-thirty and, after a quick drink, we went to Calton Hill and reconstructed some ancient publicity shots that Jon Gillam had brought along. Then we went back to the hotel for a few more beers. I was relaxed and in a strange sort of way I felt immediately cleansed of all the other shite that had happened since I left the band – it was like we'd never been apart. At midnight, having spent nearly six hours reminiscing, drinking and having a really good time, I realised I'd had nothing to worry about – the guys were brilliant. I was so fired up I suggested that Threshold should think about a reunion tour in Scotland. There was also a fan event planned in Atlanta for the following June, and I asked them if they'd like to come to that with me, too. Everyone thought it was a great idea and before we knew it, the *Edinburgh Evening News* headlines were announcing a US tour. Sadly, the distance between our homes and other commitments made it impossible to get together and rehearse, but the guys carried on without me and are making music again.

So I'd cut loose from Threshold and was officially a Roller, so help me God. Almost immediately I found myself in London for the first time. Bell Records had got us an appearance on *Crackerjack*, a popular kids' TV show that went out every Friday at five o'clock. The request to appear had come at the last minute, so Jake rushed us down to London in the trusty van.

This was the winter of '73, and it seemed that most of the country was on strike. With unemployment topping one million for the first time, inflation at 18 per cent and with the miners having gone on strike the month before, a state of emergency had been declared. It was that bad.

The BBC had not escaped the power of the unions and, as a result of the TV workers' solidarity, some programmes were being recorded at the Shepherd's Bush Empire, a theatre near the Wood Lane headquarters and studios. When we arrived there, all keen and eager, we were told that more of the BBC workforce had gone on strike and that *Crackerjack* wouldnae be on that week. We generally sympathised with the workers but it didnae stop us being fucking gutted at Shepherd's Bush and we weren't very sympathetic at that precise moment. But luck, fate or whatever was on our side – just as we were about to turn round and leave to drive all the way back up to Scotland, a call for Tam came through at the theatre's stage door. They wanted us on *Top Of The Pops*, due to be recorded the day after next. We prayed the strike wouldnae get in the way of our biggest break so far.

'Remember' had been getting a fair bit of airplay. Radio Luxembourg made it a featured disc, which meant it was played every hour. People had started buying the record and we were hovering just outside the charts, which was what led to us being asked to appear on *Top Of The Pops*. Bands that appeared in that slot nearly always broke into the charts soon after.

Making an appearance on *TOTP* was not as straightforward as you might think. You didnae just show up and mime. This was the '70s and the unions reigned supreme. The Musicians' Union had managed to bring in a ruling that said that bands had to re-record their songs for television broadcast. So, although at that time most of the *TOTP* numbers were mimed (or 'lip-synced', as it's called today to sound more technical), they were at least lip-synced to specially recorded versions of the song.

I was taken to what appeared to be a derelict theatre somewhere between Trafalgar Square and the Thames to do the deed. This state-of-the-art recording facility consisted of a Neumann microphone and a 60-watt light bulb. At least, that's all I could see. It wasnae a bit like REL in Edinburgh, which was the only other studio I'd ever been in.

Dick Leahy was there.

Being in that creepy old wrecked theatre full of shadows and strange men ogling me made me feel a bit nervous. I felt the weight of responsibility for the first time in my life. I continually cleared my throat, fiddled with my fingernails and generally ponced about to hide my nerves. At the same time I was high on adrenaline and excitement, which has to be one of the best natural highs you can get. I was uncomfortable but exhilarated; paradoxically petrified and euphoric.

Before I knew it I was in front of the mike, 'phoned up, and ready to go. A nice little catchy intro, backing vocals to remind me what the song was called, and I shimmy-shamied into 'Remember'.

I'd always been one for poring over lyrics trying to guess the hidden meaning, but it didnae take long to work out there wasnae any in that song!

So there I was, on a dirty old stage with my mike and my greasy 60-watt light bulb, my knees shaking so much that when I started singing I found I had developed a fast vibrato that would do Feargal Sharkey proud. Apparently Dick wasnae bothered by the strange sound. Afterwards, he told me that Nobby had the same vibrato and he was relieved that the two recordings of the number would sound similar. Obviously Nobby thought so too, because years later he said that on the Rollers' first *Top Of The Pops* appearance, I was miming to *his* voice.

There was more singing to be done before we went to mime

63

'Remember' for *TOTP*. It was off to Mayfair Studios for me.

I was less nervous having got the *TOTP* recording out of the way, which meant that I could pay more attention to my surroundings and what was happening. Now these were *proper* studios, more like REL but bigger and better equipped, and I was relieved that all London studios weren't like the derelict theatre.

Knowing that I would be singing into a microphone previously spattered with the spittle of Eric Clapton and Marc Bolan was almost too much for my wee head to take in. The Mayfair Studios had been used by all the big names – hit after hit after hit had been recorded and mixed right there on South Molton Street. Later, after Mayfair had waved goodbye to the Rollers and the likes of the band Kenny, Hello and Bucks Fizz, they went on to look after top names throughout the '80s and '90s. Midge Ure (with both Slik and Ultravox), Kate Bush and Tina Turner all made hits at Mayfair.

When I got there, I was greeted by Phil Coulter, who was in charge of production that day. I relished being in the presence of a real songwriter; a songsmith who wrote mega successful songs; a songwriter who had written songs that I now had to sing before him. Phil was a kind, gentle, softly spoken Irishman and he put me at ease straightaway.

The agenda that day was to re-record the vocal for 'Remember' yet again, and to attempt 'Shang-A-Lang', which was intended to be the follow-up single. The priority was to get the new version of 'Remember' out in the shops pretty damn quick. It was selling and selling but the lead singer on the single was no longer in the band! Literally as soon as I finished singing, the tape was couriered off to the record factory so that my version could be pressed and Nobby could be efficiently replaced with the sleeker, smoother model.

With 'Shang-A-Lang' done and dusted faster than anyone had dared hope, we were left with studio time to spare. By then, the other half of Martin/Coulter had arrived, like a bull in a china shop, and suggested we should re-record 'Saturday Night'. It seemed to me there was little point in doing that because the song had already been released – and flopped. It had also been recorded by Tam's other band, Bilbo Baggins, the band which Alan Wright had dumped Threshold for. We did it anyway, and thanks to Bill Martin jumping around, stamping his feet, clapping his hands and screaming out the 'S-A-T-U-R-D-A-Y . . . NIGHT!' chorus, which resulted in the song's affrettando, anthemic quality, the record later broke the States for us. It got to No. 1 there and ensured that many more people would make many more millions out of the Bay City Rollers.

Thanks, Phil and Bill, for the great memories.

shang-a-lang
shang-a-lang

We Sang 'Shang-A-Lang'

Next stop: *Top Of The Pops*. We'd had about 48 hours to think about what to wear for our first national television spot.

Luckily for me, it had been decided that the hideous cabaret look had to go by the time I joined the Rollers. They had a new look which was better but really nothing special. It was basically a street look mucked around with a bit.

In Scotland, a retro Mod craze had just ended and the kids' clothes were made up of a weird mix of Mod and skinhead influences, but as well as that there was a heavy-metal element. Taking a bit from each look, the mixed-up kids around Edinburgh – some long-haired, some crew-cutted – were wearing faded Levis that had to have been bleached and slashed a bit. They also had to be shorter than normal, so that when you wore them with a pair of Dr. Marten's boots, other kids could see how far the boots came up your legs and how many laces you had. The higher your laces, the cooler you were. On the top half we wore braces over a Ben Sherman short-sleeved shirt.

We took this trend and exaggerated it by getting some flared trousers and shortening them to mid-calf length. The DMs were substituted with softer, friendlier baseball boots, or platform boots from the King's Road, as worn by any other glam rock star of the day worth his salt. The V-neck skinny-rib sweaters we wore at the beginning were knitted for us by my mum and other relatives of the band.

Bill Martin decided this mish-mash of clothing wouldnae do for *Top Of The Pops*. He had us all decked out in red-and-white American college-style sweatshirts, each with a different team-member number. These were supposed to be our ages, but as Derek ended up with 41 and Alan with 5, someone – presumably Tam – clearly didn't agree with that idea, probably because he didn't want people to know that Alan was knocking on 26. We weren't too keen on the look but there was no time to argue. After *TOTP*, we went back to our skinny-rib jumpers, short trews and platform boots, and stuck with them until after our first album came out. Bill Martin hung on to the concept, though, and a year or so later Slik, also written for and produced by Bill 'n' Phil, appeared on the scene clad in white baseball gear.

Arriving at Shepherd's Bush, we were taken to our dressing-room and then straight to make-up where we were plastered with pancake and prettied up. Our hair was washed and blow-dried, teased and lacquered – the whole process took about five times as long as the filming, which was over and done with in a flash. We wanted to hang around and soak up the scene, but once we'd mimed our bit, it was back to the dressing-room to scrape off the make-up and then back out into the real world. Tam didn't think it was a good idea for us to mix with any degenerate rock musicians that might be lurking in the bar. We drove straight back up to Edinburgh in good time to see ourselves on our black-and-white tellies the following night.

There was a big shock from Tam a few days later when he announced that John Devine had quit and that a wee young gadge called Stuart John Wood – 'Woody' – was coming in. Tam said in his book that he knew John wanted to leave but kept it from the rest of us because morale was low. At the same time that we were all supposedly suffering from low morale, he said elsewhere in his book that the band had become optimistic and fired up by my presence and positive outlook. I think it's safe to assume that John's face just didn't fit any more and that Woody's chipmunky grin did. Plus, of course, Woody was a lot younger than John and therefore was much more suited to Tam's ideals.

Compared to the hassle and re-recordings that went on when I took over from Nobby, the switch from John to Woody was seamless and the line-up that would conquer the world was in place.

After *Top Of The Pops*, 'Remember' entered the charts on 9 February 1974 and climbed steadily. A couple of weeks later, the Rollers were back at Shepherd's Bush to record another appearance – this time, thankfully, minus the baseball shirts, and with 15-year-old Woody on board. By then, the TV workers' strike was off because the Labour party had just about wrested power from the Tories in a general election, so we could now do *Crackerjack* as well. After that, it seemed that every kids' TV show going was gagging for us – you name it, we were on it. I particularly remember doing *Lift Off With Ayshea*, because Ayshea had a fantastic smile and tits I couldnae keep my eyes off. *The Basil Brush Show* and *Blue Peter* never excited me in the same way.

All these TV spots helped 'Remember' on its way and into the Top 10. It finally came to rest at No. 6 and was in the charts for a total of 12 weeks. We got a silver disc for sales (which means more than 200,000 in the UK) – not bad going for my debut single.

Within four weeks of joining the Rollers, on £10 a week, I'd earned enough money to buy a tumble-drier for my mum for Christmas. She'd always wanted one and it was brilliant to be able to get it for her. Within eight weeks, Mum and Dad were the proud owners of the first fridge-freezer on the estate, and their youngest boy was the singer of a song in the 'hit parade', as Mum told her pals.

Life was good, but already the pressure was on to repeat the success of 'Remember' with our next single, 'Shang-A-Lang'.

'Shang-A-Lang' is actually an old Gaelic battle cry first used by Robert the Bruce. The rest of the song was about the hero's battles and his eventual triumph at Bannockburn in 1314, where Bruce 'ran with the gang' (his army), who would 'rip up' and 'lay down' their foes. At least that's the story that should have been put out when the single was released on April Fools' Day!

The song, in truth a nostalgic little number about rock 'n' roll and good times in the '50s, charted on 27 April. A week later, we were back on *TOTP*, which sent the song rocketing to No. 2. We were over the moon and on top of the world, to use just a couple of suitable clichés. We were presented with another silver disc each. I can't remember what I bought my mum and dad next.

By the time 'Shang-A-Lang' started to go down the charts after about eight weeks, we'd recorded our next two singles and their B-sides. Tam decided we all needed a holiday and we did – we were knackered. Tam, Woody and Derek blew a good few hundred (pounds, that is) in Jamaica. I went back to the south of France with my mum and dad, and it was good to not have to worry about grape-picking to finance my stay this time.

While we were all scattered around the globe recharging our batteries, Bell Records released our third Martin/Coulter number, which was called 'Summerlove Sensation'. It captured the imaginations of thousands of young girls all over the country as they dreamed of hunky fellas strolling hand-in-hand in the evening sun on a sandy beach; hunky fellas who bore little resemblance to the underdeveloped teenage misfits who sang the song! It was pure escapism – most of them would in reality be spending their 'vacation' (clever – cool American vibe!) stuck in a caravan in a muddy field overlooking stormy, grey seas if they had a holiday at all. By the end of July, 'Summerlove' was in the charts and we were soon all back in Shepherd's Bush once again. The song didn't fare as well as 'Shang-A-Lang' and only reached a disappointing No. 3. I started to worry that we might have had our day, but there'd been another TV workers' strike which had kept *TOTP* off the air for ten weeks. As a result, 'Summerlove' had only been on once – on a show hosted by The Osmonds who were in town that week and really maxing up the TV appearances. Tam told the press it was nice for the Rollers to be able to have a soft drink with the brothers after the show, as they didn't drink alcohol either. We were assured that this one performance, which was a bit overshadowed by our Mormon friends' domination of the media that week, was the only reason for the song not doing at least as well as 'Shang-A-Lang'. We relaxed a bit when we got our third silver disc and I bought my mum and dad a mansion and a matching Mercedes.

With three Top 10 hits under our belts, it was decided that it was time to make an album.

What should be on it?

The three hits to date, for a start. Everyone agreed on that, at least. Bill 'n' Phil wanted the next single, 'All Of Me Loves All Of

You', and all four B-sides, too. Most of the money to be made in the record industry is in the publishing, that is, the writing and registering of a song, so that you can earn royalties from that song forever. That's why Bill 'n' Phil wanted as many of their songs as possible on our album. As did Eric Faulkner, who was starting to get twitchy because he'd not been allowed any songs on B-sides so far. The compromise was six Martin/Coulter tracks, four Faulkner/Wood tracks and two covers. Somehow 'All Of Me' got left off, in favour of 'Saturday Night', Les-style.

So four of the tracks were already done and dusted. The eight remaining songs that would complete the album *Rollin'* were recorded over just four days in August. Bell wanted that album in the shops as soon as possible, if not sooner, so to speed things up, session musicians were brought in. We just showed up to record the lead vocals and backing vocals. Even with the help of the session musicians, it was still an impossible amount of time to make an album. It was basically a case of do it once and that's it.

Eric wasn't happy, despite the fact we had four songs on the album. Not being allowed to play his guitar for real was a serious kick in the teeth for him. It didn't matter about the three Top 10 hits and the cash that seemed to be flooding in; what was the point if he couldnae play his guitar? As far as he was concerned, we should have been given as much studio time as we (or he) needed to get it right.

He seemed to be directing his frustrations my way. There was a noticeable drop in the temperature of a room when one or the other of us walked in. Looks that could not only kill but would also torture and maim beforehand were thrown my way because my voice remained, whereas his guitar and even his backing vocals on some tracks weren't up to scratch. Often the backing vocals had to be re-recorded by me and Phil Coulter.

One of the two extra Martin/Coulter songs on *Rollin'* was a raunchy little number called 'Give It To Me Now', and I half expected Mary Whitehouse to come down on us like a ton of bricks for that one, even though it wasn't quite as blatant as Gary Glitter's 'Do You Wanna Touch Me' which had set her off the previous year. 'Give It To Me Now' had already been released by another Martin/Coulter act, an Irish singer called Kenny, with a B-side called 'Rollin'' which, funnily enough, we never recorded, despite its apt title. Kenny the Irish male vocalist is not to be confused with the band Kenny, who later had a hit with 'The Bump' – but only after we'd recorded it and used it as a B-side on our fourth single. 'Jenny Gotta Dance' was the last Martin/Coulter track and that had also been recorded elsewhere before its appearance on *Rollin'*. It was all so incestuous.

'Ain't It Strange' was written by Eric, Woody and me at Eric's Craigmillar flat. The other three Faulkner/Wood numbers were called 'Angel, Angel', 'There Goes My Baby' and 'Just A Little Love'. The first one had me and Eric on lead vocals, and the last one was supposed to be sung by Woody. It wasn't until the album came out that we discovered that my guide vocal, recorded only to help the others with the backing vocals, had been used instead of Woody's voice. If I sound a bit like I can't be bothered on that track, that's why.

The two cover versions that completed the album were 'Be My Baby', the classic '60s Ronettes hit written by Phil Spector, and 'Please Stay', an early Bacharach composition originally released by The Drifters in 1961. The song had been a Rollers favourite since the very beginning.

It wasn't a bad collection of songs; we just wished we'd been allowed a little bit more time to put them together – Eric to the point where he'd probably still be in the studio today.

In September 1974 the album *Rollin'* was released, although it wasn't really. That is, it was released, but you couldnae get it, because Bell held it back. It was advertised and publicised from mid-September, so record stores were taking orders. As a result, when it was finally shipped nearly a month later, it went straight in at No. 1. Bell's clever tactic ensured *Rollin'* was the first debut album to achieve this. It knocked Richard Branson's baby, *Tubular Bells*, from the top spot – the album which, together with another one of Mike Oldfield's, had been at No. 1 and No. 2 for the previous four weeks. Before that, *Tubular Bells* had been at No. 2 for a further six weeks, held off by Wings' *Band On The Run*.

Rollin' stayed in the official British Market Research Bureau (BMRB) charts for 62 weeks. In *Melody Maker*'s alternative charts, it entered at No. 12 on the same day it entered the real charts and

71

never made it to No. 1. It stayed in their Top 3 from early November till after Christmas, though.

Before the album came out, we'd had some pretty good press in the music journals. As most of our coverage was in the teen mags, it was encouraging when we got mentioned in the 'proper' music press. *Melody Maker* did a nice little feature about the Rollers and Mud, under the headline 'Bringing Back The Good Times'. It wasn't in any way in-depth, but it's significant that while lead singer Les Gray was allowed to speak for Mud, it was Tam who spoke for the Rollers. Soon after that, we did an interview with a lady called Jan from *Record Mirror*, who clearly had the hots for us. She all but ignored Tam throughout and subtly encouraged us to speak for ourselves. We all bitched about not having had enough time to make *Rollin'* and Tam stuttered around the edges, nearly having a seizure about what we were saying. His feelings about 'females' took a turn for the worse and from then on, all interviews had to be conducted by males.

The favourable press was short-lived. It was absolutely horrifying that *Tubular Bells* could be taken out by the likes of *Rollin'*; that a bubblegum band like the Bay City Rollers could outsell 'proper' music. The intellectual music hacks gnashed their false teeth and sharpened their wits.

They'd had plenty practice. The problem was that our brand of pop music was too real for them, it gave them nothing to analyse or pass deep-and-meaningful comment on, so all they could do was bitch, just like no-hopers who never made it past the start line always do.

Here's some of the constructive criticism we received for our first few singles:

'Remember': 'Who the devil are these fresh-faced punks, with their la la la?'

'Shang-A-Lang': 'The doe-eyed kids babble on with their weak-kneed codswallop, this time stringing what sounds like a series of ancient rock tune titles together to create some lyrics.'

'Summerlove Sensation': 'Walking in the sand and summer nights, baby talk and treacle.'

It used to make me laugh. No one was trying to say Bay City Rollers songs were any more than feel-good pop tunes, but for some reason we were seen as a threat to the likes of legends like

Deep Purple and Led Zep. Our only crime was to shed a light on the pomposity of some of the other acts around at that time.

Rock versus pop. A simple case of musical snobbery. It was exactly the same as the dissing that Will and Gareth attract today and there are several reasons for it.

One of them is a general resentment towards artists that achieve success through talent shows and have not done the apprenticeship – they've not trawled the pubs and clubs and faced humiliation and rejection like most of their rock contemporaries have. Ignorant critics felt this way about the Rollers, which was unfair, because before I joined them they'd been doing the poverty and rejection scene for years.

The snobbishness comes from the arrogance of some of the 'proper musicians' who in our day were all busy trying to out-serious each other by not releasing commercially oriented singles and concentrating purely on albums. These were no longer called albums, by the way, but 'bodies of work'. Most 'bodies of work' were albums with some sort of well-hidden theme, and as far as I'm concerned the only act that produced 'bodies of work' in the true sense was Pink Floyd. *Rollin'* was neither a body nor a work and went against everything the musos of the day stood for. The Rollers represented rock's doom. We thought 'about time too, so move over you old farts, and let us young 'uns rip it up'!

Of course it was all bollocks because there was room enough for all of us and no competition between rock and pop. I believed then, and still believe today, that pop has its place. If it makes kids happy that's great, but, more importantly, it might get them interested in music and the music industry generally. Catchy little pop tunes can arouse interest and get kids hooked where serious rock can't. The problem is that most artists, once successful, will always cite The Beatles, Mozart, Bowie and other legends as their biggest influence. No one will ever say it was S Club or Steps that made them want to be a singer or musician!

Back then, all of us wanted to be part of a fantastic industry, and make music. We were keen to learn, improve and entertain. Today, there are still kids out there with the same ambitions, but there are far, far more that just want to be pop stars because they are greedy for fame and celebrity and riches. Couple this with the ambitions of the Watermans, Fullers and Cowells of this world, their apparent egos and need to control on a far greater scale than Tam Paton could ever have dreamed of, and you have to wonder where it's all headed.

The sheer volume of manufactured music in the charts and the never-ending stream of identical boy bands is creating an anti-pop attitude that will turn more and more potential buyers off the 'genre', and on to alternatives. At the same time, the major record companies are putting more and more money into promoting the artists that generate the most income and less and less into finding and cultivating real talent like they used to. As a result, today's stars have very short shelf lives and there are fewer alternatives. The indie record labels usually can't compete on budget or in securing airplay, so everyone loses out – apart from the cartel of top boys who continue to rake in the millions at everyone else's expense.

One last comment before I get off my soapbox. Anyone who says Will or Gareth or any of their successors can't sing needs their hearing tested. Of course they can sing, and sing well. But so can lots of other people; people who didn't make it through the first round of auditions or, better still, chose not to audition in the first place. These are the ones who aren't chasing fame for the sake of it and who have artistic integrity and respect. Some people will insist that all singers should be able to read, write and play music too, but that's just another form of snobbery that usually comes from people who know a chord or two. Being able to play doesn't have to be a prerequisite. One of the guys from Blue said recently that he was tired of people who diss the band because they don't play instruments and that, as far as they were concerned, their voices were their instruments. I agree with that – when you think of people like Sinatra or Tom Jones, all they do is sing, but there's so much more to legends like those than the boys in Blue, or Westlife, and it's that 'so much more' that record companies have given up trying to find or cultivate in favour of short-term profits. And that's why you don't get classics any more, and 'Top X Records Of All Time' surveys rarely include anything less than ten or 20 years old, apart from maybe the No. 1 at the time the survey was taken.

Now, if you think you want to be an international pop idol, ask yourself an important question: what's your motivation? Money? If so, think about a job behind the scenes in production or promotion. You're far more likely to make a fortune in those jobs than as a short-lived pop act. If it's the concept of fame that turns you on, think about how you'd deal with having no privacy, being slated in the press (maybe not at first, but inevitably at some stage) and make sure you understand what you're signing away before you sign up for *Pop Idol* or *Fame Academy*. You could well end up in therapy. If you crave appreciation and a sense of worth, find another more worthwhile area to do it in, like medicine. If you have a genuine love of music, then cut a great demo, take it to some classy independent labels and focus at all times on your fundamental need: making music. Don't prostitute yourself, whatever enticements are offered to distract you.

I don't know what Eric Faulkner would have to say on the whole issue but he took all the press criticism of *Rollin'* badly, finding it difficult to accept when we'd been given so little time to make the album and had so little input. The thing is, even if we'd had four weeks or four months instead of four days to make it, the end result would have been the same – a slating in the music press. If we'd scrapped all the songs and recorded 12 musical masterpieces, it would still have been slated, because we were the fresh-faced, doe-eyed, baby-talking Bay City Rollers.

Also, we'd still have had to use the session musicians, so it would have actually been quite hard to fill any extra time had it been available. It wasn't as if the others could have used more time to dabble with different chords and effects – it was as much as they could do to get the few chords they did know right. I'm sure Eric thought more time to practise would have got him a musical as well as a vocal presence on the album, but it's arrogant to assume that would have made a better end product. It definitely wouldnae have lessened the criticism.

The more I think about it, the more it seems that all Eric's many problems with me, the Rollers and his musical heritage stem from that age-old conflict between rock and pop. He'd wanted to be a rock star but ended up a pop idol. For tour programme photo shoots, while the rest of us did thumbs up and waved scarves, he had to appear to be in mid strum on a guitar, left hand fingers positioned for a really complex chord. This need stayed with him right till the very last album, *Ricochet* (check out the cover). He was a rock guitarist; I was a pop singer. He wanted to write rock; the Rollers sang pop. He even referred to BCR music as 'happy rock', never quite able to utter the word '. . . p . . . p . . . p–p–p– pop'.

At the time I didn't give a shite what the critics said. The album ended up being the seventh top-selling album of the year, and would've scored way higher if it had been released earlier. What did worry me was the way the critics' scorn and hatred crossed over into everyday life. Roller-bashing became cool, particularly with acne-ridden teenage boys who couldnae get a date, let alone a shag, because most girls of the same sort of age were saving themselves for me or Eric (and you watch, it's those same boys with half a ton of King Edwards on their shoulders grown up who will slate this book).

Although I was aware of some pretty heavy confrontations going on in the teen mag letters pages from one week to the next, it wasn't until years later when I started to get letters from fans telling me about evil stepfathers throwing out records and posters, and brothers setting fire to magazines and scrapbooks, that I realised how serious it had all become. But there was also a positive side to it. Our fans' loyalty and dedication helped them learn to stand up for themselves and what they believed in. One American girl who didn't like us to start with ended up spray-painting 'BCR ARE THE BEST' on a wall where the local in-crowd – her former friends – hung out. She'd found more friendship, loyalty and identity within her new circle of Roller fans than she'd ever had before. More importantly, I've received loads of letters telling stories that have moved me to tears – potted life histories from abused kids who found an escape and an optimism in the Bay City Rollers' music that in some cases was the only thing stopping them killing themselves. Even today, fans write to say that putting on an old Rollers album has helped them cope with a loss, divorce and all sorts of other stress. And that, at the end of the day, is far more rewarding than any faceless, brainless music critic's praise might have been.

So what was it that made the Bay City Rollers so successful?

Was it me on lead vocals? Was Dick Leahy's vision the crucial factor, or was it Bill Martin and Phil Coulter's songwriting genius?

Were Tam's mass mailings the catalyst, or was it his unique management style that paid dividends? Maybe it was just that we made nice, happy pop songs that took kids' minds off their teenage angst and their mums' minds off a serious economic depression for a few minutes every now and again.

Probably the most sensible attitude to take is that it was a combination of all of the above, although on days when I'm feeling a bit more obnoxious than usual, I'll swear blind it was all down to yours truly's charisma.

The question of whether Tam Paton was a PR guru of Freudian proportions, or an opportunistic bullshitter, needs to be looked at quite closely. In my opinion, Tam Paton wanted to get rich and to satisfy the craving for fame and fortune he'd had since he tried to become a pop star in the '60s. He didn't set out to create the world's first mega successful boy band; he chanced upon Alan and Derek and the rest of them and went with the flow. He thought he knew all about image, but showed inexperience in his ability to put theory into practice and develop an image suited to the band's audience, as proved by the cabaret phase. The later tartan-trimmed, stripy-socked look for which the Bay City Rollers are remembered came from a drawing sent in by a fan, not Tam. What he *did* have was an ability to manipulate.

Another factor that I think is important which isn't often talked about is the band's accessibility. This might sound stupid when you look at how untouchable Tam made us seem, but compared to the likes of David Cassidy and The Osmonds, we were local boys. The US acts came and went – all hell broke loose when they toured in the UK, but when they left again for the other side of the world, it was quiet. Being a home-grown band, it was much easier for the Rollers to become the focus of the Brit girls' fantasies; much easier for them to feel close to us. There'd been nothing like it since The Beatles in Britain and the market was ripe for another mania.

Tam's manipulative skills came into their own as *Rollin'* continued to bring us more and more media attention. He realised very quickly that the power of the PR word could be much more effective than clothing. For a man who was inclined to flirt with the truth occasionally, and who also had a bit of a power thing going on, the world of PR was Utopia for him. Sometimes his announcements and stories were so ludicrous that it seemed that he was testing the press to see just how much bullshit they'd swallow.

Bell Records had decided to pitch us at the younger end of the market; Tam took it a stage further and decided the Bay City Rollers would be the sugary-sweet antithesis to the likes of the Stones and all those other dirty long-haired rockers (cue more derision from the music press).

'The Bay City Rollers only ever drink milk!' was probably one of his most famous creations. After that, at every press conference we did, there'd be bloody glasses of milk set out on the table for us. We had to go to ridiculous lengths to uphold the myth – like not being seen in the bar after a *Top Of The Pops* recording, as I said earlier.

The milk story demonstrates Tam's management skills very well. It was a great headline and it got us loads of coverage. It was a fantastic marketing ploy because the kids' parents were happy to buy our records for their children because we set them a good example. It was just a shame that his inconsistency won through and he forgot the milk thing when he checked the sleeve notes for *Rollin'*. There it was clearly stated that my favourite drink was Cointreau with lime and lemonade, Eric's vice was vodka and Alan's was dark rum and peppermint.

'The Bay City Rollers don't smoke!' was picked up and used by an anti-smoking campaign in Scotland. It was like being back at school when we all had to hide in the toilets to have a crafty fag, or should I say a sneaky cigarette. We were never very comfortable with the blatant dissembling that went hand in hand with Tam's myths. Poor Woody had a real problem getting the words out when he was called upon to state that he had never smoked and couldnae stand girls that did. Or perhaps he was still quaking from the embarrassment of Tam's press release which told the world that he, Woody, was afraid of the dark and still slept with a teddy bear. However far-fetched the stories were, they achieved what they were created for – to make more money. Fans reading this crap about teddies thought we were even cuter than they had previously and rushed out to buy more records and merchandise.

'The Rollers don't have time for girlfriends' proclaimed another story, but this was more than a case of not wanting to lose record sales because a bunch of hormonal 13 year olds might feel rejected if Alan suddenly had a bird. It was a case of saving lives. It had been printed somewhere that Eric had a girlfriend called Jenny – presumably the name came from the *Rollin'* track – and over the next few days the mountains of mail at the fan club were higher than usual. Allegedly one of the fans had threatened to commit suicide if it was true, so Tam had to put out an official statement that Eric did *not* have a girlfriend. Presumably the lassie put away her noose for another day and peace was restored in Prestonpans.

While on the subject of the fan club – little mail ever reached us. Unless Tam needed us to be photographed reading it or dealing with it, or opening presents, the mail and us never met. You see, it was all precious, priceless market information to be sorted, analysed and acted upon. It gave Tam another means of control; he could put the fear of God into any given Roller by making him think he was on the way out. For instance, he might say something like, 'Woody, you're not getting so much fan mail this week, we'll have to get you some more camera shots.' Or: 'Derek, you're not very popular right now, you'll need to be extra-friendly to me – sorry! – the fans.'

It was never me who needed my profile increased. As the lead singer, I naturally got the most fan and media attention – the latter not always intentional or positive. I don't mean that to sound big-headed, but it's a fact of band life; a fact that sadly many guitarists or other band members never seem able to grasp. It's been the same throughout time and won't ever change – Brian Connolly and Andy Scott of Sweet at the same time, Liam and Noel later. If there's so much as a touch of jealousy or resentment towards the lead singer or any other member of a band, that band's as good as dead. It's always just a matter of time – sometimes one of a song-writing duo might wait until the other one's been dead for more than 20 years before swapping the order in which the names appear, but it's still the same syndrome.

This was the time that Tam also started to work on the 'sixth Roller' syndrome. Having found fame at last, and revelling in his new-found profile and power, his PR efforts were focused just as much on himself as they were on the Bay City Rollers. He went to great lengths to set himself up as the sixth Roller and one of the lads. He even had poster-sized photos of himself included in the annuals and was never one to miss out on a photo opportunity. Even today, I sometimes see him described as the Rollers' 'guiding light and father-figure', a description he gave of himself in his 1975 book. This angelic persona must have been created to counteract the Svengali-type comments that were beginning to be whispered on the fringes of Rollerland. Whenever Tam has been interviewed, back then and more recently, he has always denounced the Svengali label as unfair and inaccurate, but I have to agree that it was. To refer to Tam Paton as a Svengali is to do him an injustice – in my opinion, you need to add in Napoleon's megalomania, the Marquis de Sade's obsession with control and a caring nature on a par with Pol Pot's.

I've just read back through that last paragraph and asked myself whether or not to leave it in. Does it make me sound bitter and twisted? I don't want to come across like that, but if I do it's not surprising, really.

The one thing I've realised since I started writing this is that I've always been in denial about how Tam has affected me. I've continually told myself and other people that I was the one he couldnae dominate or control; I was the one that stood up to him. And while there's some truth in that, I can see now that it's not 100 per cent right. To say I was immune to his games would be a lie. At the time, I really did think I was untouched by his power, but looking back, there are a number of events where my judgement was more than questionable, and while I'm not looking for someone to blame, I believe his influence was a major factor in most of them. I may have thought he couldnae get to me at the time, like he did with the others, but I can see now that I didn't escape unscathed. He did get inside my head, and he did cause disruption there.

For a start, there's the Tourette's . . . I blame Tam for the fact that I can't stop saying 'fuck' and 'shit' and 'arsehole' whenever I open my mouth . . .

In spite of all that, my relationship with Tam from the moment I joined the Rollers was *felt* to be different to the relationships he had with the rest of the band and I'm sure that was the biggest single reason why I never became really close to any of them. The special relationships that you might think would start to develop between five young guys on the verge of superstardom just didn't happen. I'm sure it was because I was less dominated than the others and that affected the way they were with me. Who knows, maybe that was yet another situation that Tam engineered. Perhaps there was some benefit in keeping me distanced from them. With me out on a limb, was there less chance of us all ganging up on him? Less chance of mutiny?

Another factor that made it difficult to form normal friendships was that the band's environment and lifestyle was not conducive to normal social intercourse. We never sat still; from 'Remember' onwards we spun around in a frenetic whirlwind of activity that numbed the senses. When we came to a halt, usually only ever in a hotel room for the night, we had no energy to talk. We just slept.

It would have been so much better if we could all have been best mates, but even in those very early days, my sixth sense was telling me there was something odd going down. I couldnae put my finger on it, but it was as if there was a secret that everyone knew except me. It was like they'd all had their initiation, and I still had to slice my finger and become a brother. I used to have a recurring dream that I'd walk into a room where they were all sat chatting, then they'd just stop, look at me sideways, and look back at each other, remaining silent. A nightmare I'd had as a child also came back to haunt me: I'd be alone on a dark mountain in the dead of night, surrounded by hideously malformed black sheep with evil glinting in their eyes as they looked at me sideways through thick, matted lashes. They'd begin to close in on me but I always woke up, in a cold sweat, just in time. I'd forgotten all about that dream until it resurfaced in early Roller days.

The only Roller I can remember ever having a real conversation with was Alan, probably because he was older and wiser. Al was a straightforward, nice guy. You knew where you were with him. Derek was inoffensive, another 'nice guy'. There was no malice in Woody either – he was still a kid after all – but from day one he and Eric were mutually and exclusively best buddies and may as well have been joined at the hip. Poor Woody missed his mum and Eric looked after him. Each one on his own was OK, but when they were all together, with Tam controlling them, they were a different entity altogether.

I used to stand back and watch the interaction between Tam and the guys and try to figure it all out. I'd never seen compliance like it. His size and strength played a big part, definitely. He had been known to kick down a door or two when he lost his temper. Worse, there was a rumour that when he was in the army, in Cyprus, he'd had an altercation with a couple of Greeks and had to be smuggled off the island. That might have been part of his own image creation but it was believable. He certainly came across as a real hard bastard. That, together with the fact so many former Rollers had fallen by the wayside so far, made them a wee bit twitchy. The implication was usually unspoken but clear – toe the line or you're out; there's plenty more where you came from. I think his problem was that he knew as well as I did that as the lead singer I wasn't as instantly replaceable as other band members so he was a little bit less powerful with me.

Obviously, I was nervous around him too; I was a skinny wee kid and he was a big fucker. I just wasnae as scared as the others. Maybe my in-built disrespect for authority kicked in and prevented him from having total control over me. It was obvious he didn't tell me what to do as much. The only thing he ever instructed me not to do was smoke botanical substances in front of the other guys – I could do it in private, but not with them. (None of them smoked weed at the time, but that doesn't mean that, apart from me, the band really was as clean-living as they were portrayed. They just hadn't discovered skunk yet. There were enough 'pervy pills' popped by Bay City Rollers in their heyday to fill the Grand Canyon, but more of that later.)

The control freakery didn't stop with the implied threats that you'd be out if you didn't behave. One of the guys told me quite early on he'd seen Tam following him when he wasn't working, going to and from the pub and around town. The Roller never let on he'd seen him and said nothing. Tam had got the message across that he was omnipresent, always watching, and would know if you misbehaved.

Even at the top of the charts, the band was literally living in fear and there was no way they'd risk anything that might make Tam angry. The fans were getting more devious in their attempts to get into our knickers. I was, as ever, eager to please and would run the risk of Tam finding out. The chance of one of the other guys risking a post-show liaison was non-existent. I think it vexed them that not only had I made the most of the groupie scene for nearly a year with Threshold, I was still out there seeing action while they, finally at the top of the charts, continued to live in a state of forced impotence. Maybe they didn't like it that Tam couldnae control me in the way he controlled them. Maybe they couldnae handle me getting the most attention – in every sense. Maybe I'm being too philosophical and I just irritated the shit out of them!

Rollermania

We began to find ourselves on TV more often than the news and then we were on that as well.

We were recording appearance after appearance and how we wished the promo video had come into its own before 'Bohemian Rhapsody' instead of after it.

At the same time we were trying to find time to record songs and play gigs all over the country. We even started going abroad – to far-flung, exotic places like Northern Ireland, Eire and the Isle of Man. By then, I'd spent many nights and journeys learning lyrics so that I didnae have to dive around the stage throughout the set like I'd had to at that first gig. As a result I felt a lot more comfortable on stage and I could concentrate on other aspects of my performance. I wanted to entertain as well as sing, and I started to think about the artists I'd grown up with and what it was about them I'd admired. I thought back to the concerts I'd been to in Edinburgh and what the best performers did that made them stand out. In all cases I found it was the sheer confidence that they exuded; the absolute certainty in the artists' minds that they were born to do what they were doing. That and an innate ability to connect with their audiences.

At the very early gigs, most of which had been booked weeks or months before we were on *Top Of The Pops*, we would usually be performing in small chicken-in-a-basket-type venues, often with nothing more than some sort of rostrum for a stage. At one gig, they tried to have us perform on the dance floor. Within minutes of coming on 'stage', we were besieged and the gig was stopped almost as soon as it had begun.

Soon the size and quality of the venues began to increase and rostrums grew into real stages, some even with safety curtains. Before we knew it, we'd played a gig on a real stage with a barrier between the audience and us. Then the barriers started to get moved farther and farther back from the stage because fans had started trying to climb over them and onto the stage to get at us. When that didn't work, increasing numbers of lines of security guards were brought in.

The way the stages we performed on grew higher and further removed from the fans sums up how the band's following was growing, and how quickly. We went from small-rostrum-in-a-club to cordoned-off-and-removed-by-about-20-feet-and-three-rows-of-security over a period of about eight weeks. I think it was that progression that helped my connectivity with an audience to grow in proportion to the size of the audience, so I was never fazed by the sheer volume of people in front of me.

The few weeks after *Top Of The Pops*, when we were playing the gigs we'd committed to before we'd been on the show, gave us our first taste of how it felt to be physically under threat. The fans were starting to join together to form an ever-increasing mass. They weren't at all malicious, but the proximity of more than a manageable few of them was unnerving. During that time when we were playing gigs that had been booked before things took off, I probably felt more uncomfortable than at any other time during the course of Rollermania. No one had really anticipated the reaction and there were no procedures in place to deal with it.

Increasingly, we would find more people outside a venue than inside it. Even when they didnae have tickets, they'd come along anyway just in case they could catch a glimpse of us. After a wee while, though, the chance of a glimpse wasn't enough for your average fan; there was no point in just going along to a venue unless you were going to go the whole hog and try and come away not only having touched a Roller, but having removed a bit of one. Somewhere around this time, the term 'Rollermania' was coined but it was nothing compared to what was to come.

Tam decided we were big enough to need our own proper

security. He got in touch with a firm called Artists Services, run by a guy called Don Murphy. The company, the only one of its kind, specialised in event security, and had been set up to deal with crowd control when the likes of The Osmonds or David Cassidy were in town. We were due to be making an appearance at Brands Hatch – a Radio One Fun Day, I think – no gig or anything, just an appearance, and Artists Services were to protect us.

Don sent one of his top men, Patrick Callaghan, to Brands Hatch, along with a couple of other heavies and the comment that his charges that day were 'a bunch of woofters'. When they arrived at the location, the security guys were warned with a nudge and a wink to 'stay away from the manager'. They wondered what the hell they'd let themselves in for and were relieved to find that the lead singer, at least, was cool and a great guy.

That day at Brands Hatch was the first time I met my good friend Patrick Callaghan, or 'Paddy the Plank'. From then on, Paddy and combinations of his colleagues Fat Fred, Wally (or 'Molly') and Patsy were always around to look after us. Although the others were interchangeable, Paddy was a permanent fixture because he was a right good-looking geezer – he reckons Tam fancied him.

By the time Rollermania was in full swing, we were forever grateful for the presence of security – not only because we were in fear of straightforward physical attack, but also because the fans had now taken to hurling things at us on stage. The younger fans would normally throw teddy bears and flowers. Knickers and bras with details of the owner's fantasies scribbled on were par for the course from their older sisters. And while I don't want to give any substance to the myth that my kinsmen and women can be less than forthcoming with their cash, I have to tell you that at one gig in Edinburgh, we couldnae believe it when the wee girls started throwing their jewellery onto the stage. After the gig, there seemed to be slightly less hysteria outside the stage door than normal. Later we found out this was because the jewellery-throwers had scrambled up onto the stage once we'd gone to try and get back the stuff they'd thrown at us!

In the summer of '74, we played an open-air concert in a park somewhere in Essex. Because it was outside, there was no restriction on numbers so there were probably more than 10,000 people there, mostly Roller fans. There were some hefty barriers in place and, better still, a pond between the stage and the audience. But that wasn't enough of a deterrent. They managed to break through the barriers and then started falling and jumping into the water in an attempt to get to us. It seemed that maybe things were getting a bit out of hand.

Whenever there was an occurrence of mass hysteria, fainting and not enough St. John's Ambulance crews to cope, the newspapers were full of anti-Roller reports and references back to poor wee Bernadette Whelan who'd had a heart attack in the middle of a crush of Cassidy fans earlier that year. It was this 'shock horror' reaction that provided Tam's greatest inspiration to date.

He studied Cassidy, who was surrounded by fans wherever he went, as were The Osmonds. There were always a few thousand fans outside the Churchill Hotel when David was in residence. The bigger the crowds around the artist, the more popular they were perceived to be, the more publicity they got and the more records they sold. You don't need too much of an IQ to work out that times and places were being leaked by record companies and publicists.

Tam watched and learned and resolved to do better. He rubbed his hands with glee when the newspapers started talking about Rollermania, and decided that from then on, the hysteria would be whipped up wherever and whenever possible, whatever the cost and whatever the risks.

I found out only recently that one of the ways he did this was to instruct Paddy the Plank to make sure that whenever there was a hysterical mass, for instance around a venue's exit routes after a gig, the Rollers were driven right into the heart of it. It was actually worked out beforehand where the fans were likely to accumulate so that the so-called escape route would be sure to be as manic as possible. Paddy sums this up by saying 'when it was wrong, it was right'. He basically had to look at the safest and quickest way out for the band, and then do the complete opposite. It was an ingenious scheme that never failed; a photo of a couple of Rolls-Royces or a minibus covered in clambering, screaming girls would always, always appear in the press the next day. Never mind that we ran the risk of being lynched every single time we went somewhere and that totally wrecked get-away vehicles were an everyday occurrence. Brilliant! Someone, and I'll wager ye it wasnae our concerned manager, even had the presence of mind to make sure that our escape vehicles had layers of foam and cushions on the floor and around the sides, so that whoever threw us from the venue into the van would be reasonably sure they wouldnae hurt us.

The first time we were in Canada, the chaos was contrived, as per usual, and the police went ballistic after we were mobbed by thousands of hysterical fans in a basement car park. It was out of control and they were out of their depth. In Australia, we had the use of an armoured vehicle not far short of a tank to make it look as though we were being kept safe. Thirty or forty girls jumping up and down on the roof almost caved it in while we cowered, shitting ourselves, inside. That was probably the worst occasion because, on top of the noise, panic, and feeling that we were about to die horrible deaths, it was about 500 degrees outside and we found out what it must feel like to be microwaved.

There would always be questions asked after a riot and poor Paddy was always being interrogated by police about how and why a situation could have been allowed to happen. He became skilled in bullshitting his way through it, blaming some non-existent security or promoter guy for having fucked up and promising it wouldnae happen again.

Ironically, the most manic and hysterical event throughout the Rollermania years happened without any manipulation from Tam whatsoever. As Paddy says, this one was just *too* good and there was no way that even Tam could've dreamt it up.

The event in question was a Radio One Fun Day at Mallory Park, the race track.

Throughout the '70s, Radio One hosted loads of live events all over the country. Their Roadshows were the most frequent, held throughout the summer, and the Rollers attended several, but the Fun Days were something else. These took place at race meetings and were billed as a family day out where you could see a host of Radio One personalities, star guests, bands and celebrities. The first ever Fun Day was held at Mallory Park, and the event returned there from Brands Hatch in 1975. The Bay City Rollers were invited to perform live, on a boat, in an ornamental lake in the middle of the race track. The publicity attracted the largest ever Fun Day audience to date of around 47,000.

A broadcasting tower and hospitality tent had been put up on the island, which you reached by means of a small wooden bridge. Radio One's security were having problems at the bridge before we arrived, but when the helicopters carrying us and The Three Degrees appeared in the sky, all hell broke loose. We'd just managed to land when the bridge was stampeded and in no time at all the island was covered with fans. Others, seeing that it was possible to get to the island, started running across the racetrack, regardless of the fact that there were souped-up Ford Escorts driven by top-name DJs racing around it at the time. Once safely across the track, they jumped into the water for the final leg. Meanwhile, a waving and grinning Tony Blackburn was whizzing around the lake in a speedboat being driven by a Womble. The police were in the water trying to get the girls to safety, but they only managed to throw a small percentage of them back onto the banks.

Oblivious to the degree of commotion outside, the Rollers were in the tower being interviewed live by David Hamilton. As the fans closed in on the tower and windows and doors were kicked in, it was impossible to carry on and we were taken off the air. Plans for us to do a 'lap of honour' around the racetrack were quickly abandoned.

Paddy decided we needed to get the hell out of there and fast, but Tam and the radio people weren't having any of it. Paddy persuaded them with a few carefully chosen and forcefully delivered words, and the helicopter was called back. The problem was that it couldnae land because the island was blanketed with fans. Instead, we were put on a boat out onto the lake but that just resulted in another surge of fans wading and swimming towards us, all the time trying to keep their heads out of the water so their make-up wouldnae get spoiled and their hairstyle wouldnae be ruined. Some of them got to the boat but were so hysterical and knackered by that point they were in real danger. We pulled a few of them onto the boat because they really seemed to be in danger of drowning, but there wasnae enough room for more than a couple. About 40 girls were rescued by the police who had taken to little rowing boats, which was all that was available to them. It was like a D-Day scene. Nearly all of the rescued girls needed treatment and four were hospitalised.

Finally, we managed to get back to the island and the tower, and the various security teams were able to keep the screaming hordes at bay. The helicopter finally landed and we got on board, but as it tried to take off there were still fans hanging from the bottom of it, being prised free by the police and security guys. Paddy fell off and was left on the ground teeming with rioting girls who were by now more than a little bit vexed about having been so near and yet so far.

DJ John Peel later said that if he lived to be 200 he would never see anything more bizarre than the events of that day.

Rollermania swamped us, not just at gigs, but everywhere we went; Tam made sure of that. Even when he wasn't orchestrating some sort of mayhem, the percentage of UK girls between the ages of ten and eighteen that were fans of the Rollers ensured that the shortest excursion drew an instant crowd of tartan. When the fans found out we were due to be recording a TV show, the studios in question would be under siege for hours before we arrived. One time at the London Weekend TV studios, the screaming was so loud that poor Maggie Bell, who was trying to sing inside the studio as we arrived, was completely drowned out.

It was madness and the feeling of imprisonment was growing. Tam built on it by making sure that we were always in our beds with a pint of milk by ten o'clock – for our own safety and well-being, of course – in our shared rooms, with guys from Artists Services stationed along the corridors to protect us from wily women. We never had the same roommate twice in a row; we always swapped around, the unlucky fifth one having to share with Tam. It was another way to make sure none of us got too close.

Meanwhile, Tam's parents' house in Prestonpans was nearly disappearing under the pile of fan mail and gifts that arrived there daily. It was thanks to one of those fan letters that the Bay City Rollers ended up with the tartan-trimmed image that became our trademark.

Eric had started adding a bit of tartan trim to his shirts and a wee lassie had picked up on that and sent him a picture of a fan dressed in jeans with tartan down the sides and around the hems. She also wore a waist-length jacket with tartan trimmings on that, too. I'm not sure if Eric actually got to see that drawing or whether it was just intercepted by the Paton police and pounced on. Whatever, it was sent to a costume designer in London who set about making our first set of new-look clothes. It didn't happen in time for the photo shoot for our first album where, with the exception of Eric's tartan shirt, we're all still in various styles of skinny-rib. By the second album, there was a mixture of both, with Eric and the Longmuirs in full Roller gear, Woody still in that skinny-rib with a big red W on it (and starting the scarf round the wrist trend), and me in white denim with blue stripes. The fans immediately began copying the look and wearing it on the streets to identify themselves. By album three, it was uniform.

Another advantage of the new image was that as our records climbed the charts, it was easy to apply it to a whole range of highly saleable merchandise which we were probably told would generate thousands in extra revenue for the band. Tartan and the Rollers' logo was successfully imprinted onto hundreds of items, from socks and underwear to pillowcases and curtains. Woolworths had one of the largest stocks of BCR merchandise. Most fans owned at least one pair of their knee-length white socks with the tartan print and logo up the side, and were gutted when they were told they weren't allowed to wear them to school. Most mothers complained that the pattern faded after a few washes and that they had to keep buying replacements, and most people involved in the merchandise marketing marvelled at how much cash rolled in.

During our first tour, there were masses of people hawking tat that they liked to call 'genuine BCR merchandise' outside every venue. They got away with charging stupid money for rosettes that looked like they'd been made by a two year old because the kids just had to have *everything* that had tartan or a logo on it to prove they were the band's No. 1 fans. This pissed off the kids' parents and the press, who blamed us personally for the rip-off. To combat the problem, Fan Fare Rollers Ltd was set up and managed by Artists Services, in an attempt to fend off the touts.

By the time our second tour programme was printed, Fan Fare Rollers Ltd was offering 'a fabulous Roller wrist watch', 'great colour printed T-shirts', 'BCR stationery kits' or 'a pair of those crazy Roller socks'. If those failed to entice, you could get a beautiful sew-on patch, a rosette, badge, scarf, or any one of the dozens of exclusive Roller products offered in the free brochure. The ad went on to say how pleased the Bay City Rollers were now that 'their very own sales company' was up and running.

The official merchandise didn't only come from Fan Fare. It was all over the place, and presumably licences were paid for and issued for everything from the jigsaw puzzles to the 'tour game' launched by a company called Whitman Publishing. A deal was also signed with C&A, the high street giant, allowing them to develop and sell their own range of Roller gear. It's rumoured that one million square yards of unique Bay City Roller tartan were made up for that range.

As with every aspect of the Bay City Rollers, we should've taken more of an interest in what was going on with the merchandising but, as usual, we just didn't have the time to deal with it. In any case, we honestly believed that everyone else was looking out for us and protecting our interests. Our naivety cost us millions in financial terms and dearly in terms of the effects on our lives. Tam consistently claims he was as ripped off as the rest of us because he was out of his depth when the band finally took off. So far, nobody has found or done anything to show otherwise; although he was the only one that managed to hold on to his house and talks about how rich he now is thanks to his 'property' business.

Time for a tour.

The hip young glam promoter, Jef Hanlon, was approached by Bell Records to do the same for the Bay City Rollers as he'd been doing for Gary Glitter, the New Seekers and Barry 'Dancing On A Saturday Night' Blue. Jef was respected in the industry as one of those people who loved the biz and not just the glamour. He'd done his musical apprenticeship playing guitar on Hamburg's Reeperbahn like The Beatles, and had worked with Herman's Hermits where he'd learned how to manipulate a fan following and make it really work wonders for the band.

Jef came up to meet us at Tam's parents' place and there we sat, surrounded by sacks of spuds, listening attentively, while he explained the major differences between doing one-off concerts and club gigs and a fully fledged national concert tour. Jake – previously in charge of gear, transport, sound, lights, stage, the lot – suddenly got a team four times the size of the one guy he'd been till then. He was now officially tour manager as opposed to roadie, with one guy to look after the gear, two on lighting and himself on the mixing desk. Any apprehension was outweighed by the prestige of now having a whole team of techies, even if it was a minuscule team by today's standards.

Friday, 18 October, saw the opening night of the Bay City Rollers' first concert tour at Birmingham Town Hall. To make sure the whole country knew about it, Jef arranged for a lorry to break down in the middle of Birmingham soon after five o'clock, just as everyone was leaving work and going home. Coincidentally, at the same time, we were on our way to the Town Hall to do a sound check. Fans around the venue mysteriously found out the Rollers were on their way but that they were stuck in traffic just up the road. They started to surge through the streets. To the casual observer and any reporters in the neighbourhood, the traffic had been halted not by the broken-down lorry, but by the stampeding fans. The next day's headline – 'Bay City Rollers fans bring traffic to a standstill' – was easily achieved.

The newspapers lapped it up because by then they'd discovered that as soon as those three little words 'Bay City Rollers' appeared on a placard outside the newsagents, they'd sell an extra few hundred thousand copies to fans, so they were happy to have us on the front page as often as possible. Furthermore, the nationals knew that many of those few hundred thousand had never bought a paper before, so the chances were that those kids would develop a brand loyalty and keep buying their paper for years. If they advertised a poster of the Rollers on the front page, sales went through the roof. Throughout that first tour, the amount of coverage obtained by the Rollers just kept on growing.

Jef's plan was to create as much of a furore around the Rollers as possible at the first few gigs, knowing that after that the momentum would build on itself and carry the tour along without the need for any more input. This would leave him free to concentrate on the more mundane aspects of his job, like collecting cash, dealing with venue management and keeping the kids as safe as possible.

The venues were contracted to provide their own security, which, depending on how up to speed they were, would consist of anything from a bunch of pensioners to teams of firemen. In most cases, these impromptu protectors of the young would concentrate on trying to maintain order for the first number or two, but more often than not they ended up watching the show instead of the crowd. Having come across the problem before, Jef Hanlon also brought his own security professionals along – Black Bob and his mates from Glasgow's notoriously hard Sauchiehall Street. Bob and his crew were tasked with watching what was happening *under* the audience, in case anyone fell down and couldnae get up again.

The second gig was in Taunton, Somerset. The fans there, desperate to show they were bigger fans than the Birmingham posse they'd read about in the papers that morning, screamed louder and waved their scarves more frantically. By the time we came on stage, they had worked themselves into such a frenzy that hundreds of them just passed out. The headlines the next day exaggerated the number of Roller fans that needed medical treatment after the concert, so the next night at the Rainbow Theatre in London, hundreds of St. John Ambulance crews were drafted in along with massive amounts of security, which in turn led to more headlines about the size and scale of Rollermania, and more determination from fans in towns and cities further down the tour schedule to outdo those at the earlier gigs.

Being only the third date of the tour, in London and therefore with mega publicity potential attached, the Rainbow Theatre gig was ripe for hype. Our most dramatic escape to date was assured by making sure that there were enough breakdowns in communication to make BT look efficient. Decoys were placed at all exits so that Paddy could convince the police investigators the next day that every possible measure had been taken to minimise the disturbance. As usual, the getaway vehicle was positioned to attract maximum attention and was soon surrounded with screaming hordes. With Paddy and Fred left outside, the driver attempted to move away but couldnae go anywhere. The arrival of the police on horseback made for spectacular photographs in the papers the next day and outrageous headlines. Everyone declared the operation a great success.

It wasn't just the people working around the Rollers who contrived and manipulated; the fans were getting good at it, too. While Jef was having lorries break down and Tam and Paddy purposely bungled attempts at protecting us, the fans started to fake the fainting. This was because at the first couple of gigs, when girls at the front were overcome or getting squashed, Jef made sure that security got them to safety *via the stage*. It didn't take long for them to catch on that if you passed out, you'd get rescued and carried off backstage within a hair's breadth of a Roller. It took much longer for them to suss that after those first few shows, fans in need of resuscitation were carried to the sides and then out of the auditorium. No doubt they quickly recovered when they realised their ruse had failed.

After the first three gigs we had the Monday and Tuesday off, but not so that we could rest. The gap was intentionally left so that more publicity could be generated. Someone leaked where we were staying, so the Holiday Inn at Slough was inundated with fans and phone calls. On the Monday, someone suggested going to the cinema in Leicester Square. Great idea, we thought, stupidly not spotting the reason. Obviously there was a near riot when we got there and we were forced to go back to the hotel and watch *The Guns Of Navarone* and *El Cid* on a projector. Cine films at the hotel became our standard form of entertainment on nights off. *The Colditz Story* or *Escape From Alcatraz* would have been more appropriate.

One night, during a stay in Slough, Tam had arranged for us to go and judge a Bay City Rollers lookalike contest nearby, hosted by one of his Radio One cronies. What a clever way to get a lot of lads, most of whom wanted to be pop stars, all in one place and in awe of the pop people around them! The winner was a wee guy called Jimmy Pursey, who knew Tam and the others from the Walton Hop, his local disco, but who'd not been sucked in by their ploys. He went on to front one of the UK's biggest punk bands, Sham 69.

After that two-night break, we had a gig each of the following 12 nights, starting up north in Halifax and Southport, then around the country via Oxford and Cardiff before going back up to Edinburgh on the 31st. There were two shows that day, but Jef had to stop the second one halfway through because the Odeon's security crew of firemen were getting a wee bit wound up by the fans' behaviour. I think that was the first gig where GBH was done to the venue – some of the seats had got broken (or pulled out, as the papers said) during the proceedings.

shang-a-lang

The management of the venues still to welcome the Rollers were probably beginning to question their sanity in having the band appear knowing what might happen, but there was no escape by then. Contractually they were tied, and they would have been sued by Jef Hanlon, the band and God knows who else if they'd try to get out of a gig. They knew what was coming their way – we weren't the first band to attract a hysterical following that broke things – so instead they included 'damage budgets' in their calculations and pricing. Some of the more cunning venue owners, when they found out about seating being destroyed, actually loosened nuts and bolts to make sure that their decrepit old seats *would* collapse under any degree of pressure, and then go on to claim the costs of new seating back from Jef. As a matter of course, Jef would need to spend an hour or two with owners after a gig viewing alleged damage and thrashing out some sort of settlement. The time and costs were budgeted for.

After Edinburgh we stayed in Scotland for three more nights, ending with a concert at the Glasgow Apollo from where we had to be rescued once again by the police. By then we were ready for our three nights off, then it was back on the road with gigs in Gloucester, Lewisham, Manchester, Newcastle and Hull.

The 12th was a day off for my 19th birthday. Something like 2,000 teddy bears arrived in Prestonpans.

The last leg of the tour started with a gig in Hemel Hempstead, but only after we'd been to see a fan in hospital who'd been in a road accident and was distraught about missing the show. Five more nights and we ended up back in the Midlands at the Wolverhampton Civic Hall on Tuesday, 19 November – just over a month since the tour began.

In case anyone's interested in what the set was on that tour rather than the hype and hysteria that surrounded it, it was an hour long and opened with 'Shang-A-Lang'. 'Summerlove' and 'Remember' were included, of course, along with some rock 'n' roll numbers like 'CC Rider', 'Let's Have A Party', and Alan singing lead vocals on 'Great Balls Of Fire'. There were some tracks from *Rollin'* – 'Just A Little Love' and 'Be My Baby' among them. The set ended with 'All Of Me Loves All Of You', which had been released two weeks previously. Our last Martin/Coulter single went to No. 4 and earned us our last silver disc. As the B-side of that single later went to No. 3 for Kenny, there was some speculation that if we'd released it we'd have had our first No. 1.

With a successful tour under our belts and a debut album that by now was at the top of the charts, there was no let-up in demand. One minute we were jetting off to Yugoslavia to take part in a pop festival and a TV show; the next we were in Germany for a week doing TV and promo for our first German gigs in December.

The week before Christmas, we performed our first German concert at the Hamburg Musikhalle. The next day we toured the city on a bus and did the Musikhalle again that night. The audience, if a little *kalt* the first night, had warmed to us a lot by the second. I liked it in Germany and have always felt comfortable there. I love the beer, and that whole *Cabaret* vibe. Let me give you an example.

In most places, fans would send us wee presents. They'd send dolls they'd made, cute little latex Leslies all dressed up in tartan. The difference in Germany was that the dolls sent by the fans were dressed in PVC, wore rubber masks and held whips. I quickly came to understand what it was about Germany, and Hamburg in particular, that had attracted and inspired the likes of The Beatles.

Back in England it was time to record a number for another one of Mike Mansfield's TV shows, this time dressed up as choirboys. Mike and Tam probably came up with that one between them.

Throughout all this manic activity, I was experiencing levels of sexual frustration greater than any man could ever imagine. There I was, surrounded by hot girls and women, and I couldnae get near them. No wonder then that as soon as we got any time off to go home, I was at it like a rabbit on speed.

During tours, Tam did everything he could to keep us and the fans apart. Sometimes a few were allowed backstage after a gig but they were hand-picked by Tam and were usually the ones he fancied himself. Unfortunately, they weren't the right gender for me. He used to jokingly say things like 'Be nice to them!' or even 'You might need these one day!', which went way over my head. 'What for?' I said.

The shared rooms and guarded corridors were the biggest

problem, and that practice continued for years. Even with such measures in place, he'd still come prowling in the night to check we were alone, and we all feared he might be rifling through our rooms when we weren't in them. As we began to slowly break free from him much later, he would still come checking, especially when we had our own rooms.

When it all got too much, which was often, I ran the risk of humiliation and many times all I could do was watch in amazement as he literally dragged girls from my bed and threw them out the door. Outfoxing him became a sport and I started hiding my companions in wardrobes and under my bed – but he soon caught onto that. I started anonymously booking rooms in fake names so that I could install girls in them and sneak out later on when he thought I was safely tucked up in bed. He was obsessed with keeping me away from women; I was obsessed with getting to them. He was convinced that the Bay City Rollers had to be untouchable to maintain their popularity; I was determined to enjoy the fruits of my popularity. It was a never-ending war which drove us both to distraction.

In Stockholm once, I hid a girl out on the fire escape. Along came Tam, who decided the middle of the night was a good time to sit and chat for a while. As his nose was trained to detect that slightest whiff of perfume, I'm pretty sure he knew I'd hidden a lassie somewhere and was just trying to force her out. By the time he eventually left and the girl could safely come back in, she was literally blue with cold. A few more minutes and I could have been up on a charge of death by hypothermia, but it turned out OK because we had a great time while I warmed her up again.

At first, I was the only one willing to risk a sexual liaison while working. I had to keep my activities secret from the other Rollers, too, because I couldnae take the chance that they'd maybe grass me up to Tam. On tour, I would have to wait for them all to go out, or claim exhaustion or sickness before I could even think about getting any action. Then, as soon as the coast was clear, I'd dig out my stash of phone numbers – a stash that would normally consist of a few hundred names and numbers left at the hotel before we checked in. Added to those were the photos and bits of paper I'd been slipped by fans at airports and in crowds. Finally there were the notes that had been stuck under my hotel room door. The numbers left with receptionists at the hotel were discarded because I'd no idea what they looked like. The others, who passed me notes directly or under the door, were much more creative and able to promote their own particular talents more precisely. In other words, they described very clearly exactly what they would do to me should they be selected, and often this was written on the back of a photo which wouldnae have looked out of place in a porn mag.

For foreplay and to heighten the anticipation, I'd do eenie-meenie-minie-mo on a shortlist of candidates for a wee while, then start phoning around the numbers and literally binge-shag, not knowing when the next opportunity might arise.

The main thing I had to look out for was the nutters. I used to pride myself on my ability, courtesy of my sixth sense, to spot them a mile off and filter them out in the initial stages. For example, if they were swinging an axe as they handed me their number in the vicinity of the local psychiatric hospital, I probably wouldnae have followed that one up. I chuckled to myself when Robbie Williams was on TV recently, saying how amazed he was when one of the birds he'd shagged started talking as though they were now boyfriend and girlfriend. *Hello??* OK, maybe she wasn't wearing the latest Versace strait-jacket, but you can usually get the gist by looking into their eyes or engaging in about ten seconds of basic conversation beforehand!

A new way of evading Tam presented itself soon after arriving in Australia for the first time, late in 1975. I had really bad jet lag to the point of being barely able to function in any way, let alone sexually. My mum had given me a couple of Mandrax sleeping pills to take on the flight in case I couldnae get to sleep and they'd succeeded in doing that, but the jet lag was still there soon after I woke up again. A local doctor was called in to sort me out fast.

'Look, my mum gave me these before I left home,' I said, showing him the label on the empty bottle. 'They work really well. Can I get any more here?'

'How long are you in Australia for?' he asked, not batting an eyelid.

I told him, and he wrote out a prescription for another hundred.

'Hopefully, that'll fix you,' he said, handing it over.

Perhaps he was hoping I'd take the lot at once.

The Mandrax were very, very effective. Within half an hour of taking one, I was out like a light. Then it occurred to me that if I could get Tam and the others to take them, I would be free to explore the local delights without fear of being discovered. So, I got them all taking the tablets and off I went. After the first few excursions, I decided it was safe to let Alan in on the secret and from then on the two of us went out sharking together. There was no point in telling the others because (a) they'd have not wanted to take the risk, and (b) we couldnae trust them not to tell Tam.

If that sounds devious, it was nothing compared to some of the schemes dreamed up by the girls trying to get to us. They all must have been equally, if not more, frustrated because the ruses they came up with made mine seem pretty poor. The less imaginative would book themselves rooms in the same hotels in the hope of bumping into one of us in the lift or in the lobby. The ones slightly higher up the evolutionary scale would try and get hired as chambermaids or receptionists in the relevant hotels, and in some cases the hirers were stupid enough to take them on. One time in America, I made a date with a cute wee chambermaid for that evening, and when she arrived, she called my room from the lobby. I went downstairs to meet her and was gobsmacked to find her seated at the wheel of a Rolls-Royce, dripping in diamonds and designer-dressed. It transpired her daddy had given her the car as a present and the chambermaid job was not exactly the mainstay of her family's income. There were loads of similar rich kids in the States, and it never ceased to amaze me how much money would get blown on Roller-stalking. There was a couple of fans from Ohio that literally followed us around the world – from the States, to Japan, to England and back again. Every night they were there in the same hotel as us; it must have cost them, or their parents, thousands.

The most unimaginative but effective scheme, particularly in America, was to pretend to be a journalist. We were doing so many interviews all the time that it was impossible to have all the interviewers' credentials checked out, and if they'd had cards and badges printed up, they usually succeeded in getting to us.

Unfortunately, most of the girls using this method were, shall we say, the less attractive of our pursuers. Realising that nude photos of themselves might not achieve results, they needed face-to-face contact so they could win us over with their wit and intelligence – or so they thought. Far more likely to succeed was the full frontal approach or getting hold of a lift key and riding the elevators until a Roller got in. The lift then got jammed between floors while the lucky Roller got jammed against the wall.

The constant hounding by fans wasn't always welcome, but I kind of accepted it as the downside of the benefit of being able to get sex without preamble whenever the opportunity arose. During that same tour of Scandinavia when the wee lassie had her brush with hypothermia, our Viking ancestors certainly lived up to their reputation for a bit of rape and pillage. In Copenhagen, I was accosted by about ten of them in a hotel corridor. I legged it back to my room and while I was fumbling with the key and lock, they managed to literally rip off all my clothes. After what seemed like forever and a few well-placed stamps on toes that I was able to make seem accidental, I finally managed to get into the room. In Helsinki, after a gig where the wooden barriers *and* the stage were brought down by the fans, about 40 girls got wind of us back at the hotel and the chase was on. Up and down corridors, staircases, even through the sauna. I'll never forget the expressions of sheer disbelief on the faces of the big old boys trying to soak out the strains of the day in the sauna, as a bunch of tartan-clad lads followed by a horde of hormonal teenagers fell in, realised they'd picked the wrong door and fell out again.

I'll probably get slated in various places for having taken advantage of gorgeous, silk-skinned, eager girls and women so indiscriminately. That could start one hell of a debate which is probably best left alone. Suffice to say that it was never me that made the initial approach; they all knew what they wanted and we all wanted the same thing. It's the essence of being a pop or a rock star – always has been, always will be. It was fucking wonderful, and I'm not going to admit to any kind of retrospective guilt about my behaviour. I'd always liked sex and the diversity and quality on offer at that time was mind-blowing. Knowing that I shouldn't have been doing it and the ever-present danger of being discovered by Tam, made the thrill of it all indescribable. I guess it was a bit like the feeling someone gets when they're having a passionate, illicit affair, but magnified a million times.

shang-a-lang
shang-a-lang

The Pleasure and the Pain

Nineteen seventy-five. Most significant worldwide events that year seemed to be mirrored in Rollerland. It was to start out a year of scandal (world: Watergate; Rollerland: session musicians), develop into a year of important firsts (world: first female leader of a British political party; Rollerland: No. 1 single), new beginnings (world: China's new convention; Rollerland: Phil Wainman) and peace (world: end of Vietnam war; Rollerland: the exception – absolutely no chance of peace there!).

The dawn of the New Year focused everyone on what we'd done so far and where we thought we were going. For once, the band had a bit of an input. It was agreed pretty much universally that Bill Martin and Phil Coulter had done their best with us and there was a danger we would be stuck in a rut if we did many more songs with them. So our relationship with the duo was ended after they'd kindly given us four Top 10 hits and a No. 1 debut album in less than a year. There were some mutterings about Bell Records being off their heads to finish what had been a very successful relationship, but in the end it turned out to have been the right move. Bill and Phil went on to write many more hit songs for bands like Kenny and Midge Ure's Slik. After that they went their separate ways; Phil devoting his time to his love of Irish music, Bill continuing to preside over the world of pop.

On top of the hits, we'd also just received a Carl Alan Award for being the most popular group of 1974 (but the good old city of

Edinburgh still refused to give us a civic reception). This award was the '70s equivalent of a Brit, and we were really chuffed to be presented with one by HRH Princess Anne.

There were other changes taking place at Bell. Columbia Pictures, the label's parent company, was having a shake-up. They'd brought in a guy called Clive Davis, fresh out of Columbia Records (no relationship to Columbia Pictures). Paton versus Davis. The impending clash for control would have scared the life out of us if we'd had the foresight to see it coming.

Davis' job was to start up a new label, headquartered in America, and called Arista. Bell was to become the UK branch of that label. Clive was a lawyer with a penchant for talent spotting who eventually found himself at the helm of Columbia Records. Looking for a fresh challenge, he jumped at the chance to set up the new Arista, and quickly signed a number of hugely successful 'serious' acts, including Blood, Sweat and Tears, Simon and Garfunkel, and Janice Joplin. He didn't like pop music and didn't want any pop acts on his new classy label. At the same time, he had no notion of the scale of the Rollers' popularity in Europe – that funny little continent that had spawned nothing of any importance since The Beatles.

As soon as Arista was up and running, the Rollers' contract was transferred by the parent company from Bell to Arista, but it nearly wasn't. Many other Bell artists were dropped for not meeting Davis' spec. One of the label's biggest acts, Tony 'Tie A Yellow Ribbon' Orlando, went to Elektra. Another top band, Hot Chocolate, were lost to Big Tree, who got them into the Top 10 with 'Emma' – previously recorded on Bell. Barry Manilow and the Rollers were the only names of note to survive the clearout. The fact that we did was thanks to Tony Roberts, who had replaced Dick Leahy when he left Bell to do his own thing after *Rollin'*.

This is one of those points in the story of the Bay City Rollers where you have to ask 'what if. . . ?' What would have happened if we'd been signed up by another label that really wanted us?

As usual, we didn't think about it at the time. We were told what was best for us and accepted it.

Tony Roberts had stuck his neck out for us big time. Having been able to make Davis see he'd be kissing goodbye to millions if he let us go, he was now under major pressure to come up with the goods. Enter Phil Wainman, probably the most successful producer of the day.

Phil was most respected for what he'd done with Brian Connolly's Sweet. Since 1971, the band had had eight Top 10 hits including a No. 1. Phil had started out in a band called the Paramounts and scored a minor UK hit in 1964. Then he had a touch of the Nobbys and left the band that went on to change its name to Procol Harum and released quite an important little number called 'A Whiter Shade Of Pale'. He'd then turned his hand to songwriting and a bit later, while working as a session drummer, he met Johnny Goodison. The two, who would in the not too distant future be writing songs for the Rollers, toured in a band called the Quotations, but their focus always remained on writing and publishing. The big break came when he introduced Sweet to writers Mike Chapman and Nicky Chinn. From 1973 on, they had massive hits with 'Blockbuster' (using the same Yardbirds riff as Bowie's 'The Jean Genie'), 'Ballroom Blitz', 'Hell Raiser' and 'Teenage Rampage' – all songs which brought a rebellious tone to pop long before punk was born, and respect and recognition for Phil.

All was well for a long time until Chapman and Chinn decided they wanted a different role, and become writer/producers like Bill 'n' Phil and others. This created friction and Phil Wainman was ready to move on by the time Tony approached him with a proposal and a clearly defined brief: get the Bay City Rollers a No. 1.

Shouldn't be hard, thought Phil, I've the relevant experience. But there was a catch . . .

At that point, the Rollers were in the middle of a scandal the like of which had never been seen before in the world of pop, although it happens all the time nowadays. The tabloids shat on us from a great height. They'd found out we'd been using session musicians and told the world the boys couldnae play their instruments. Manna from heaven! You could feel their sneering delight coming off the pages as they exposed the Bay City Rollers as fakes.

Let's think for a while about where they'd got their information. Was it sour grapes on the part of our former songwriters? Did one of the session musicians we'd used see a chance to make a few quid? One theory suggests that it was a certain Mr Paton who spilled the beans at a time when there wasn't really much going on in the press about us. I know some say that any publicity's good publicity and maybe someone told Tam that and he put the story out to test the advice. I cannae think of any other reason he'd do something so stupid, unless one of the band had really pissed him off somehow and he'd lost all sense of reason. Wherever it came from, the breaking of that story represented that unavoidable turning point that all celebrities dread – the point when the papers, who are so kind and encouraging to start with because you increase their sales, suddenly decide you're now worthless to them and show themselves to be the back-stabbing, lie-spewing bastards that they truly are.

The most frustrating thing about the whole episode was that it really wasn't a big deal anyway – we'd have happily admitted to using session musicians if we'd been asked. Everybody except the real musical geniuses did it; it was just a simple matter of economics and minimising expensive studio time. Less time in the studio meant bigger profits for the record company, which benefited everyone.

Interpreting that we used session musicians to mean Eric, Woody and Alan couldnae play their guitars was daft. Of course they could play . . . how on earth could we have performed over a hundred gigs by the time the story came out if they couldnae? The simple fact was that their standard was acceptable when they first started out, and later on the audience noise levels would drown out far worse than one bum note or chord. They only fell down when they had to be consistent and accurate in a studio. Logic, record company budgets and outrageous time pressures dictated that we were not going to spend a couple of days getting one track down when we could bring in musicians who would get it right first time and at a fraction of the cost.

Like the rock versus pop scenario, it's just another one of those things about the music industry that'll never change – those who can play and write and do it well will gloat about it and take the piss out of those that cannae. Paddy the Plank once told me a story from way back in his days with The Beatles. The Monkees, arguably the first truly manufactured band, were in town, as were Lennon, McCartney and co. who had taken over the fifth floor of London's Royal Garden Hotel. The four of them, all lounging around in their Sergeant Pepper outfits, stoned out of their heads, collapsed in hysterics at John's piss-taking rendition of 'Hey hey, we're the Monkees'.

Arista was determined that none of their bands should be subjected to the same derision and the order was given: on all future Bay City Rollers recordings, the band must play their own instruments. I wouldnae mind betting they thought we'd never manage it and they'd have an excuse to be shot of us once and for all.

For Eric this was a dreadful time. From the day I joined the band, he'd been uneasy about my presence. Nobby had been quiet and serious about his music, like Eric, and I was a jumped-up little kid who wanted to be a pop star. I'd come in at the last minute and hit the big time while he'd had the struggle and poverty. He resented that I had as much say as he did, which in itself was stupid as none of us really had any say at all. On top of all that, it seemed Tam couldnae control me. Worst of all was that as the lead singer, I got more attention. There was a serious popularity clash.

When the piss taking about the band's musical aptitude started, I'm surprised he didn't end up in a psychiatric hospital. With all of those problems festering away inside, he was now being forced to face the fact that I was the only one, a few backing tracks and 'Angel Angel' aside, who actually performed on the early stuff. He wanted and needed more profile and more say and he wasn't getting it.

Phil Wainman took up Tony Roberts' challenge. He came to meet us in Edinburgh at my old haunt – the REL studios. The purpose of the meeting was to find out if he thought he could work with us (and just how good or bad we were at playing our instruments), and if we thought we could work with him.

I liked that he was down to earth enough to want to sell himself to us. I'd have expected someone with his degree of success to be more concerned with putting across how lucky we were to have the opportunity to work with him. The fact that he'd been to Princes Street and bought himself a tartan bow tie 'to break the ice', was welcomed. He seemed to want us to have a productive, two-way relationship, rather than to dictate how things would be done, and after Bill Martin's heavy-handed approach, we liked the idea. Eric perked up a bit.

We were all a bit nervous the day he came to see us for the first time, not knowing what to expect. Because of that we mucked about and took the piss. Phil remembers me asking him what shoe size he wore and the rest of the guys cracking up. I have no clue what that was all about and can only assume it was some kind of in-joke at the time. If it was, I'm surprised I was 'in' on it!

Phil set about restoring a balance of power. After listening to us play a while, he told me I was singing flat. He made me stand on a chair and the mike was extended to its full height. He scratched his head and said that made no difference, so the band must be playing sharp. Next he said I was singing sharp and could I try bending my knees . . . I had been stitched up like the proverbial kipper, like all the apprentices over time who've been asked to go and get a long weight.

It was decided that Phil was the man for the job and off he went back to London. Tam gave him a lift to the airport and propositioned him on the way. Later, we laughed about the fact that Phil, a devout heterosexual, had felt strangely complimented by Tam's advances. It was the first time a gay guy had tried to pull him.

The next thing we had to do was choose some songs to record with Phil Wainman. Having spent an evening with Tam when we'd all taken along lots of different records we thought we could do, we put forward the Four Seasons' 'Bye Bye Baby'. We knew we were on the right track when Phil said he was 'relieved' when he heard it.

'That's a No. 1 song,' he said, but he was worried about the intricacies of the number and said that it was going to be a difficult record to make. It was a subtle and polite way of saying he didn't think we were up to it.

'Let's do it,' we said, and began practising.

In no time at all, our first recording session with Phil arrived. To everyone's amazement, 'Bye Bye Baby', 'Give A Little Love' (written by Wainman and Goodison), 'It's For You' and 'Maryanne' (both Faulkner/Wood compositions), were all wrapped up in just three days.

We worked long hours to achieve that, desperate to prove that we were bona-fide musicians. We didn't often stop for sleep or food. Phil kept up the momentum, and kept us awake, by pedalling around the studio on his funny little foldaway bike.

That was my happiest time with the Bay City Rollers. We were all fired up with enthusiasm; we had a feeling in our bones about 'Bye Bye Baby' and we knew Phil and Johnny's 'Give A Little Love' was a winner too. Eric was ecstatic about having a guitar solo on 'Bye Bye Baby' and having not one, but *two* of his and Woody's songs on B-sides at long last. Phil brought us all together well on that track and the feeling spilled over into our relationships outside the studio.

The atmosphere was so good that the guys were even able to laugh at their over-publicised musical inadequacies. One time Phil had to call in a session guitarist to fine-tune their Fender Strats, because they'd been trying to do it with the bridge saddles. When it was explained that this was the cause of a bit of sharpness at the 12th fret, they were nonplussed: 'Oh well, we know fuck all about guitars.'

'Bye Bye Baby' was rushed out in February, charted immediately, and helped along with a few *Top Of The Pops* airings, was No. 1 by 22 March. It replaced Telly Savalas's 'If' – a ballad spoken rather than sung by the actor who played *Kojak*, the top cop series of the time. The music critics obviously hated such an outright piece of commercialism and although they weren't exactly over the moon when it was knocked from the top spot by a Rollers song, it was the lesser of two evils. Some of them have, in later years, even been brave enough to say things a little bit positive about the song. One reviewer said that the earlier BCR hits had been 'charming in their naivety' but 'by "Bye Bye Baby", the Rollers were coming on like a proper pop band, all big harmonies and guitars'. It was so rare to get some positive feedback, we didn't even bother to question what they'd thought we'd been before we were a proper pop band.

At one stage, the song was selling 60,000 to 70,000 units a *day*. Barry Perkins, who looked like he had serious sunburn most days, appeared to be about to explode as the sales data filtered through.

'It's a big pie, a big pie!' he would chortle, fingers dancing over the calculator buttons. His blood pressure must have gone through the roof when, after six weeks, the song was still topping the charts. On 29 April, we were ousted by Mud's 'Oh Boy', which must have made Phil's former colleagues Chinn and Chapman feel a bit better about their sad loss.

'Bye Bye Baby' *is* a great song and it got the kids waving their tartan scarves with abandon at school discos across the land (by this time, they'd also made up a not-too-complex little line dance to go with it). Workmen couldnae help whistling it in spite of themselves and to this day, that first chord immediately prior to my resolution to tell my bit on the side it's over, is instantly recognisable. In the UK, it's probably the best-remembered Rollers number. It's the one the audience waits for at gigs today; the one I normally save till last. I've recorded loads of different versions of it over the years but my favourite is a haunting acoustic interpretation. Everyone else's preferred version seems to be the '90s-style raved-up recording.

If things had been hectic before, 'Bye Bye Baby' made the early months look peaceful. Having had a No. 1 song, the Rollers were now a product with serious export potential and all the stops were pulled out to get us maximum exposure abroad. Videos that looked more like home movies were made to promote the song in Japan and Australia and there was even talk about trying to break America.

Europe and the UK were becoming more and more demanding. One day we flew to Germany to record a TV show, then flew straight back to England for a gig that night. That was followed by a major press conference the next morning in London, then another gig up north. The spring of 1975 was one long appearance – Capital Radio, *London Bridge* for LWT, *Roskoe's Round Table* and *Saturday Scene* were just some of the shows we did over a ten-day stretch. Tempers were getting more and more frayed and we all just wanted to be away from each other. Still sharing hotel rooms, we couldnae even get away from it all there.

There wasn't much time to dwell on it, let alone say or do anything about it, because we had another album to make. We were scheduled four weeks at Chipping Norton studios in Oxfordshire to record ten songs. A European tour would start one week after that, so there was no margin for error. As if that wasn't pressure enough, recording was interrupted twice so that we could film *Shang-A-Lang*, the Granada TV series due to air in the spring.

After such a good start with Phil, things took a turn for the worse when Eric found out from Phil Wainman's 'song peddler', David

Walker, that they wanted five songs on the new album. Now it was Eric who was coming on like the proper pop star, protesting that his and Woody's songs should dominate. Phil said he just wanted the best songs on the album, which he obviously didn't consider the Faulkner/Wood compositions to be. Eric didn't want anyone else earning royalties that would be the band's if his songs were used, which was admirable but not very practical. He flounced off and wrote 'Money Honey', which was about the greed he perceived in the industry and the people around him. One of those was Barry Perkins, who was, ironically, his only ally in the debate because of his own publishing interests in a company called Carlin Music, which meant he also stood to make money from having Eric's songs on the album. Tam wasn't happy with Eric at all, mainly because he was making a stand and showing he had balls . . . though hopefully not literally. Our manager was working on the book with Michael Wale by this time and his inability to conceal his frustration with Eric's stance on the matter is clear – either that or he was making a deliberate effort to shame Eric. He tells all the band's fans how difficult his lead guitarist can be: 'You see, with him there's no compromise.' The point is that contrary to Tam's textual declaration that in rows with Eric 'we always end up doing what I say in the end', Eric got his way on this and lots of other occasions.

The number of Goodison/Wainman tracks on the album went from the five originally requested to three – 'When Will You Be Mine?', 'Let's Go' and 'Rock And Roll Honeymoon'. A whole seven tracks were allocated to the dynamite Faulkner/Wood duo, two of which were also credited to me so that no one could say the lead singer couldnae do anything but sing. For similar reasons, Eric sang lead on 'When Will You Be Mine?', which was already a bit naff lyrically (it was about not having sex before marriage). Alan sang the out-of-place 'Rock And Roll Honeymoon'. I say out of place, because 'Honeymoon' was a great rock tune delivered by Al with oomph and talent. Next to Eric's insipid 'When Will You Be Mine?' and other stuff like 'My Teenage Heart' and 'Angel Baby', it stood out a mile. 'La Belle Jeane' and 'Marlina' were a nice pair of Faulkner/Wood numbers (we had to print a statement on the album cover that the names Jeane and Marlina were purely fictional, lest some of our less-stable fans took the song titles to represent girlfriends of band members and felt life to be no longer worth living). 'Bye Bye Baby' and a re-recording of 'Keep On Dancing', erasing Nobby Clark from the Roller psyche once and for all, completed the album which was, when all's said and done, much better than *Rollin'*.

Despite the early trauma over content, the *Once Upon A Star* sessions started well. We were beside ourselves when Phil – no doubt anxious to restore harmony – suggested on the first day that we should go to a nearby pub for lunch. *Pub??* We thought he was winding us up as there'd been such a massive effort to make sure our recording location was kept secret so we weren't disturbed. Of course we now know that no such thing happened – it was just another line we were fed – so Phil wasn't being as controversial as he appeared to us at the time.

He suggested it would be best if we didn't wear our Roller gear to the pub. He couldnae believe it when he found out that with the exception of my one pair of tartan-free jeans, no one else had even one item of clothing that *wasnae* Roller gear. He decided that, in the absence of normal clothes, we would just have to sneak to the pub for grub and a pint at quiet times when there'd be less people there. It wasn't long, of course, before word spread and then every fan within 50 miles of the studios knew where we were working. Our cover was blown and from then on we were trapped again. Those few outings were heaven while they lasted; a taste of reality in an unreal existence.

At this point a lot of people in the same situation would have started to resent the trappings of fame and wish they could 'just walk down the street without being recognised'. It certainly got Alan that way. Eric resented the intrusions which stunted his creativity. Personally, I accepted it as the price you paid for success. It was kind of like that crucial point that many pop, rock and film stars reach when they come up against excesses and where they either go the sex and drugs route or find another type of religion. It was love-it-or-hate-it time, and still, I loved it. Probably it was the contemplation of the levels of that success and the adulation and what a good time I was having that started to increase my confidence to levels I'd not previously experienced. Obviously this affected my thought patterns. For instance, I found myself thinking about that rule that we had to wear our Roller uniforms at all

My Les McKeown Scrapbook

Leslie Richard, fourth and final son of Florence and Frank McKeown.
(courtesy of the McKeown family)

The McKeown brothers – me, Brian, Hari and Roni.
(*courtesy of the McKeown family*)

I loved school . . . at first. Luckily
my hospitalisation with meningitis
came during the hols so I didnae
miss any.
(*courtesy of the McKeown family*)

Broomhouse (the 'Irish Ghetto') – bikes,
birds and babbies. A cycle of life.
(© *Lynne Wilson*)

Edinburgh, 1973: a pair of thin white dukes.
By now I'd formulated my escape plan.
(© Les McKeown)

My first band, Threshold; me on the left.
(© Pete Gillam)

Threshold, 1973. Left to right: Alan, me, Jon, John and Alex.
(© Pete Gillam)

Threshold, 2001. Left to right: Alan, me, Alex, Jon and John.
(© Lynne Elliott)

March 1975 – a year after the Bay City Rollers' first
Top Ten hit and the gold discs were rollin' in.
(© MSI)

Show us some leg, lads! Wonder who said that? Could've been any one of a
number of industry professionals involved with the Rollers at the time.
(© MSI)

By January 1976 we were top of the US charts . . .
(© DC Thomson)

. . . and I was on top of the
world. *(© Les McKeown)*

ROLLERMANIA

At the Radio 1 Fun Day at Mallory Park, fans nearly drowned trying to get to
us, and Tony Blackburn raced around in a speedboat driven by a Womble.
(© MSI)

In April 1976, Alan Longmuir was replaced by Ian Mitchell (back left). After about six months, Ian was replaced by Pat McGlynn.

(© DC Thomson)

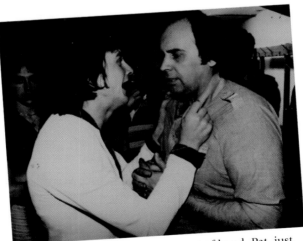

By 1977, things were getting out of hand. Pat, just visible behind me and looking dazed, hid in my hotel room to escape the unwanted attentions of 'Tattie Tam' Paton (right).

(© unknown)

By late '78, I had to hire local security in Japan to protect myself from
Tam and the other Rollers, whose hotel rooms I bugged to find out
what they were saying about me.

(© unknown)

1979: free of the Bay City Rollers and free of the tartan! My first solo venture, Ego Trip, was wrecked in the UK by an ITV strike, but we did really well in Japan and Europe.

(© MSI)

MY FAMILY

My family in 1993. I married Peko, the daughter of a Buddhist monk,
ten years earlier. I had to have my head shaved for the ceremony.
(*© unknown*)

One year old Jube with Peko
in 1985. A lot of new dads
find the first year hard, but by
this time my friend Charlie
was around a lot.
(*© Les McKeown*)

Back in the US of A in 1995 with my new band and family – Kev, Si, Jube, Russ, Peko, Ross and me.
(© Akemi Kinouchi)

That's my boy!
(© Peko McKeown)

1997 at the Hard Rock Cafe, Atlantic City – one venue brave enough to book us under the threat of legal action from Eric Faulkner.
(© Patty Simmons)

REUNITED?

1985: Woody, Alan, Eric, Derek, Pat, me and Eamonn Holmes, who was running a competition in which the prize was a day out with me, ten years after the height of our success. Same old problem – me in prime position; Eric looking pissed off.
(by permission of Eamonn Holmes)

Late 1998 – Derek, Alan, me, Woody and Eric filming for a BBC documentary about our lost millions.
(© Lynne Elliott)

GOING BACK TO MY ROOTS

Going back to my roots, 2001.
(*© Lynne Elliot*)

My lovely mum and dad, who both died
just over a year after this was taken.
(*© Lynne Elliott*)

Raving with the Legendaries in my US home town, Atlanta, 2002 – Si, Kev,
me, Mike and Russ.
(*© Lynne Elliott*)

Who knows what the future might bring!
(by permission of Frank Boyle, Edinburgh Evening News*)*

times, and the next time I was in London I treated myself to a silver suit from the King's Road. I was subconsciously telling myself as I bought that suit that it could be used, if and when necessary, to make a subtle 'fuck with me and I'll rebel' statement to Tam. I was getting a bit of that feeling of power that in Rollerland had been his unfairly exclusive domain so far. But what I definitely wasn't aware of was that I was also sending out 'I'm different to/better than you' vibes to my bandmates which, along with various other actions, led them to start worrying about the size of their lead singer's ego and where it was headed.

Phil Wainman made a breakthrough early on in the *Star* sessions. Not only did he have us all playing instruments to everyone's satisfaction, but he'd invented the '*schnitzer*'. The schnitzer (which Phil says is German for cheat, though it actually means carving, or cutting) was a means of recording and mixing just one chorus of a song, and then running the quarter-inch tape around the studio, with all of us supporting it with pencils, so that it could be re-recorded back on to the master tape. Phil's technique did away with the need to sing and play the chorus as many times as it was in the song, which had been the only way to do it previously. Fortunes were saved on time and budgets and, needless to say, the record company people were having orgasms over the savings. You could say that Phil Wainman's schnitzer meant that was the first time pop music was 'manufactured', technically speaking, at least.

There were still pockets of tension during those sessions, probably down to the time pressures which, despite the schnitzer, were still there. Phil, although he must have been immensely relieved that we were pulling it all together, was sometimes a wee bit lacking in the patience department. Sometimes I'd only get a few lines into a song before he'd shout '*No!*', stop the track, and make me start again. This could happen time after time and each time I got more and more frustrated. At Chipping Norton studios, the control room was high up and it doesn't need a shrink to work out why I had a problem with Phil sitting up there looming over me. His continual stopping and starting was really making it hard to concentrate on singing and as I festered about him being belittling rather than encouraging, I'd keep doing it wrong. Being 19 and not well equipped to deal with the conflict in a mature and reasonable way, I took to trying to wind *him* up back by being argumentative and acting like I knew more than he did.

We got there in the end and *Once Upon A Star* was released in early April. Bell kept it back like they'd done with *Rollin'* before and it charted in May, going straight in at No. 1 again. We got presented with our gold discs at the start of our second tour. It was only when our third album came out later in the year that *Star* dropped out of the charts, after 37 weeks. The three successive albums kept us consistently in the album charts from October 1974 until the spring of 1976. There was then a short reprieve and by the autumn, we were back in with our fourth album. *Once Upon A Star* was the second top seller of 1975, after a Stylistics greatest hits album, and we sold more copies than *Tubular Bells*. So bollocks to anyone who says we were a five-minute wonder!

Five-minute wonders don't get their own magazines or TV shows. The mag may have been shite, but at least we had one!

The Official Bay City Rollers magazine was launched early in 1975 in glorious full colour and crammed full of bullshit. It was written by editors and copywriters with a PR brief to satisfy and big expense accounts to cover. One week you'd find me supposedly talking about how the fan club received letters from parents worried about the band's influence on their kids, followed by my concern and reassurance that it was good to love the Rollers. Following the BCR special in *Music Star* claiming Eric had a girlfriend, the magazine provided the ideal vehicle in which to vehemently deny such scandal. Eric said he could never even think of having a girlfriend because he thought too much of the fans. Give me a bucket. Tam used the magazine to say anything and everything that needed saying, for example that there was no fear of the Rollers using drugs or booze as an escape like Hollywood stars did because they were too happy and too well balanced. It was the sheer quantity of the bullshit that made the magazine so bad.

The TV series *Shang-A-Lang*, which we started recording in March, was a lot better and aired for the first time on the first of April. In Britain, we were the first band in pop history to have our own programme. It had been done before in the US with the Monkees and the Partridge Family, which launched David Cassidy, but never at home.

The show had far-reaching effects. No self-respecting teenage girl in the land misbehaved at school on a Tuesday and risked a detention which would cause her to miss the show at 4.20 – a slot that gave the audience just enough time to rush home from school.

Like everything else, *Shang-A-Lang* was hastily thrown together. The 13 half-hour programmes were recorded over just three sessions of two days each. The producer, who kept us all sane – most of the time – was a fantastic lady called Muriel Young, who we'd met before when we'd appeared on *Lift Off* and *Lift Off With Ayshea*. It was so refreshing to work with a lovely, kind woman for a change.

Apart from the two or three songs we performed for each show, there were tons of other footage and features to entertain the fans. On *Shang-A-Lang* you could get a fix of the Rollers at work, rest and play.

In the first few shows, you could watch Eric and Woody having guitar lessons with Big Jim Sullivan, one of the most talented session musicians of the day. That feature was cut along with the show's director when the row about session musicians blew up. In came Mike Mansfield who introduced the 'bum shot'. I was never quite sure if that was for his benefit or the audience's. Features with more longevity included Derek's interviews with guest celebrities and a bit about the history of rock 'n' roll. This was all padded out with tons of footage of us doing absolutely anything that could be used on the show, preferably showing what a great bunch of happy-go-lucky guys we were. They'd have us riding Raleigh Choppers around the studio or riding horses in the woods. I'd not been near a horse before, and my colleagues thought it would be a laugh to make sure it was me who got the most spirited one. After a bit of an initial panic, I managed to take control and from then on, I loved the challenge of being astride a difficult or powerful beast and bending it to my will.

They also filmed us swinging on ropes and mucking about on a farm. By this time Eric and Woody had bought *their* doomed farm, near Edinburgh. It was supposed to be their little sanctuary, their haven where they could write classic songs undisturbed, so Tam had the *Shang-A-Lang* crew go visit and film them there. Eric and Woody had used a company name to apply for planning permission to convert part of the farm into a studio and, thanks to the programme showing images of the farm throughout the land, it came out at a council meeting who exactly it was applying for permission for the studio. The fans invaded and Eric and Woody's short-lived peace was shattered. While we were away on tour later in the year, four fans moved in and lived there for more than a week before anyone found out. The final straw came when the place nearly burnt down. It was a good publicity story for Tam, though, as was Eric checking into the Forest Mere Health Farm in Surrey for a rest. That too was filmed for *Shang-A-Lang*.

Not surprisingly, the fact that we had two days to record four or five shows put everyone under pressure. We should have been used to working like that by then I suppose, but it just seemed that the more we coped, the more they expected from us. Even Tam not being around much because he was off sniffing out and grooming others for superstardom didn't help. Still having to re-record songs for broadcast because of the bloody unions was the worst bit. Sometimes, as our roadie Jake Duncan remembers, we got away with switching tapes so that the man from the union unknowingly took away the master, but violence finally broke out when Bill Martin was momentarily back on the scene to produce the re-recording of 'Saturday Night'.

Being the perfectionist he is, and no doubt still seething from being replaced by Phil Wainman and wanting to make sure we – the band – paid for it, he took an age to set up the sound to his satisfaction. Every time we started the track, he got all Wainman-like, said something was wrong and made us start again. I questioned the need for Bill's presence in a way that caused offence, and as we were scrapping, Muriel and Barry Perkins came in. Barry tried to calm things down and found himself on the end of a punch from somewhere which sent his glasses flying across the studio. The others watched and laughed at what must have looked totally mental. At least the ruck prompted Muriel to try and do something about the union situation, and she managed to use her feminine wiles to negotiate some sort of deal with them for us, minimising the chance of the same thing happening again.

All the hot acts of the era were guests on *Shang-A-Lang*. They might not have given us the time of day anywhere else, but in the same way that Elton John has the vision to record a song with Blue today, they knew being on the Rollers' show would do their careers no harm. Some of them just performed their latest hit on their own; others were brave enough to interact with us. With Lulu, we did a top-hat-and-tails song-and-dance number and Eric foolishly kissed her at the end, resulting in an avalanche of mail. I think we stuck with male guests after that. Slade, Alvin Stardust, Sparks, T. Rex and Gary Glitter all appeared on the show.

On the day that Cliff Richard guested, tragedy struck. After Cliff had done his bit, he left the Granada studios to go back to his hotel. The fans, not knowing who was inside the van leaving the studios, assumed it was the Rollers and stormed it. The police, who were always there to keep the crowds under control when we were recording, moved in. One of the policemen had a heart attack and died. The dreadful news filtered through into the studio and we were all devastated. We felt responsible and useless, but we were made to carry on recording the other shows scheduled for that day. There was no room for tragedy in our schedule, but none of us realised exactly how unfeeling the Bay City Roller machine had become until some months later in the year.

The fans seemed to be as immune to what had just happened as everyone else. If you'd separated them and talked to them individually they might have displayed a degree of sadness, but en masse they were oblivious and uncaring.

Shang-A-Lang was one of Granada TV's most profitable exports. By now you'll not be surprised to hear that the Bay City Rollers didn't personally make any money out of the show, nor out of the video of highlights released and sold worldwide in the '90s, nor from the repeats of the show a couple of years ago on Granada's satellite channel.

While we were making an album and a TV series, Jef Hanlon worked on organising our second UK tour, which would begin less than five months after the first one ended. Venues throughout the land clamoured to be included on Tour Number Two's schedule, and the owners started thinking about which areas of their halls needed refurbishing so that they could make sure those bits got suitably damaged at the gig.

Everything was bigger and better for this one, including the tour convoy. It consisted of Tam and the band in a couple of cars, followed by a vanload of security including Paddy and Fat Fred, driven by Billy 'Up Front' Francis. There was a three-ton truck containing the light crew, Jake and his team of roadies, all their equipment and the band's instruments. Jef Hanlon and his security guys had another car, as did the Irish support band called Chips. They also had their own van. Dave Eager was called the 'compere' but his main function was to calm the audience so that they could actually hear him announce the acts. He had a car. There were two merchandise men from Artists Services, their two assistants and a mobile shop. A transit van stuffed full of programmes completed the procession. There'd not been much time to get new photos done for the programme, so Jef and Tam pulled old ones out of files in an attempt to fill it. The centre spread was a poster of us surrounded by sacks of tatties at Tam's house, and with the exception of the front-cover shot and a couple inside, many of them showed us in our old skinny-rib jumpers, bereft of tartan. Jef filled one page with a futile plea to the audience to behave themselves during the concert and not get carried away – while no doubt thinking up a plan to kick-start and build up the mania once again.

This time it started way before the tour did. It began as soon as the tickets started to go on sale. To be a real fan and prove it, it wasnae good enough just to get a ticket any more; that ticket had to be for a front-row seat. So desperate were the fans to get themselves in pole position, that in Edinburgh the police had to be called in to keep the fans orderly while they queued waiting for the box office to open. They had to try and stop them all crushing each other as they surged forward when it did. In Cardiff, it was reported that the venue was stormed by fans who rushed in after the cleaners at five o'clock in the morning, in an attempt to be first in line for tickets. I'm not sure whether these events were contrived, but given that the only reports of ticket mania seemed to happen in major cities, I'd guess they were. The coverage created a demand for tickets that meant that a few weeks before the tour started, the Rollers were heroes for adding dates to try and minimise the rioting and despair that occurred when hundreds of girls couldnae get hold of them. Extra nights were added in Glasgow and Edinburgh, so where we should have had a break of three nights, we only had one. No doubt we were never intended to have that break in the first place. We did get three days off between 12 and

15 May, but only so that we could record another four *Shang-A-Lang* shows on the 13th and 14th. From 27 April until 3 June, we had only 6 nights off.

And so the tour opened in April with six nights in Scotland, the first at the Glasgow Apollo. The Scots Guards played bagpipes and drums up and down the aisles of the theatre, then there was bird-song, for some reason, played through the speakers. Dave Eager announced us. We came on stage and stood, backs to the hysterical mob, while the word 'ALIVE' lit up the drum rostrum and the stage erupted into a rainbow of coloured lights. 'Bye Bye Baby' ended the show, not that anyone could hear it, and by then many of the fans had already left the theatre so that they could get a better position outside.

The tour progressed much as we'd expected. It was the same as the first one but better or worse, depending on how you look at it. There were more fans suffering from hyperventilation and needing treatment during gigs, and many more forced stoppages. One of our hometown shows had to be stopped not once but twice, while Dave Eager tried to restore some sort of order. The same happened a few nights later in Newcastle and police reinforcements were called in to restrain the thousands outside the venue who hadn't been able to get tickets (this time, Paddy and Tam's attempts to keep the police away were falling on deaf ears). Our getaway vehicle that night was an old van on the brink of falling apart. It skidded, or was skidded, on a roundabout as we made our escape and was immediately besieged. There would have been more left of it if it had been parked overnight in the baboon enclosure at Windsor Safari Park. The manager of Newcastle's City Hall graciously told the newspapers that Rollers fans were worse than those of The Beatles or The Rolling Stones.

Talking of the Stones, I'm pretty sure it was during this tour that Joe Seabrook, one of our security team, somehow managed to burst a main artery in his leg. Drawing on what I'd learned in the Boys' Brigade, I quickly made a tourniquet out of my tartan scarf to stem the flow of blood until an ambulance could get there. Funnily enough, there was a story that didn't make it into the papers. The act was acknowledged in a much more meaningful way more than 25 years later though, when I was invited to attend Joe's wake. After working with us, he'd gone on to be Keith Richard's personal bodyguard for 15 years, and it seems all The Rolling Stones knew about the tartan scarf incident.

Talking of tartan, in Swansea, the name of our hotel was leaked and the endless screaming and chanting from hundreds of tartan teenagers outside trapped the other poor guests for hours. Somehow, in Southport, some fans managed to fight their way past the security and almost pulled Eric and Alan off the stage. The show was stopped for 15 minutes and the audience was threatened with us not coming back on unless they cooled it. That made great headlines so the next night in Stoke-on-Trent, Eric was nearly ripped in half as the fans tried to pull him off the stage and I tried to pull him back on. At Manchester's Belle Vue, we had to leave the stage twice and the show was cut short by Tam, who seemed just for a moment to be tiring of the monster he'd created.

Jef had been unable to get us a gig at Earls Court in London because it was considered too dangerous to have a venue of that size full of Rollermaniacs. Instead, the Hammersmith Odeon was booked for Saturday, 31 May and Sunday, 1 June. The press reported that 250 fans were treated for shock and that a passing motorist had the door pulled off his Rolls-Royce because the fans had thought we were inside. When Parliament reconvened on the Monday, Marcus Lipton MP accused the Bay City Rollers of deliberately 'whipping up' hysteria and demanded that we change our act. Tam responded appropriately – appropriately, that is, if you want to cause maximum controversy and make the story run. 'No fucking way,' he said, and told us to concentrate on whipping up hysteria. A couple of days after that, a pianist named Tony called for an emergency meeting of the Musicians' Union to ask for session musicians to be banned from working with us, in an attempt to get us to behave. That same night, in Oxford, the audience included Peter Marsh, a psychologist who had been studying the behaviour of football fans. He'd gone along to compare and contrast football hooligans with Bay City Roller fans, and backed up Lipton's comments by telling the press that the band members *were* purposely inciting the girls to riot by getting as close as they possibly could to the fans without actually touching them, then jumping back again to send them into a frenzy. He didn't mention any acts of hooliganism; he just slated the band. After a gig in Great Yarmouth, we were given the next 24 hours off. I went home to Edinburgh.

A few hours before I had to be at the airport to fly down to Bristol for the Thursday night gig, I was driving my girlfriend at the time and my brother Hari around in my brand-new Ford Mustang. We waited for ages to turn out of a side street onto the main Corstorphine Road, which was then a dual carriageway on that stretch. Seeing a gap coming in the outer lane, I put my foot down and pulled out quickly into it, keeping my foot down so that the car coming up behind wouldnae have to slow down. Once going with the flow, I slowed down and pulled into the inside lane. By now the traffic had thinned and it was then that I noticed an old lady up ahead a bit at the kerb. She looked as though she was about to step into the road so I hooted and she looked up. In that split second, I thought, 'OK, she's seen me', and then she stepped off the kerb. I swerved and missed her, but then she changed direction. The next thing I knew the car was embedded in someone's front garden wall and I couldnae see where the old lady was.

A nurse who was walking along the Corstorphine Road helped me out of the car through the window.

I'll never forget and I'll never get over seeing that old lady lying in the street. An ambulance and the police were called, and my girlfriend, who had head injuries, was taken to hospital to be fixed up. The people whose wall I'd demolished took Hari and me into their home and tried to calm us. This they did in the usual Scottish manner – they gave us a cup of tea and a shot of whisky. As the glass reached my lips, the police arrived.

After the press had tired of printing the speeding, drugged-up, pissed pop-star stories which most readers were happy to subscribe to, I was charged. My court appearance was set for November, a few days after my 20th birthday.

Needless to say, the gig that night had to be cancelled. Jef Hanlon had to tell the fans as they queued at the door. The TV cameras got it all for *John Craven's Newsround*. The *Edinburgh Evening News* managed to get the basic details in that evening's stop press column. The next morning's national headlines were predictable if nothing else – both *The Sun* and the *Daily Mirror* guaranteed themselves thousands of additional sales by being able to write 'Bay City Roller' and 'Death [Crash]' in the same headline. Tam concentrated on making sure everyone knew the lassie that had been in the car was Hari's girlfriend and not mine.

I felt as if I was not in my own body but our manager insisted that the best thing I could do the following night was go ahead with a gig in Southampton. I shouldn't have been surprised by that – Alan and Derek did *Top Of The Pops* the night after their beloved mother died. The problem was that there was no way the momentum could be allowed to stop. It was felt that if we cancelled the rest of the tour (there were only three or four dates left to play), we'd lose a hell of a lot of fans and that could be curtains for the band. I don't know why he didn't just come straight out with it and say, 'It's not the rest of the band's fault you fucked up. Why should all the rest of us suffer because of your stupidity?'

A statement was issued by our spokesman, Tony Barrow, who said that although Les McKeown was still badly shaken he didn't want to disappoint any more fans. The next day the papers made sure everyone thought I was a cold, unfeeling bastard for going ahead with the gig. That night, as the fans carried on screaming as though nothing had happened, I couldnae take it any more and finally cracked. I broke down and ran from the stage. The rest of the guys didn't know what to do so they carried on playing and by the time they started the next number I'd been pushed back in front of the audience, still crying, like them, and brainwashed into believing the show must go on. Somewhere outside my head I could hear some of them shouting 'don't cry, Les, please don't cry'. I just wanted to curl up and die.

I was 19 years old, I'd just killed someone, and it seemed like everyone around me was pretending it hadnae happened or it didnae matter. There I was on a stage in front of a few thousand screaming girls who, for the most part, didnae want the concert they saved and waited ages for to be anything less than perfect. Tam was worried about contracts and commitments and getting us to the US. The other guys in the band didn't know how to deal with me. How could they? They stayed away and I didn't blame them. None of us had a clue about how to care for and support someone in my situation. What the hell were they supposed to say? The only people that did say anything were the journalists and they just kept making everything worse.

I got through the two London gigs in some kind of haze and the gig after those was the second-to-last gig of the tour. By that time the press hype and the build-up of fans trying to outdo each other had reached its peak. This was the Oxford gig, the one attended by our friend the psychologist. There were security guys and photographers in the orchestra pit, and the girls were clambering into it as they tried to get onto the stage. It looked to us like the guys in the pit were being really rough with the girls in their attempts to stop them. In my unthinking, unstable state of mind I hit one of the photographers with the mike stand. Next, Eric and I were off the stage and in the pit, trying to stop these guys from hurting our fans. Eric, once back on stage, explained to the rest of the audience that he had seen men beating up a little girl and that he didn't like it. We carried on with the set and when we came off stage, we found out that one of the guys Eric had smacked in all the confusion was not part of the theatre's security or a photographer, but a St. John Ambulanceman. A hefty donation was made to ensure the organisation's continued assistance at future gigs and to keep the story out of the press. I ended up with another court appearance set for November and Eric walked away.

The newspapers the following day carried many different versions of events. People that had been in the orchestra pit said that we'd been swinging our mike stands around throughout the show, deliberately trying to hit them. Others just reported that the lead singer had hit a photographer. One thing was clear and indisputable – that maniac McKeown who'd run over that poor old lady was out of control. It felt like everyone hated me, and I felt that way because my only source of information was the papers which, in my naivety, I believed. On top of that was the guilt when I thought about the old lady's daughter, then there was the concern and sadness in my mum's eyes and the helplessness in my dad's – just as hard to deal with. I don't usually have much truck with therapy and counselling but, God knows, I wish there'd been something back then. I wish I hadnae been expected to keep a stiff upper lip and get a grip. And I really wish someone could have told me how I was supposed to say sorry and how my life could ever be the same again.

The guilt doesn't fade; it grows. The more I think, the worse it is, so if I start to think, I usually end up having a drink. I'd like to be able to put some blame for that feeling elsewhere, especially on

Tam. But at the end of the day, no matter how you're forced to behave, or how your individuality is suppressed, you still have to answer to yourself. I know I shouldn't have gone on stage so soon after the accident. I know I should have gone with my gut feeling. I should have had the strength of character to say no, enough is enough. I know it was wrong to take it out on the Oxford photographer, but that wasn't a reasoned action so I can at least excuse myself for that one.

I sometimes wonder what would have happened if I'd had the balls to quit there and then? At the very least, I might not have acquired the 'heartless bastard' label and people's recollections of me and their perceptions today might be different. After a time I might have gone on to have a more successful solo career. Maybe taking positive action would have allowed me to lay that old lady's ghost to rest and feel a little bit easier about it all than I do now.

shang-a-lang

The Scots Invade America

After the hell that was the spring of '75, Tam told the newspapers that he was giving us all some time off, even allegedly cancelling appearances, so that we could all chill out a bit. Eric and Woody were going to a health farm in the south of England, I was moving into my new house at Torphichen and learning to fly, and Alan was going fishing in Inverness. There was no mention of Tam's or Derek's plans.

Tam took the opportunity to moan, like very famous people usually do, about lack of privacy and pressure. He'd reached that point where, having courted the media and publicity for so long, he'd decided he didn't like the invasions that went with them:

'Often the public ask how can these young men with the world at their feet be suffering, but they don't seem to realise that the pressure comes because they can't get away from it all. When you ask the fans to ease off a bit they tell us "we made you!"'

What Tam's describing is what I call the IOU syndrome, which I'll talk a bit about later.

The important thing here is that despite what Tam was saying to the press, he was making plans to put us under more pressure than we'd ever known.

That pressure was called America.

But first, we had another album to make and another No. 1 to notch up.

During the summer, we were allowed another four weeks to record our third album, *Wouldn't You Like It?*. Our second with Phil Wainman, again under the musical direction of Colin Frechter. Routinely by now, there were fights over which and whose songs would be on the album, made worse by the fact we'd all recently had smallpox jabs for a tour of Australia which, we were told, was making us more argumentative than usual.

In the end, with the exception of Phil and Johnny's 'Give A Little Love' – the only single to come off the album – all the songs on *Wouldn't You Like It?* were written by my friends Mr Faulkner and Mr Wood.

Now you might think that Eric would've been happy about that. Not a chance.

Having secured a near 100 per cent songwriting presence on the album, he started querying why some of his songs were included and others were left off. 'Money Honey', his favourite, wasn't there, nor was another one of his stronger numbers, 'Rock 'n' Roller'. It was probably considered too similar to 'Too Young To Rock And Roll', which *was* included. Eric complained that songs he clearly considered classics, such as 'Another Rainy Day In New York City' and 'You're A Woman', didn't make it (until albums six and four respectively) while the anaemic 'Love Is' and 'Lovely To See You' passed the test. It was easy to see why – while we were being allowed a certain amount of rope – sorry, scope – to expand and develop our style, it was felt that too hasty a departure from our sing-songy roots would be dangerous.

The result was that *Wouldn't You Like It?* was, in my opinion, the weakest of all the albums, and most people, with the possible exception of some Faulkner/Wood devotees, have agreed. One thing that was not open to debate as the album was released was that Eric Faulkner was never going to change. He'd got his own way with an album of virtually all his own stuff, and then said that it wasn't the right stuff. Was he ever going to be satisfied?

Just as with *Once Upon A Star*, the weakest link as we went back into the studios to start *Wouldn't You Like It?* – according to Tam's research – was Alan. Once again he was given a track to sing, this time a ballad called 'Here Comes That Feeling Again'. The song wasn't of the calibre of 'Rock And Roll Honeymoon' but it was well sung (he always was well sung, Big Al . . .). By the time you got to

'Derek's End Piece' you felt relieved at having reached the end of the album. But it didn't do to contemplate the strange choice of title on that one. That could make you feel as bilious as you did listening to 'Shag Hide' ('Shanghai'd In Love').

The excellent 'Give A Little Love', which saved the album, was rushed out as a single as soon as it was recorded – unusually for those days, months before the album's release – and our second No. 1 spent nine weeks on the chart. It was No. 1 for three weeks and the song of the summer for most teenage girls in Britain. It was knocked off by Typically Tropical's (Whoa! I'm Going To) 'Barbados'. The four songs that topped the chart in between 'Bye Bye Baby' and 'Give A Little Love' demonstrate the eclectic nature of the charts at the time: Tammy Wynette's 'Stand By Your Man' was a rare country success, followed by a godawful TV-related song, 'Whispering Grass', sung by Windsor Davies and Don Estelle from the comedy series *It Ain't Half Hot, Mum*. Next came 10cc's classic 'I'm Not In Love', and 'Tears On My Pillow' by Johnny Nash.

Three albums into our career, worldwide domination was ours for the taking. Throughout Europe, we were consistently No. 1 in both the singles and albums charts. Word had spread to Australia, and even Japan – a country that, in my mind, was even more distant than Oz and New Zealand.

From August onwards, the Japanese had an album-releasing frenzy the like of which had never been seen before. Our first two albums were released there by CBS/Sony, under licence from Arista, but in reverse order – *Once Upon A Star* was our debut album in Japan. One month after *Rollin'* they brought out *Bay City Rollers,* which was the same as the US debut album except that the Japanese added 'All Of Me Loves All Of You', missing from the UK LP. As *Bay City Rollers* was made up of a mix of *Rollin'* and *Star,* there was nothing on there that hadn't been on one of the first two. Most people would call that market saturation, but not in Japan. To meet the incredible demand for the Rollers, CBS/Sony then immediately released *Souvenirs Of Youth,* a double album released only in Japan that included everything ever recorded by both versions of the Rollers. Even 'Mañana' was on there, along with 'We Can Make Music', and 'Saturday Night' for the third time in four albums – but with Nobby Clark's vocals on this occasion. They also threw in all the B-sides for good measure. Just over two years later, *Souvenirs Of Youth* was reissued under the name of *Early Collection* with a couple of extra tracks. By *Wouldn't You Like It?* the licence had been transferred to Toshiba/EMI, who added 'Saturday Night' to their version, just in case anyone had missed it on the previous three. The following month they reissued identical versions of *Once Upon A Star* and *Rollin'*.

In spite of the record-releasing mania in Japan and record-breaking sales of albums by a band who hadn't yet set foot in the country, America was the priority.

Just before Tam's press release about what a well-earned break we were all going to have, an American Bay City Rollers manager had been appointed. That means an American had been hired to look after our interests in the US – not that Tam had been replaced by an American, unfortunately.

His name was Sid Bernstein and his credentials were unbeatable. He'd been responsible for introducing The Beatles to America, giving them sell-out shows at Carnegie Hall for starters in 1964, followed by record-breaking shows at Shea Stadium in 1965. He specialised in breaking British acts in America and delights to this day in talking about his responsibility for the 'British invasion'. It was Sid's assistant, Dave Stein, who first put him in touch with the Bay City Rollers phenomenon. Dave got a hold of Barry Perkins's number, who wasted no time in putting Bernstein's office directly in touch with Tam.

On 15 September, Arista released 'Saturday Night' in the US. Five days later, we made our American television debut on a show called *Saturday Night Live with Howard Cosell*. Before the spring tour, it had been rumoured that one of the Glasgow Apollo shows was to be filmed for an American show called *Wonderama*. I'm not sure if it was actually filmed or not, but I'd guess that getting us on the *Cosell* show was a right result compared to a bit of pre-recorded gig stuff on the other show.

Our first appearance on American television was to be no ordinary song-and-bit-of-chat affair, this was a highly orchestrated manoeuvre with the subtlety of a George Dubyah speech. The attention to detail reminded me of my own highly orchestrated manoeuvre back at Forrester's School. It was incredible that it was only four years ago that this kid on the verge of international superstardom had been so distraught and destined for the scrap heap . . .

Thanks to the latest satellite technology, our appearance on *Cosell* was a live link between the early evening show and a one-off special late-night gig at the London Weekend Television studios, staged with the sole purpose of grabbing America by the balls. The gig was called 'Night Flight' and opened with us bursting out of a massive tartan gift box, labelled 'From Scotland, With Love'. Everything about it suggested that our performance was 100 per cent live, but of course in reality there was no way the powers that were would take such a risk with the most important gig of the band's life to date. The combined genius of Phil Wainman and Jef Hanlon ensured that the big event was cunningly engineered so that the performance seemed as live as it possibly could. It was all done with tapes and recordings of the audience that had been made earlier, but no one sussed it. Even when one of the amps fell over during the show, nobody noticed that it crashed to the floor without a sound. Even more telling is that at one point I was pulled into the crowd by the girls, yet the vocals didnae miss a beat!

The audience was only about 500 to 600 strong and on this occasion, because nobody wanted to take responsibility for little girls roaming the streets after midnight, there'd been an age limit set of 16. Also, it wouldnae have done us any favours to have American parents throwing up their hands in horror at the sight of so many little Brit children totally off their trolleys. Apparently, young teens in a state of hysteria was acceptable. Luckily the link had been cut by the time the post-show riots broke out.

The next day, the *Daily Mail* reported that the show, which also featured Shirley Bassey and Frank Sinatra, had been watched by 25,000,000 viewers. Apparently, I'd gone into hiding in Edinburgh, having been knocked unconscious afterwards by fans, and Tony Barrow said that much as I loved the girls, understood their excitement and appreciated their devotion, I strongly objected when they went over the top. I was, of course, at pains to point out that despite the injuries I'd sustained, it was the safety of the audience that I was most concerned about. The 25,000,000 bit was probably true, but that's about it.

Again, the Bay City Rollers were being accused of having been deliberately provocative. A bunch of undernourished Scottish kids

129

jigging around in fancy dress was provocative? It was clear that the British media's attitude towards us over the session musicians saga was not temporary and they were now going all out to flatten us.

Well, fuck 'em. We were off to the States, anyway.

We flew first class to America on 30 September. We were served champagne, caviar and canapes. I was starving and scoffed the lot. The others, preferring their down-to-earth pie and chips, weren't impressed. On future trips, we'd have to take McDonald's on the plane with us, picked up by someone in a limo from the golden-arched restaurant nearest the airport and delivered onto the plane at the last minute. We marvelled at the treatment we were getting and thought it was great that everyone was so good to us. If we'd known how pricey all those Big Macs were going to work out once all the associated costs had been added in, maybe the caviar and canapes would've been easier to swallow.

There were to be no gigs on this first visit, it was just a promo tour – one appearance after another, after another, after another. There'd also be some interviews, but not too many, because apparently the Americans had difficulty understanding our accents.

When we touched down at JFK, I felt like I'd arrived in more ways than one. There was a pipe band lined up and playing on the tarmac, and limos on the runway. We were whisked off to the luxurious Westbury Hotel on Manhattan's Upper East Side and no one commented on the fact that there were maybe a few hundred girls to greet us at the airport and probably a few thousand waving us goodbye back at Heathrow.

I liked the Americans and laughed at the way they called Woody 'Stooart' and me 'Less' (over there Les is usually short for Lester and Lez is short for lesbian). We came from 'Edinborrow'.

Tam obviously felt like he'd finally made it and wasted no time in spending $9,000 on getting his teeth capped. He tried to get me to do the same. I told him I didn't want my crooked but perfectly healthy teeth mucked around with just because his idea of the day was that we should all have Donny Osmond smiles.

We were bundled off for our first photo shoot at the Rockefeller Center in Manhattan. The Center, in all its massive sky-scraping glory, brought together all my feelings and expectations about America. Standing on a site once peppered with hookers and pimps, the complex was built by John D. Rockefeller Jr for the new radio and TV companies of the '30s, like RCA. By 1940, 'Radio City' was made up of 14 buildings around a plaza with a skating rink and a gold statue of Prometheus. The Rollers had to pose for photos in front of the statue. I wonder if people in the throng were sniggering to themselves for having us pictured with a mythical figure who was condemned to endless punishment?

One of my clearest memories from that trip is of the crabs . . .

I caught crab lice from a bed. Can you believe that? Well, it's true. We stayed in a hotel in Chinatown, I woke up in the morning and I had crabs. Simple as that. I'd always been told that they couldnae live away from nice warm genital areas for very long so, as you can imagine, I was shocked to learn that they can in fact live away from the body for some time. From then on, I always asked for the bed sheets to be changed while I was actually in the room if there was any chance at all that someone with crabs or some other condition had been using it a bit earlier, which, of course, there always was.

I don't know where the idea came from, but I laughed to myself as it took shape. I quickly collected up as many of the itchy little bastards as I could into a glass and covered it over. A wee while later, I managed to sneak into Tam 'my door is always open' Paton's room and plant them in his bed. Later, Alan slipped some more into his drink. The ones in the bed obviously survived and took hold because Woody, Alan and I could hardly contain ourselves as we watched him permanently scratching his balls for the next few days. The funniest thing was that in all the bullshit put out about us and how it was always said that I was the joker of the band, that particular tale was never used to demonstrate just what a cunning rascal I was.

That reminds me of another confrontation I had with crabs in Munich. After a show, I was chatting with a really gorgeous bird who wanted to sleep with me. We had a shower together and I saw them.

'*Was ist das?*' I asked, pleased with my grasp of the German language.

'*Was?*' she answered.

'*Sie haben die Krabben!*' I stated. The literal translation of what I'd said is 'they have the prawns', and she was a bit confused. I called my friend Bubi to ask him what German for crabs was.

'*Filzlausen!*' he informed me.

'*Filzlausen!*' I told her, pointing at them. She understood me, and was suitably embarrassed and upset. What could I do? Avoiding any entanglement, I managed to remain crab-free. Looking back, it was incredible that I didn't spend half my life at the VD clinic, all things and quantities considered. Apart from the one crab infestation that wasn't down to me, I didn't catch anything worse than a bit of non-specific urethritis, which could have been caused by any number of things other than shagging.

By the time we made it to America, we were taking various medications to help us sleep at the right times, be awake at the right times, and do everything else at the right times. For a fair wee while we'd had a stash of stuff to help us out as and when we'd needed it, and now it seemed we were needing it more and more often.

I'm fairly sure it was the cocktail of drugs on that promo tour that caused me to have the weirdest and most horrible dream I'd had in my life, on our third or fourth night there. Looking back, it's easy to see that this latest nightmare had the same latent content as the earlier ones of deformed sheep and black nights, but that the horror was scaled up in line with my career progression and the continually growing unease between me and the others in the band.

There we were – Eric, Woody, Tam and me – in a hotel room, and we'd all taken ludes (Quaaludes). Ludes were the Viagra of their day, the only difference being that if you were tired when you took them, you'd just keel over and sleep for ages. We were always tired so they were safe, weren't they? Dreams being what they are, on this occasion we'd taken them when we weren't all that tired. Maybe we'd had some speed just before to keep us awake. We were just sitting around chatting and laughing, and I can clearly remember feeling like I was in a dream – in the dream, if you know what I mean. Then there was some kind of blank, like a cut between scenes in a movie, and suddenly I was witnessing a bizarre sex tableau like a *ménage à trois* I must have seen at some time in the *Kama Sutra* or some other erotic literature. I couldnae believe what I was seeing; I just sat there watching. Although in the dream I was in a trance-like state, I remembered the new camera I had with me and, feeling safely disconnected from the situation, I began snapping away, chuckling to myself. Soon I'd finished the film so I sneaked off back to my room to get another one. There was another cut between scenes and I was back in the room with the others, but the scene had ended and the three of them just sat there looking at me with exactly the same expression as those fucking sheep. I went back to my own room and found my roll of film pulled from the reel and stretched all over the bed . . . that's all I remember before waking up. I wonder what Freud would have had to say about that?

I spent most of the rest of the week looking skywards with my mouth hanging open. We went to a New Jersey shopping mall that was bigger than Wales, restaurants that served dinners for one that would feed fifty back home and drove around in limos that were longer than the Firth of Forth Bridge. On the fourth of October, one week after our first US TV show, we were on *Saturday Night Live* again, only this time we really were.

We flew home the next day, knowing nothing could ever be the same again.

Having already released 'Saturday Night' as a single, Arista went into overdrive and rushed out an album, imaginatively called *Bay City Rollers*, one week later. It was made up of the 11 best tracks, in their opinion, from *Rollin'* ('Shang-A-Lang', 'Be My Baby', 'Summerlove Sensation', 'Remember' and 'Saturday Night') and *Once Upon A Star* ('Bye Bye Baby', 'Marlina', 'Let's Go', 'My Teenage Heart' and 'Keep On Dancing') together with 'Give A Little Love' from *Wouldn't You Like It?*, our third album, which still hadn't been released in the UK. When you look at who wrote those tracks (four from Martin/Coulter, one from Goodison/Wainman, two from Faulkner/Wood and four cover versions), the allocation seems fair, given the band's history to that point. It's only when you look at the songs that weren't included that you see that while 'the professionals' were equally rejected with a brace of tracks each not making it onto the album, a total of *nine* BCR-penned numbers were overlooked. With that one simple statistic in mind, it's easier to subscribe to Eric's theory that everyone was out to line their own pockets with publishing royalties at our expense. But then again, you could still argue that the Faulkner/Wood songs just weren't good enough, especially in America where we had yet to build a major fan-base. The point is significant mainly because it was the first time Eric wasn't able to stamp his feet and influence the outcome of an album's track listing.

Back at home, 'Money Honey' was released and it charted on 22 November. It reached No. 3. If you've been paying attention, you'll remember that this was the song that Eric wrote at the height of his fury with Phil Wainman over the tracks to be included on *Once Upon A Star*, and his feelings come through loud and clear:

> Money Honey you ain't got no respect
> Sly like a fox, yeah
> Just to see what you can get . . .

While the lyrics were never going to set the world on fire, it made a change for a Rollers song to echo real emotion instead of the sugar-coated stuff of 'Summerlove Sensation'. There was also a nice little riff in there which, in my opinion, not only contributed largely to the song's success, but also conjured up a brilliant wee vision of Eric in a temper, with a platform boot stomping up and down and sparks flying from his tufty hair.

The success of 'Money Honey', coupled with Arista's reluctance to have too many of our own songs on our first album, wound Eric up to such a level that it was impossible for the rest of us to just shut out his rantings any longer. His theory was that because 'Money Honey' had made it into the Top 3 (and to No. 1 all over Europe and in Japan), it proved that his songs were good and that we shouldn't be lining other songwriters' pockets by doing cover versions. We all thought it was a good song and our collective ego had grown to such an extent by then that it was easy to think we were better than the rest. Eric was right; we should stand up for our beliefs and not be dictated to.

In reality, of course, fans bought the record simply because it was sung by us. Many of them have said as much since, and that it was their least-favourite Rollers song because it wasn't the 'happy rock' they were used to. On the other hand, some say they welcomed the rockier number because it showed the band was growing up, but in

shang-a-lang
shang-a-lang

most cases that's just what they say now, having developed their musical appreciation over a period of 20-plus years. There can't be many people on the planet who would argue that the Bay City Rollers wouldnae have had the same success if they'd released 'Ring-A-Ring O' Roses' at that time. If the song was so good in its own right, how come no one else has wanted to record it since?

Tam dealt with Eric's points of view by trying to bring him back down to earth, or crushing his self-esteem, depending on whose viewpoint you take. Unfortunately, the words and tactics used by Tam just made Eric feel inadequate, and making you feel inadequate was Tam's most effective and frequently used weapon. After 'Money Honey', it wasn't a case of 'well done, lad, you've written a hit song', but 'look what you've done, we only got to No. 3 because of you – the Rollers are finished!'. He pressed the point home when the album *Wouldn't You Like It?* also reached No. 3 in early December and only stayed in the charts for a meagre 12 weeks.

I think Eric feels that this was the crux time when we should have gone it alone and done our own thing. But if we had, the music mafia would have disowned us, we would have been unable to work anywhere in this solar system and, more importantly, the songs would probably have been predominantly naff.

Eric says that we were all brainwashed by Tam, especially Woody. I've thought long and hard about that, and really I think to say we were brainwashed is a bit of a cop-out on our part. It's kind of like an admission that we didn't have the substance to resist it; that we were weak and naive. Naive, without a shadow of a doubt – but weak? Sometimes, some of us probably were, and that was definitely exploited by our manager. Like I said earlier, at the end of the day you answer to yourself and you have to accept responsibility for your actions – or inaction. I think that Eric's belief that we were all programmed and brainwashed is his way of subconsciously putting the blame somewhere else for things that he feels he did wrong or went wrong in his life.

He seems to blame the rest of us for never having sat down and taken control of our own destiny, despite his attempts to make us do it. With hindsight it's very easy to say we should have taken the time to think about exactly where we were going and plot a route, but we simply didn't have the time, energy or experience. Having any kind of a group discussion would have been an achievement in itself. We were so caught up in our manic day-to-day existences and ensconced in our own little worlds, that we were really not that much interested in anything more than what we were doing that night or the next day. We just had too much on our minds. On top of that, we seemed to be doing all right and we were being looked after by people who we were constantly told knew far more about the record industry than Eric did, so why worry?

Knowing what we know now, of course, we should have paid more attention to what was going on. None of us could disagree with that. When Eric started to write down some of his thoughts on the Rollers' career, he said that 'the way Tam manipulated Woody was one of the most pathetic things to happen during the band's existence', and that Woody was brainwashed against writing songs with Eric. Apparently, after *Once Upon A Star*, Woody put forward no new songs until the sixth album. So what does that mean, then? That all the Faulkner/Wood numbers on *Wouldn't You Like It?* and the next two albums were written before and during *Star*, or that they were in fact written solely by Eric? Given that there's seven Faulkner/Wood songs on *Star* and all but one on *Wouldn't You Like It?* were attributed to the two of them, I'm having a wee problem working out exactly how Tam had brainwashed Woody against working with Eric.

Clive Davis, meanwhile, having been forced to take notice of the Bay City Rollers now they'd notched up a No. 1 single and hit album in the States, began to take an interest. By that I mean he began to recommend what should and should not be released and recorded. He required that a phenomenon as big as the Rollers would have to have his stamp on it for the world and the future to see. His secondary consideration was to rake in as many dollars as possible, and the quickest and safest way to do that was to release the likes of 'Shang-A-Lang' and 'Summerlove Sensation'. Songs that were proven winners in Europe were probably likely to have the same success in the US.

Eric was driven to distraction. He, along with others, resented Clive's change in direction for us and found the accompanying butt-kissing and bullshit hard to swallow. In the UK, we'd broken the mould and moved on. In his eyes, the bubblegum stuff was firmly in the past now we'd had a hit with 'Money Honey', the earlier songs' merits and undeniable place in our history ignored and derided. In America, Davis's desire to release the old stuff threatened to knock us back a good couple of years, artistically. It was a classic case of one step forward, two steps back.

After a while, Clive gave in to our demands and we won, getting 'Money Honey' released as the next US single in February 1976. It reached No. 10.

We'll never know what would have happened if 'Bye Bye Baby' or 'Give A Little Love' were released as singles in America, which they never were. There was a promo release of the first one and I don't know why it stopped there. Likewise we'll never know how we managed to get our own way against one of the most important, knowledgeable bosses in the music industry. If it was a ruse to help us on our way to self-destruction, it was one hell of a tactic.

Eric just went on and on and on and in the end the rest of us agreed with him just to shut him up. The arguments with Arista went on for weeks – 'we' were adamant that we would record our own songs which were as good as anything Phil Wainman or anyone else could come up with, and not be told what to do. Eric and Woody would be the next Lennon and McCartney and God help anyone that got in the way of that dream.

Phil Wainman, who'd gone to America with us, had enough and left us all to it. He just wanted to make records and the level of politicking going on drove him crazy. Clive wanted him to stay and produce the band but his mind was made up – 'I didn't want to get involved in the politics of it, so I just walked away . . . that was when they [Arista] stopped paying me.' Phil pissed off the Yanks a second time when he produced the Boomtown Rats' 'I Don't Like Mondays', a song about the playground massacre in San Diego in 1979. Today he has little interest in the music industry and, like so many other people, believes that there is no future for it.

Phil feels that Clive Davis was one of the people most responsible for the band's eventual demise, saying he wanted to 'assert his authority' and that he 'Americanized an English [sic] pop band'. He says that if he and the band had been left alone, 'we could have gone on for another five or six years'. It's nice, though, that he still feels that way after all the trials and tribulations he endured. Obviously the job satisfaction counted for more than the number of tracks he got onto albums.

Things may have looked pretty dismal on the surface but, as is often the case in America, there was shite going on behind the scenes of which we had no knowledge at the time.

When Arista was being set up by Columbia, Tam appointed a New York attorney called Marty Machat, who was Phil Spector's lawyer, to renegotiate our contract which until then was with Bell. His fee for 'selling' the band to Arista at a time when every record company in the world would have signed us, was allegedly $50,000, or at least 10 per cent of the value of the deal.

This was when Tam was probably feeling out of his depth for the first time, hence the appointment of Machat to protect his and the band's interests, and to increase his importance in Davis's eyes. If Tam is to be believed then it seems he was in a different league and allowed several clauses in the renegotiated contract that should preferably not have been included, or else he was selling us down the river for a few dollars more. One such clause, which I know Eric feels was the biggest mistake to date, allowed Arista to retain 50 per cent artistic control. That might seem excessive but I'm not sure what was standard in record contracts back then. But even to me, it doesn't sound too clever for Arista to retain just 50 per cent when presumably we had the other 50 per cent, which would explain why the rows over what we should or shouldn't record dragged on – neither party had the final word, legally speaking. Meanwhile, Clive continued to act like he was everyone's best mate and especially mine.

Another of Tam's appointments was that of a Mr Stephen Goldberg to the position of the group's – and Tam's – accountant. On his spate of appointing a team of expensive experts, Tam recently explained his actions in a TV documentary by saying 'if we paid the best, we got the best', which presumably means he believed that you got what you paid for.

Goldberg immediately set about creating no less than 13 companies under the banner of ALK Enterprises, Inc. to ease the tax burden on the band, and also to ease a nice fat fee into his pocket for doing so. We were told all this top-level financial manoeuvring was essential if we were to avoid the outrageous 90 per cent tax bracket we'd be in otherwise. It was a very complex and sophisticated network, which of course it had to be. Even the names of the companies seemed confusing to us – one was Deals Music Management (Overseas) Ltd, while another was Delsa Publishing Management (Overseas) Ltd. There were at least another two companies for Tam's money. We were to rest assured that our interests and long-term security were everyone's top priority.

To demonstrate how effective the corporate network was, one of the 13 companies set up was called Bay City Music. It was formed to collect royalties from Eric's songs and allocate them equally between the five members of the band, on the basis that the songs wouldnae have made any money if the band as a whole had not recorded them. With just the four Faulkner/Wood tracks on *Rollin'* to look after at the time in question, it appears that the running of Bay City Music was then transferred to another company, Carlin Music, who earned 15 per cent for looking after it. The Bay City Music coffers should have swelled nicely as the 'Money Honey' money (honey) started to come in, but it seems that wasn't the case.

Much later, after Eric moved to London (with Tam not far behind, finally accepting that despite his hatred of the place he needed an office there), he employed someone called Colin to look at the band's complex web of finances. The copyrights of the songs which had passed to Carlin reverted to Bay City Music and Eric says that Colin then began selling the songs worldwide, but to whom it's not clear. He says that I refused to sign some sort of contract which would have given us a £600,000 advance and that Colin quit in exasperation.

The newly appointed Stephen Goldberg immediately endeared himself to the BCR team by cutting the security guys' wages. Paddy the Plank, thankfully, only rarely affected by the politics and in-fighting, wasn't too bothered though. He was having a very nice time benefiting from the on-going competition between Roger at Polydor (The Osmonds' label) and his opposite number at Bell, to outdo each other on no-doubt-legitimate expenses.

'I spent £1,000 on dinner at X restaurant!' one would say.

'That's nothing – I did £2,000 last week at Y!' would come the response, or another similar remark.

shang-a-lang
shang-a-lang

More often than not, Paddy and his colleagues would be invited along to dinners and parties. It's ironic, isn't it – those guys were out boozing and living the high life while we bands slogged around the world and crashed two to a room in hotels, without a clue how the other half were living and with even less of a clue that we were paying for it.

That's why I get a wee bit riled when I read something that Tam said in his book with Michael Wale:

> Sometimes I wish more of the group would be interested in the business side of things and not just the creative side. I'd certainly value their criticism. Maybe this may happen as they get a little older. At the moment, money doesn't seem to bother them very much. They just like doing what they're doing. In 1975 each Roller has been getting £35 to £40 pocket money a week. In addition, money is drafted into their accounts every year, and they've got their own bank accounts. So if we do a tour and draw £50,000 about £8,000 will go into each of the Rollers' own account. But, as I said, they don't seem to worry. Money just doesn't seem to bother them, which, in itself, is quite strange.

As if all of Eric's bitching and the battles of wills in America wasn't enough to stress me out, soon after we got back from our US promo tour I had two court cases to deal with.

I had to go to court for hitting the paparazzi guy in Oxford who I'd thought had smacked a fan. Apparently it was a 'fairly violent and unprovoked attack'. I was fined £1,100 and given a three-month suspended prison sentence. I celebrated my 20th birthday two days later by doing nothing except worrying myself sick about my next court appearance in six days' time . . .

On Tuesday, 18 November, I was at the Edinburgh Sheriff Court facing a charge of causing the death of Euphemia Clunie by reckless driving or, alternatively, of driving without due care and attention, (that's how they do it in Scotland – there's a major and a lesser charge for the jury to consider). The details of the next three days are a bit hazy in my mind.

The whole thing was a media circus. Since the accident happened in May the press had been hyping it up, so by the time I actually arrived at the court, I felt like a serial killer. One day back in July, there'd been a crowd of fans gathered outside the court just because I'd been 'expected' to appear there that day. I was touched that they'd turned out to show support, but sickened that someone had probably leaked my so-called appearance.

I knew as I finally walked into that courtroom that everything was stacked against me. The media had found me guilty long ago. The members of the general public, as always, found it easy to believe what they'd read in the papers and wanted to see the reckless yob swing. Probably Tam's 'fans favourites' charts reflected changing trends between May and November.

When the first witnesses were called, I was sure I'd be jailed for life. One of the vehicles in the inside lane that I'd overtaken when I came onto the Corstorphine Road was a van full of Scottish National Orchestra musicians. They were adamant I'd been driving my sports car too fast. It was more of the same from other witnesses. It seemed to me at the time that everybody thought I was a pop star with loads of money and a flash American car, who had obviously been drunk and was probably high on drugs, too. I needed to be brought down a peg or two and anyone who could help do that was only too willing to oblige.

At the 11th hour, the nurse who'd helped us from the wreckage at the scene appeared from nowhere and convinced the court that there was absolutely nothing I could have done to avoid the accident. On Thursday, 20 November, I was found guilty of the lesser charge of reckless driving because it was decided that I had been driving at 40 in a 30 limit. I was fined £100 and banned from driving for a year. Naturally, I was relieved at not being taken down to the cells, but I didn't feel any better, and I still don't. The media coverage of the whole sorry story lies deep in many minds and even today I'm told by legal people that there's nothing I can do when some ignorant hack writes that I killed an old woman when I was pissed and stoned out of my head.

I did derive a morsel of pleasure from the fact that Derek Jameson, then the northern editor of the *Daily Mirror*, along with the deputy editor of the *Glasgow Herald*, were both bollocksed for being in contempt of court when they printed photos of me that they shouldn't have. Apparently it could have prejudiced the jury who otherwise might not have known what I looked like.

Eight days later, we were on our way to Australia for our first ten-date tour in the southern hemisphere.

When we arrived, Tam was beside himself to discover that the promoter had called in a herd of girls to welcome us and cater to our every whim. He'd just assumed we were like all bands they handled and that our needs would be the same as the others'. I'd been bordering on celibate while waiting for the court cases to come up and just the sight of these drop-dead gorgeous birds got me going. It was then that I put together my Mandrax plan that I talked about earlier, but not before I'd engineered a trip to a department store with Paddy, on the pretext of needing new clothes, and shagging one of the store assistants in the changing rooms. I decided I loved the Australians and their devil-may-care attitude to life.

My pill-induced sleep brought on a whole new type of dream. There was no malice like before, just comedy. In the one I remember best, I was sharing a room with another Roller, and was shocked when I went back to the room one day to find him sitting on the floor at the end of the bed, watching a porn film and having a wank. I asked him what he was doing, which met with the response you would expect to such a pointless question. I said, 'I know, but why are you doing it now? Can you not do it later?' The Roller in question was completely nonplussed and said it didn't matter. 'What's your problem? Everybody does it,' he sneered. OK then, fair enough. In the dream I remember thinking how he obviously thought it was completely normal to masturbate, irrespective of the presence of someone else, and of the same sex, at that. It fascinated me and I wondered how I'd grown up sharing two rooms with three brothers and never come across any of them having sex, either with themselves or anyone else.

Halfway through the tour, in Melbourne, Woody collapsed and was taken to hospital. They checked him over and let him out, but he took a turn for the worse on the way to the next gig, in Canberra. He went to hospital again where nervous exhaustion was diagnosed but heat exhaustion was publicised, along with a quip from Woody about it just being too damn hot in Australia. We did the Canberra gig minus one guitarist, and then went on to Sydney, but there it was decided we'd have to call it a day. The New Zealand leg of the tour was postponed indefinitely and we all flew home on 10 December.

How thrilled we were to arrive back in London after a 24-hour journey – with a seriously crook guitarist and *all* of us on the verge of collapse from exhaustion – to find hordes of pushy, parasitic paparazzi in our faces. I let fly a stream of abuse and called them all vultures, which was a mistake, but only because it drained me of the last drop of energy I had left. I had to be helped onto our bus like an old man.

I went home to my Edinburgh house and crashed for ages. I was completely knackered, jet lagged and stressed out. My brothers came round but I wasn't on the same planet. As usual, the phone was ringing all the time and people kept turning up on the doorstep. As usual, there were a hundred or so fans camped outside the front gate and if I could have had them all gathered up and safely transported to somewhere warmer and more comfortable, I would have done it. The problem was that they would probably rather freeze to death than be somewhere else. As usual, it was impossible to relax and unwind.

I gave up trying to rest on the basis that you should join them if you can't beat them. I ended up with a house full of hangers-on and people vaguely connected with the music business: roadies, techies, studio people, anyone with an 'in'. Because of my job, most of my guests weren't friends like most people's party guests are. I couldnae tell you their names or any more about the people there that night than Michael Barrymore could've told you about the guests at his house the night one of them died. I felt sorry for Michael when it all went tits up at his house, because I could see how that kind of scenario could happen. Have people in your house you don't know, throw in drink and some drugs, and you put yourself in the lap of the gods. It's a bit like when you're a kid and you have a party as soon as your mum and dad are away and can't keep the gatecrashers out, but on a much bigger scale.

The next morning, some officers from the Lothian and Borders Police knocked on the door and woke me up. I opened the door bleary-eyed, still half-pissed and not too coherent. They asked if I had a gun. I remember thinking it was a strange question and thought someone was having a laugh, then I thought something along the lines of how I must have moved on in life because here I was chatting with the Lothian and Borders cops instead of the

Costorphine bastards of old. Then my eyes focused on the air rifle propped up by the door. I briefly wondered why I kept it there because a baseball bat would've been more effective had the need for self-defence arisen.

'Sure, I've got a gun, an air rifle,' I said. 'Right here.' I pointed down at the rifle.

The cops explained that a 15-year-old girl had been treated at hospital the night before for a head wound caused by an air rifle pellet in the vicinity of my house. They said they were investigating what might have happened and would be sending a report of their findings to the Procurator-Fiscal.

After Christmas but before Hogmanay, the Procurator-Fiscal ordered further investigations and the press just couldnae believe their luck. That drink-and-drugs-ridden thug who'd only just murdered an old lady was now being done for shooting one of his fans! It was beyond their wildest dreams and beyond my comprehension. What the *fuck* was going on with my life?

It all went sour for the poor press when one of my 'guests', who turned out to be the boyfriend of a well-known television personality, came forward and confessed it was him who'd been pretending to try and take out a few fans when the gun went off. The media, gutted that their main story had run out of legs, started to speculate that maybe Tam had orchestrated a dodgy alibi and, as expected, the general public were again only too pleased to believe that was fact. But it didn't help that Edward the Confessor was later given a job within the Rollers organisation as a reward for having the decency to come forward and own up.

Like the accident, the shooting at Torphichen is another experience that is obviously going to haunt me till I die. It's the second most memorable thing about Les McKeown, after the fact that I kill old ladies. However, at least in this case there is an amusing twist in the tale:

In 1994, I was doing a gig at the Cavendish at Tollcross in Edinburgh. As I came out of the sound check, there was a group of women hanging around the entrance. They spotted me as I walked to our tour bus, and then one of them came charging over, wrist scarfed up, shouting, 'Hi Les, remember me? I'm the one you shot in '75!'

Now what was I supposed to say to that? For once, I was

speechless. All I could think was, if even the girl that got hit was convinced it was me that did it, then what chance did I have? I said something back and made my escape.

I thought that after all that time I understood the levels of passion that fans felt, but that episode proved I'd been wrong. Shit, you could even be accused of trying to kill one and they'd still come back for more! My friends today have a name for it, this emotion that is more than unconditional love or undying devotion. They call it ABWS (Acute Battered Wives' Syndrome). They philosophise that I am like the ultimate evil husband or lover and that there will always be some women who have so little respect for themselves that they can just laugh it off when I'm rude or obnoxious to them. Easy – it's because they really love me – or at least they did, or thought they did, a long time ago. Sufferers of ABWS usually suffer from other forms of mental illness, too.

Towards the end of the year, another band with a Scottish lead singer called Midge Ure was trying to woo away our fans and get that same devotion and love for themselves. They were called Slik, and in December they released a Martin/Coulter song called 'Forever And Ever', which had previously been recorded by Kenny, who'd ended up doing 'The Bump' after we did. Funnily enough, their image was US-style sportswear a bit like ours on our first *TOTP* show. The papers proclaimed that Rollermania was dead; long live Sliksteria. Sadly, it wasn't to be. Their next single, 'Requiem', was released the following April and then they too dispensed with the services of Bill 'n' Phil. After that they could never again perform in the UK under the name of Slik. Not that Midge gave a toss. It was probably the best thing that could have happened to him.

We finished off 1975 with a gig just before Christmas at the ABC Theatre in Belfast. It was an inter-denominational event (that is, Catholics and Protestants mixing together peacefully), and with my mum having been born just down the road in Banbridge, it felt good to think that in some small way we might be lightening things up, if only for a short while. That night, our support band were called the Young City Stars and one of them was called Ian Mitchell.

Our two No. 1s that year earned us two Christmas *Top Of The Pops* appearances – 'Give A Little Love' on the 23rd; 'Bye Bye Baby' on the Christmas Day show. We watched it in one of the hospitals we spent the day in, with kids who were able to smile despite being ill and away from home at Christmas. It was good to end the year on a positive note and helped to bring happiness to those who needed it most.

During 1975, we'd started to do our bit for charity and through various competitions we must have raised hundreds of thousands of pounds, mainly for the Alexandra Day Fund. The charity, whose president was Princess Alexandra, helped a wide range of less-fortunate people including the disabled, the old, and under-privileged kids. The first competition, launched during the spring 1975 tour, was run in association with Gale's (the peanut butter and honey people), and followed the same lines as most competitions of the time, in that you had to collect tokens or something by buying ten times more of a product than you normally would and *then* pay to enter. No one really minded, though, because the money was going to charity. The first prize was 'a fantastic once-in-a-lifetime chance to be with the fun-loving Bay City Rollers on a fabulous, thrill-packed, all-expenses-paid week at the super luxurious Coral Island Hotel in Bermuda', with 50 runners-up prizes of a chance to meet the Rollers in London, at the Grosvenor House Hotel on Park Lane. The prize the following year, as we'd more or less emigrated to the US by then, was to spend a week with us in New York. It felt great to feel we were helping others and the time we spent with the competition winners was always good fun (although of course there were always interviews to do and photo shoots to go to throughout the prize trip) and, at least the money must have made a difference in some way to some people's lives.

Clash of the Titan Egos

On the third day of 1976, we learned that the Bay City Rollers' song 'Saturday Night' had finally reached the top of the US *Billboard* Hot 100. It had taken nearly four months to get there but that didn't lessen our pride. Only four other bands in the history of the US charts had ever gone to No. 1 with their first single and, of those, none of them had been unheard of just three months earlier. The song had failed to do anything in the UK, but then again it was released when Nobby Clark was still the lead singer. At the same time, the first US Rollers album reached No. 19. That might not sound too hot by European standards, but in North America, where the album charts list the top-selling *two* hundred albums, it was brilliant.

Two weeks after we hit the top spot, we arrived back in New York, and this time the crowd was about five times the size of the one we'd left behind at Heathrow. Rollermania US-style had hit and, like everything else, the Americans did it bigger, better and louder.

Our third appearance on the Howard Cosell show had us singing 'Saturday Night' one more time along with 'Money Honey', which went down well, reassuring Arista that it was the right song to release three weeks later. We stayed in New York for a couple of nights, at the Hotel Pierre on Central Park, and then we were off to various East Coast and Midwest cities like Philadelphia and Detroit, and down south to one of my now favourite towns,

Atlanta, for TV shows and radio interviews. The heavy promo paid off and a few weeks later, 'Money Honey' charted and climbed into the Top 10 in most US charts.

Our second US album, *Rock 'n' Roll Love Letter*, charted in late March. It got to No. 28. Like *Bay City Rollers* before, the album was made up of a mixture of the British albums, taking the title track and 'Money Honey' from our fourth album, which we hadn't even started recording yet. It also included two of the Faulkner/Wood tracks, 'La Belle Jeane' and 'The Disco Kid', from *Once Upon A Star*, which had been left off the first album. And no less than seven tracks from *Wouldn't You Like It?*. In contrast to the first album, with its two Roller-written tracks, this one more than redressed the balance. In fact, the only song not written by Eric and Woody was the title track, which had been on an album called *Behind The Eyes* by Tim Moore. Clive Davis had put forward the song and we'd liked it. It looked like Eric was getting his own way again and one Davis-recommended track must have been his idea of a compromise.

A few months later, in Japan, Toshiba/EMI also released an album called *Rock 'n' Roll Love Letter*, not realising that an album with the same name had already been released in North America. It was a compilation that didn't have much in common with the US version, and included 'Love Me Like I Love You' (like 'All Of Me', never on a UK album) and, for a change, 'Saturday Night'. As soon as the record hit the shelves, the record company realised what they'd done and quickly reissued the album under the name of *Rollers Collection*, with the same catalogue number and everything.

On April Fools' Day 1976, two years to the day after 'Shang-A-Lang' was released, Alan Longmuir was sacked from the Bay City Rollers.

Although Al had been questioning whether or not he was happy with his lifestyle in the band and had been thinking that maybe he'd be happier spending more time on his farm and with his girlfriend, the decision was made for him. He's said since that he'd been happier as a plumber than he was as an international pop star, but at the same time it was what he'd always wanted. It was why he'd put the band together with Derek in the first place – to be a pop star and be famous. But maybe not that famous.

Tam says he was left with no alternative but to suggest Alan hang up his tartan after he began to let the image slip and had been seen – shock, horror – unshaven. Never mind that he was a founder member of the band, he was nearly 28. Tam told anyone who would listen how depressed Alan had been and how he'd wanted his life back. He even used the age-old excuse from years ago about how Alan had wanted to 'spend more time with some female' once again. Absurd and false rumours went round (started by whom, I wonder) that Alan had tried to take his own life, apparently by sticking his head in a gas oven. Anyone who knew Al could only see the funny side of that. If Alan was going to do himself in he would have done it with whisky, not by sticking his head in an oven. Tam's priority was to make sure Alan's fans felt positive about his departure and that they understood Alan would be much happier out of the band.

Alan's departure left the rest of us paranoid. Who was going to be next?

I felt the resentment towards me grow even stronger because as the lead singer I was the least likely to be ousted, as far as the others were concerned. Little did they know.

The new Roller who took Alan's place was a wee guy called Ian Mitchell, who'd caught Tam's eye just four months earlier when we were in Belfast. Ian's band, the Young City Stars, supported us at a gig just before Christmas. At some point after that, and before joining us, Ian had moved into Tam's house, 'while awaiting the possibility of forming a new group in Scotland'. Ian later told a journalist that he thought he may have accidentally got Alan out by telling Tam about some photos showing Alan kissing a girl. Now *that* sounds far more likely to have caused Tam to react than some bollocks about forgetting to have a shave.

Born in 1958, Ian had a ten-year advantage on poor old Al. I saw the others cagily eyeing him up in the same way that the deformed sheep watched me in my dreams and I felt sorry for him. OK, he wasn't Alan, but there was no need to make him feel like a leper. I knew how it felt to be the one that was left out so I made a point of looking out for wee Ian.

'Love Me Like I Love You', the Rollers' ninth single, was released in the UK a week after Ian joined us. We made a cheesy promo video for the song which had us all, arms linked, around a globe, with Alan there one minute and Ian the next, like some kind of metamorphosis. It was supposed to be positive and uplifting, but it just made Alan's fans cry even harder as they watched him fade into oblivion before their very eyes. And they'd already had to swallow the pathetic press photos of Alan and Ian shaking hands; the new Roller decked out in BCR uniform, the old one in a pinstripe suit.

The 'Love Me' promo was shown twice on *Top Of The Pops* because we couldnae be there to mime it live. The song climbed to No. 4, but it only stayed on the chart for six weeks. Maybe it was a sign of the times and that the charts were changing, or maybe it was because our popularity at home was on the wane. In the States, the simultaneous release of *Rock 'n' Roll Love Letter*, as per Clive Davis's suggestion, and produced by our old friend Colin Frechter, only made it to No. 31, which seemed to confirm the dreaded decline. It took quite a while for us to get to grips with the fact that there was no comparison between 31 at home and 31 in the States because the charts in the two countries were so different.

Eric was suffering. He was obsessing about lack of control and input when in fact he had loads of both, as we've seen many times so far. At the same time he was starting to have problems with his weight and Tam was constantly on at him to lose the extra pounds he was piling on. Eric didn't see that it mattered how fat he was and thought Tam was using the weight issue as a diversionary tactic to change the subject from his continual 'we should be going heavy' comments. In Australia, Eric had got hold of some speed (amphetamines). The speed was supposed to suppress his appetite. It also played havoc with his sleeping patterns, which were already fucked by the Australian time difference, so it wasn't long before he was taking downers like Secanol and Valium to help him sleep. On 14 April, he took an overdose at Tam's house.

One of the best-remembered aspects of the whole incident was that Tam Paton, on finding Eric unconscious, called the press before he called an ambulance. His two completely contradictory accounts of what happened and in what order are documented in two television documentaries made in 1999. When interviewed by the BBC, he said: 'I think I phoned the ambulance first. No, I mean I definitely phoned the ambulance first.'

Just a few months later he'd forgotten what he'd said and told

shang-a-lang
shang-a-lang

VH1: 'I phoned the newspapers. Or I phoned the ambulance. I don't know which I phoned first.'

Whenever Eric's been questioned about the overdose, he's usually said it was an accident – just too many uppers and downers and not paying attention to how many he was taking. On other occasions, he's referred to how claustrophobic life as a Bay City Roller was: 'When you're locked inside a hotel room most of the time, there are three doors out: sex, drugs and booze. Some people take them all.' With the first and third not available, it sounds like he was saying he was using the drugs as a means of escape as well as to alter his metabolism.

With Eric still recovering, the rest of us set off once again for a promo tour of the States, this time on the West Coast. *Tiger Beat* magazine superimposed Eric onto photos of the rest of us taken on that visit so they could avoid the nasty overdose issue. Like everyone else, they didn't know that, by now, pill-popping to keep us going was part of everyday life and Eric's scare did nothing to abate the flow of pills.

From the West Coast we went on to Sound Stage Studios in Toronto, Canada, where we were rejoined by Eric to start work on our next album, *Dedication*.

By now, Clive Davis was really starting to assert his authority, which was making Tam insecure. He fought the insecurity by fighting with Davis. The result was that the quota of Faulkner/Wood songs dropped from all but one on the previous album to just four on *Dedication*, which made it a much better album than *Wouldn't You Like It?*. The album opened with 'Let's Pretend', written by Eric Carmen, which was great as the first track because it screamed that we'd matured and not just musically.

The song had a classic middle eight that was so obviously the writer's musical and lyrical version of the sexual climax that no one could miss the point. Even the fans who were still too young to catch the orgasm-like drift were at least aware of the heightened emotion in 'Let's Pretend' and knew something different was going on. The theme continued with 'You're A Woman' and Eric and Woody's 'Rock 'n' Roller' which, unlike a lot of our previous material with rock 'n' roll in the title, was the nearest thing to rock we'd ever done. One of my favourites on *Dedication* is the title track, written by Guy Fletcher and Doug Flett (who had also written for Elvis). While I was happy for Ian to sing lead when we first recorded it, so that he could get his own personal fan-base going, I have to admit I wasn't too cut up about having to have a crack at it myself after he left a few months later. 'Are You Cuckoo?', which was included on the US version of the album, was written by a guy called Russ Ballard, whose other songs were later recorded not only by Alan Longmuir and myself, but also by Rainbow, Hot Chocolate, Santana and Agnetha Faltskog. Most people will agree it was probably Ballard's worst-ever song and that it didn't fit with the rest of the album at all. I have another much better studio recording of that song with alternative lyrics that I might just put out as an MP3 one day!

Another track I wasn't too keen on was 'Yesterday's Hero'. Loved singing it; hated thinking about it.

Phil Wainman said a couple of years ago that *Dedication* and the album after it were 'grossly over-produced'. While I can see where he's coming from (the Americans had already redone 'Summerlove Sensation' and 'Give A Little Love' with strings, which I thought was a bit over the top), I don't think it was as bad as Phil said. It was just the way things were, and are, done in the US. A sociologist called Cornell West was asked in the mid '80s what he thought about the future of rap music. He said it would end up 'where most postmodern American products end up: highly packaged, regulated, distributed, circulated and consumed'. It was the same ten years earlier and it's the same twenty years later.

The US-produced albums did have a different feel about them. That 'feel' was what was needed for the American market. It was the same later when I was making my solo albums in Japan. There was a Japanese vibe in the music which made it more saleable there. It's just a case of knowing your market and satisfying its requirements.

The UK market, deprived for nine whole months of a new Rollers album, was finally satiated with *Dedication*. It was well received all over the rest of the world and made it to No. 4 in the UK and 41 in the US. For the first time, virtually the same album was released throughout the world. The only differences on the track listings between the different territories were that the US version had 'I Only Want To Be With You' (our next single release) and that diabolical cuckoo song on it instead of 'Money Honey' and 'Rock 'n' Roll Love Letter', which were on the European versions. In the US, both those tracks had already appeared on the previous album.

Clearly the US record execs didn't feel it was acceptable to put the same tracks on more than one album but the Japanese had no such worries, as demonstrated by their inclusion of 'Love Me Like I Love You' on their version of *Dedication*, despite the fact that it had been on *Rock 'n' Roll Love Letter (Rollers Collection)* two months earlier.

Incidentally, the fact that the song 'Dedication' had to be re-recorded after Ian left means that there are in fact two US versions of the same album, just in case you thought things were getting a little too uncomplicated on the album front!

Fan reviews of the album generally went along the lines of 'I love that song', 'That's my fave', and 'Oooooooh – listen to Eric in this bit.' An issue of major importance and debate was where the album cover's photography had been done. Was it in Canada, where the album had been recorded, or somewhere in Scotland? It sort of looked Scottish, but could have been somewhere in the Rockies. The fans in each territory were keen to find out because the photo having been taken in *their* country or territory implied some kind of permanence about the Rollers' presence. The Brit girls sensed they were losing us and desperately needed reassurance that we weren't going for good. The theory didn't pan out, though, because although the shoot took place at a Scottish loch, we were still fated to spend more than 90 per cent of our time out of our home country.

At the end of June, nine months after our first US TV appearance, we finally performed our first American gig. It was in Atlantic City, New Jersey, at the Steel Pier Music Hall, a good few years before the town was revamped and became cool. The gig went OK, considering it was Eric's first after the pills overdose. Thanks to the human decibel level throughout the set, it didn't matter at all.

We ended, predictably, with 'Saturday Night' and got the hell out. We drove to a Hilton hotel in Philadelphia, slept a bit, and were out the door again at six the next morning to get back to Toronto and carry on working on *Dedication*.

I was more than happy to get home when the job was done, but was unnerved by something strange happening to music generally back in the UK . . .

Malcolm McLaren, who'd been trying for some time to make some kind of breakthrough on the music scene, had finally done it by putting together a band called the Sex Pistols. He later said that it was the Bay City Rollers that were the inspiration behind the punk movement – he saw the media frenzy that surrounded us and wanted a taste of it. He'd also heard Sid Bernstein say Rollermania was bigger than Beatlemania. He saw page after page of press coverage and sussed how it was being achieved.

Where Tam Paton had crafted the Rollers as the antithesis to long-haired, greasy, loud rockers, McLaren took it full circle and set about creating a 'negative copy' of the Rollers; a band that would be so vile and horrible that people wouldnae be able to stop talking about it. McLaren zoomed in on the shock principle and took it to the max. It made me laugh because, all of a sudden, parents stopped whingeing about 'preposterous short trousers' and accents they couldnae understand. They all wanted us back when their kids started sticking pins in their faces and spewing up on figures of authority.

The Pistols performed their first live gig in February that year, and a couple of months later Johnny Rotten, the lead screecher, started talking about shit and hate. By the end of September, there were loads of new punk bands on the scene and a festival at the 100 Club. The Clash, The Damned, Siouxsie and the Banshees, and The Buzzcocks all jumped on the Pistols' bandwagon, and the audiences responded by throwing pint glasses around.

I watched in amusement and amazement and wondered how all this anarchy had become OK when a few years earlier the lyrics to Sweet's 'Teenage Rampage' had been censored before the record was cut because there had been some kind of obscure reference to masturbation in there.

The birth of punk rock did nothing to make me feel more secure in my job. I daydreamed about what it would be like to spit and puke along with the best of them, but I quickly realised the idea was just a hopeless dream and downed the rest of my glass of milk.

In July, we rehearsed in London's Eden Studios for our first concert tour of America and Canada, which was due to kick off the following month. Our third UK tour would come straight after it. We mucked around with some new ideas, including a song I really liked called 'When I Say I Love You (The Pie)'. It had been written and recorded by our kinsmen, the Sutherland Brothers, and has a great melody. Although it was never released as a single, it's usually in the top five of the fans' favourite Rollers songs of all time.

Conversely, 'Love Me Like I Love You', which was a UK and European single, never made it onto an album outside of Japan, just like 'All Of Me' had been left out. 'I Only Want To Be With You', our next single in the UK and the US, had been a big hit for Dusty Springfield, and was released at the end of July. This time, we managed to make it onto *Top Of The Pops*, which helped take us to No. 4 again, but the song didn't appear on any UK album.

I sometimes think we would have lasted longer at home if that had been handled differently. I mean, Rollermania was dying down and a big chunk of the market must have been thinking they'd wait for the next album for the two latest songs, rather than buying the singles. When the album (*Dedication*) came out, though, the songs weren't on there so maybe they didn't buy that, either. This was because the priority was to keep the American market and record company boss happy. 'Love Me' was never released in the US and 'I Only Want To Be With You' had already been on *Rock 'n' Roll Love Letter* so it couldnae go on *Dedication*.

In August, we began our first tour of North America. It was only short and not much was different about it to any other tour we'd done, except that the venues were further apart and we had Ian with us instead of Alan. Canada didn't know what had hit it. In Toronto's Nathan Phillips Square, an estimated 100,000 fans turned out to see us. A photo of the square was used on the inside cover of *Dedication*, and the security guys pleading with everyone to stay back at the beginning of 'Yesterday's Hero' was recorded there, too. Mixed in with the tour dates were a load of TV and radio appearances and one of our best-remembered TV gigs, on a show called *Dinah!*, was filmed at that time. Like Muriel Young a couple of years before, Dinah Shore was an oasis of feminine kindness in a world otherwise populated with money-grabbing manipulative males. We'd appeared a few times before but on this occasion the band was on for the whole show, alongside the actress Mackenzie Phillips. Ian had to demonstrate the art of making chip butties, a concept unheard of in the States and hilarious for the American

155

fans, and that was followed by a Q&A session with an audience that could barely breathe, let alone ask a question.

Our third UK tour began in Dundee on 9 September and ended ten days later in London. It consisted of ten consecutive sell-out shows but things were definitely cooling down back home. Even the range of merchandise you could get was limited to scarves, rosettes and posters. We did 'I Only Want To Be With You' on *Top Of The Pops* but it didnae feel the same any more. We were happy to get it over and done with and go straight back over to America where things were still buzzin'. *Dedication* entered the UK charts as we left and did OK, getting to No. 4 eventually. It made us feel a bit better about home, especially as the fans had still bought the album in large numbers despite the missing two singles.

Ian left the Rollers just before my 21st birthday, after just over six months in the band. It was said he just couldnae deal with the hysteria. Loads more fans were left distraught and questioning what had gone wrong.

In fact, Ian had only ever been a temporary Roller. One of Tam's plans had been to pluck him from the Young City Stars, make him famous, then put him back into the other band in an attempt to create another international supergroup, all the while growing his harem. This he needed to do because he was losing his grip on his Rollers. With Clive Davis making more and more of the decisions and gradually diminishing Tam's power and control, he was starting to feel jittery, which for Tam was not good.

The seeds of mutiny were sown. The other guys found that at last they had opportunities to go out and behave like pop stars, i.e. they could shag until the cows came home of an evening and Tam would probably never know. Even if he did find out, there was less he could do about it. With Ian gone, Tam needed New Roller Number 3,569. Enter 18-year-old Pat McGlynn, a friend of Woody's, who was in at the deep end with a trip to Australia and New Zealand for another attempt at a tour there. We played venues like the Wellington Show Buildings in New Zealand and the Hordern Pavilion in Sydney, which had a capacity of 6,500. From there, we went to Japan for our first tour in that country, so although things may have been slowing down in the UK, they were only just starting to get going in other places.

shang-a-lang
shang-a-lang

By now, the Japanese had already released eight Rollers albums in a year. The wide distribution of two further bootleg albums, *Are You Cuckoo?* and *Ka-Ga-Ya-Ke* proved that this market, like the others, still couldnae get enough of the Bay City Rollers. The *Cuckoo* bootleg featured recordings nicked from Eden Studios in the summer and from our first UK tour. The other one was a live recording where you could hardly hear the band over the screaming.

Elsewhere in the world, Rollers albums were springing up faster than Tam's wee tadger. Nearby in Taiwan, another bootleg album appeared, very soon after the release of an official *Best Of. . .* album there. Bell Netherlands released *Saturday Night* (a mix of all four UK albums) which was identical to Bell Belgium's *Joepie Presents: The Bay City Rollers*. Arista New Zealand, probably pissed off with us for blowing them out on our first visit down under, were a little later with *Bay City Rollers – Their Greatest Hits*, but made up for it by releasing *Greatest Hits – Volume II* soon after.

When we arrived in Japan for the first time in mid-December, a series of highly secret and carefully directed leaks from Tam and the record company ensured a mass of over 30,000 fans at Narita Airport to welcome us to the land of the rising sun. With the assistance of half of the Tokyo police force we were escorted to the Hilton Hotel in an armoured vehicle to do an interview talking about our first impressions of Japan and the Japanese people. It didn't matter that we'd had no time to form any impressions because they'd been written out for us before we landed. There was a bit of a panic when it was realised that, foolishly, the promoter had arranged for 'some female' to carry out the interview so we had to hang around while she was replaced with a male colleague on Tam's insistence. Photos were taken by the famous photographer Koh Hasebe, who would become a permanent fixture on the Rollers' scene and during my solo career in Japan later.

There are many differences between Japanese culture and the western world, and the one we liked the most at the end of 1976 was that there was a curfew, which meant all the kids had to be off the streets and home by five o'clock in the evening. As most of our fan-base came into the age range affected by the curfew, for once it was actually possible for us to go out and see a bit of the place. It didn't take me long to fall in love with Japan and its people. Also,

I had a fetish for technical things and electronics, so I was in my element in a country that was as obsessed with technology as I was. But I was still pleased to be home for Christmas, laden with exotic gifts and gadgets from the east.

shang-a-lang
shang-a-lang

Falling Apart

Edinburgh was nice for a break but, as always, I soon found myself champing at the bit to get away from the place. It just couldnae compete with somewhere like, say, Santa Monica in California, where we found ourselves for our first US gig of 1977. The next day we flew from the West Coast to New York and checked in to a nice hotel. By the middle of the afternoon we were politely asked to leave because the fans were causing havoc and damaging the hotel's reputation. We moved to another hotel and then did a gig at the New York Palladium, an old music hall in Brooklyn. Our old roadie-stroke-tour manager Jake Duncan, who'd left for greener grass in mid-1975 after our second UK tour, came to see us after the show. He was living in New York now and we asked him if he'd like his old job back. He agreed and will probably forever rue the day.

There was something else significant about that New York gig. I changed the lyrics of a song for the first time. Instead of 'What happened to the girl I used to know' in 'You're A Woman', I sang what happened to the *boy*. I don't know why. It might have been a Freudian slip, but from then on I would muck around with lyrics just to relieve the repetition. 'Shang-A-Lang' inevitably became 'Shag-A-Lad' (which the audiences never noticed but Tam always did) and then later 'Shag-A-Slag', when the environment had changed. If I'd taken some form of medication, I'd be a bit more adventurous: 'I fell into your open legs' instead of arms, in 'I Only

159

Want To Be With You', for instance. Robbie Williams introduced his ballad 'She's The One' as 'She's A Hun' during a gig in Cologne not long ago. A sure sign of boredom and a desperate need for a laugh.

After the Palladium gig, we hung around in New York for another week or so doing promo. Then we went to Miami to record a week's worth of the *Mike Douglas Show* on the beach. Tough job! We had to lip-sync a couple of songs each day, but they didn't hide the fact we were doing so as well as they had on *Nightflight*. One time the song was well under way before we were even up on the stage. There were other tasks to perform as well, which included limbo and trampoline contests. I did OK at limbo, but Derek was less adept at trampolining and fell off on his head. It was probably a mistake to do that kind of stuff, a laugh though it was, because I think it might have provided fatal inspiration for another show further down the line. The best part of doing that show was the evenings when I'd disappear off with Danny Fields, the editor of *16 Magazine*, to listen to Floyd, smoke some dope and talk about life.

'Dedication' the single, released in the US but not Europe, charted in February but only reached a disappointing 75. After five weeks it was gone. Fickle fans! Just because the singer – on this occasion Ian – had left the band, they didn't want to buy the record!

We punished America by taking off for the Tal & Ton studios in Gothenburg, Sweden, to record a new album, *It's A Game*. This one was going to be produced and engineered by a guy called Harry Maslin, who'd picked those particular studios because he'd liked them when he worked there with David Bowie. We rented a couple of houses nearby and drove around in a Volvo Estate, just as I do today when the Mercedes S-Class is in for repair.

Harry had produced Bowie's *Young Americans* and *Station To Station* albums. I couldnae get enough of his tales of times with the legend. I was fascinated by every little morsel of information he shared. Eric wanted to pay tribute to Bowie by including 'Rebel Rebel' on the album, which was strange, because he was usually so adamant that we should only do his songs. I think he thought people would see him as the cool, rocky, rebellious one if he sang Bowie.

I can only imagine what poor Harry must have been thinking as he listened to Eric. Probably the same sort of thing as the rest of us. When a session guitarist was used to re-record Eric's guitar solo in 'Rebel', and he found out about it, he went ballistic and demanded to be allowed to do it again. He got his own way, as usual, at a cost of several hundred quids' worth of extra studio time. Luckily, the track ended up at the arse end of side two, on an LP which really was an album of two halves. On side one there were some fantastic numbers. The best were the first two, the title track and 'You Made Me Believe In Magic'. 'Magic' and 'The Way I Feel Tonight', another fans' favourite, were released as singles in the US. 'Magic' did particularly well, making it into the Top 10. The catchy and pure pop 'Love Power' and Faulkner/Wood's moving 'Don't Let The Music Die' completed the first side. The rest of the album was a different story – four Faulkner/Wood songs (allegedly written with the aid of accomplices, including me) rounded off with the cover of 'Rebel Rebel'. 'Don't Let The Music Die' made the fans cry; 'Rebel Rebel' made *me* cry!

The best bit about making that album was watching Pat and another Roller on acid. We'd developed a knack of smuggling drugs into countries where we didn't think it'd be easy to get what we wanted – we hid it in the tartan turn-ups of our trews and laughed about how no one ever thought to look there. The fact was, we were hardly ever searched anyway because Tam's milk-drinking PR was so effective.

One night we all sat down to dinner and Pat couldnae touch his because the chicken breast was 'beating' on his plate. The next day, the other acid-ridden Roller couldnae play a note.

'My fucking guitar neck is *bending*!' he panicked. It was hysterical to behold.

We must have all been on something mind-altering when we came up with the sleeve concept for *It's A Game*. OK, the chess board and oriental chess pieces were relevant, but the Meccano-like title and yet another new Bay City Rollers logo in tartan didn't fit. If that wasn't bad enough, when you turned the album over, there were the Rollers floating naked through space and surrounded by shooting stars. Eric has one hand placed lovingly, or threateningly, around the back of my neck. Woody looks vacant and a bit scared. For some strange reason, some of the black squares on the chess board are starting to peel off. On the inside, there is nearly no

161

tartan; just a bit on Derek's shirt. Eric is in a black leather jacket, looking pensive. Derek's drumming, and Woody looks good. Someone's tried to be creative, taking pictures of me on a slow shutter speed and the result is a not very flattering fliddy shot where I'm told I look like Ann Widdecombe dressed by Oxfam, but I guess it was cool at the time.

Soon after we finished *It's A Game*, Pat left the Rollers after an episode that he was later to tell to the *News of the World*.

We were in New York. It was knackering, as usual, and one night I'd just settled down for a long sleep when the door burst open and Pat flew in, slamming the door behind him and hyperventilating. He'd been the unlucky one allocated to share a room with Tam that night, and our manager had apparently jumped him and tried to stick his tongue down his throat. Pat, who cannily slept with a bread knife under his pillow, had stuck the knife in Tam's shoulder. We could hear Tam thundering along the corridor, so I grabbed Pat and threw him in the bathroom. Then he was trying to kick the door in. We both had to put all our weight (which wasn't much – less than 18 stone combined) up against the door to keep him out. All hell was let loose but luckily the hotel security were on the scene before he got in. It all quietened down and we went to bed, Pat safe and secure in my room. The next day at the airport, Tam was literally chasing Pat around, trying to get a hold of him. He was *so* out of control by then, he didnae seem to care what the press saw or said.

Back in Edinburgh, Pat's father, who was of Romany ancestry, beat the shite out of Tam, and Pat was instantly relieved of his duties as a Bay City Roller. The story was put out that Pat had been caught shagging an Arista exec's bird – which he had. Pat, not wanting to talk about what had really gone on any more than anyone else, said at the time Tam had kicked him out because he'd complained about only getting paid £20 a week, but since then he's been a lot more detailed about what made it impossible for him to stay in the band.

Pat said earlier this year that Tam tried to rape him five times and that he'd tried to hypnotise him to make him give him a blow-job. He said Tam was constantly trying to turn the Rollers gay.

Some of the detail Pat went into was news to me. I know it

sounds incredible that we didn't all know everything about what was going on with the other ones, but we didn't. Stuff happened that wasn't talked about, obviously. It was still the same as ever on the communication front – when we did have time to talk to each other it was only superficial chat, but most times the others only really talked to me if they wanted to complain about something or argue. It's a different story today.

Whatever, Pat was out and that was that. He said a few years ago that his vocal and guitar were removed from the *It's A Game* album tapes. He also said his picture was cut out of the album photo, presumably the one on the back cover, which is feasible. At least he was still credited with having helped to write 'Sweet Virginia', and earned himself enough fame in his short stint as a Bay City Roller to get himself a recording contract almost immediately. His solo single 'She'd Rather Be With Me' came out that July, and he went on to release quite a lot of albums. There was even a bootleg Pat McGlynn album, enchantingly titled *10,000 Fucking Moist Arses*. God knows what the relevance of that is.

'It's A Game', the single, was released in the UK as soon as it was cut because it had been eight months since 'I Only Want To Be With You' and Arista realised that if they didn't do something quickly the UK market would shut down. It was already too late. Either that or the British market didn't appreciate the American over-production. I think it was more likely that the fans had moved on. We may well have matured musically, and I suppose we'd hoped they'd stick with us and we'd grow together, but there was too much competition – not just from other 'boy bands' like there is today, but whole new scenes like punk and disco. 'It's A Game' only reached No. 16 despite two plays on *Top Of The Pops*. It was clear what was happening since the previous three singles had reached three and four. The two before that were No.1s, but the first of those was over two years ago now. That was ages in pop terms. Most of the girls that bought the record did so for the nostalgia, I'm told. The Rollers reminded them of their childhood, three years earlier, and made them feel happy.

Since the first time we went to America, our home fan-base had started to shrink because we weren't around as much and communications were nowhere near as sophisticated as they are now. It was ironic that the prolonged absence of other acts such as

163

The Osmonds that had helped make us popular in the first place was now the root cause of our decline.

The Rollers' demise in the UK from 'It's A Game' on was swift and painful. The next single, 'Magic', was rushed out, peaked at No. 34 in August and was gone in three weeks. Even *Top Of The Pops* and the nostalgia factor didn't do the trick that time. The *It's A Game* album got to No. 16 which was surprising, but it only stuck around for four weeks. By September, the Bay City Rollers were gone from the charts forever.

We weren't really that bothered. It was sad, but you had to move on. In America, 1977 was the year that we peaked.

Our second coast-to-coast tour, to promote the yet-to-be-released album, was much more far-reaching than the first, and began on 9 May. For the first time in history, the Rollers were only four. We wondered how long it would be till we were only three. There seemed to be no need or intention for Pat to be replaced. New Rollers just never seemed to fit.

The first show was at the Westchester Premiere Theatre and it had to be stopped after the first few songs because of the level of screaming and fans pushing forward. This was more like it. It was reassuring for about five minutes but then it became annoying because we were trying to get away from the screaming teeny-bop scene. We wanted them to shut up and listen to the new music. The tour was successful in that it got 'Magic' to No. 9 in the charts, generated $604,000 of income and a profit of $95,000.

This was a crucial time where my emotions were all over the place. I was insecure and worried about the future. I couldnae help wondering how long it would be before the UK situation repeated itself everywhere else. I thought about what I would do when that happened and, for the first time, considered a career outside of the Rollers. In this unsettled state of mind, I began to look for somewhere to vent. The loyal fans shouldn't have been a target, but I needed to take my frustrations out on someone, or a body of someones.

After the first gig, we all went out for a few drinks and something to eat. I spent most of the evening staring out groups of fans who'd followed us. We weren't just being greeted and watched any more; we were being stalked. Don't get me wrong; I'd always been appreciative of the devotion we got from the fans, was usually happy to chat with them and accepted that lack of privacy went with the job. But a small minority of them were just downright bloody irritating. They'd ask stupid rhetorical questions and just stand there, trying to maximise their contact time with you. I found the most persistent ones to be very selfish and arrogant, they seemed to think they were a cut above the masses in some way. Today, they're the ones that come up and say something like, 'Hey, Les! I was the one who . . .' or 'Remember me? I met you at so-and-so'. Why should I?

At home, which was now London, there were 30 or so fans that always seemed to be hanging around my front door. They'd never really bothered me. I wasn't at home much, so I used to invite a couple of them in for a chat and a cup of tea. But now I was starting to feel less and less like socialising with them. I needed some space, some detachment from all things Roller-related. They didn't know that, though; I didn't communicate my needs very clearly and sometimes I'd lose it with them. Once, I tried to explain logically why they shouldn't be hanging around so much. 'I can't devote my life to you,' I reasoned. 'We can't fall in love and live happily ever after.' It cut no ice. Nor did a few heartfelt 'fuck offs', when tension got the better of me. Most of them, victims of ABWS, didn't react at all. They just fantasised about how they would be the one to help me get over this bad mood I was in. A few of them got cross when I swore and said things like 'you should be grateful we're still here' and '*we* put you where you are today'. I can see why they would think that but it *really* wound me up. I hadn't asked them to buy records or made them go to gigs. I didn't force them to ask if they could clean my flat (. . . yes, they did) and I'd never tied anyone to my bed (well, not against their will, anyway!). They did what they wanted to, not what I asked them to.

Even today, I often still come across that attitude of being owed something. After a gig, the genuine, considerate people – the ones who are not out to get whatever it is they feel owed – will come and chat a wee while, have a photo taken and move on to make way for others. I have a laugh with them and they leave happy. It's the ones that won't move on and are greedy for time, usually when they're off their heads, two inches away from your face and suffering from halitosis, that I can't handle. Just recently, after my first gig since I

165

lost my mum, the 'old faithfuls' just wouldnae let me have my space, and I lost it. I've managed to stay calm for years, but now at last I've learned that it is OK to make it clear to people labouring under the misconception that they're 'owed' something that in fact I owe them nothing. To anyone who says that celebs should always be polite and gracious to their fans I'd beg to differ on the basis that a person who is *not* in the spotlight isn't expected to be courteous with unpleasant people, so why should I be? Should Dave Glover continue to be kind and friendly with Rose West because the psycho nutter has said she's going to marry him? Nah.

By the third gig on that US tour, I was so wound up that I actually told the audience to shut up. They didn't hear, they were too busy out-screaming each other. At every gig on that tour, during one of Eric's solos, I'd kneel before him, pretending to bite the guitar à la David Bowie and Mick Ronson. I don't think one person recognised it. And then they had us performing at matinees. Bloody matinees! How considerate of the promoters to make sure the audience could all be home and tucked up in their beds at their usual time after the show. It was all getting me down.

The Rollermania, as usual, grew in its intensity as the tour progressed. By the time we got to Dayton, Ohio, the kids who'd been waiting for us since six o'clock in the morning started banging on the doors to get in and bashed them down. As they all surged through, the glass in the remaining door shattered and lot of them got cut on the way through. It wasn't going to stop them getting to the front of the stage though. During the gig, one of the girls had an asthma attack and her friend had to pull at Eric's leg to get some help. Same as it ever was. As per.

The only difference was that Tam wasn't on that tour. A guy called Larry stood in for him. Tam was cooling off and licking his wounds in Edinburgh. He told anyone that cared enough to ask that he was concentrating on his other bands, one of which was Ian Mitchell's Rosetta Stone. He'd also discovered another potential 16-year-old superstar called Gert on one of his frequent shopping trips to Denmark. Returning home, Tam went to work on the hype and publicity needed to catapult Gert to superstardom. He was renamed Baron Gert von something or other and shipped over to Britain to record some songs. Sadly, when Tam got him in the studio, it turned out that he couldnae sing particularly well.

shang-a-lang

A few weeks later, Caroline Sullivan, the author of *Bye Bye Baby* (Bloomsbury, London, 1999) apparently met with Tam in New York. He told Caroline that Eric was in Honolulu and the other Rollers were at home. They then went on to discuss the Rollers' sexuality, as you would. He said that one was more gay than straight and liked butch guys, one was bi and one was basically straight but sometimes went for older guys. What about the fourth one? In any case you can take it all with a pinch of salt because he went on to say there was 'no way' *he* was gay. What a gadge, eh?

Sticking with the issue of sexuality, I was bemused later that summer when Eric appeared in the UK's *Record Mirror* dressed as a geisha girl. He might as well have worn a T-shirt with 'I'm Tam's Bitch' printed on it. It signalled the start of a worrying trend that would see him habitually dress to distress right up to and into the new millennium.

Just over a month after the end of the last tour, the next one started, on 25 July. By then *It's A Game* was in the stores and had charted.

The Rollers hosted a TV show, *The Midnight Special*, which was a real honour and important for the band because although we'd been on the show before, this was the first time we'd hosted it, which meant we got to perform about four songs and introduce the other acts. For this critical appearance, I wore no Roller gear, in the hope of getting the message across that the times were changing. Eric chose to wear a leather jacket teamed with sexy shorts and a pair of legwarmers. On his face he wore bright-blue eye shadow. He looked a right twat. Come to think of it, that night might have been one of the first times I'd tried cocaine, I can't be sure. I know I was having a right laugh, in the midst of all that other bollocks, and it seemed appropriate at the time to launch into 'Deep In The Heart Of Texas' and try and do a southern accent. Eric sat fiddling with his flies while I continued to show off. It was the Bay City Rollers being naughty – as much of a first as when the Pistols swore at Bill Grundy on the *Today* programme back in December.

The third tour, being mainly in August, consisted mostly of outdoor shows, in the South and Midwest. The first show was in Montana, which is neither in the South or Midwest. Eric wore shorts again, this time with 'Spank Me' emblazoned across the back of them, and started changing lyrics. By the end of the month, in Detroit, it was all-out war on the lyric-changing front. In 'Don't Stop The Music', I replaced 'How can I tell her/That I really love her' with 'How can I tell her/I want to get right into her', while Eric used the F-word in a nonsensical context in 'Rebel'.

I marvelled at the lunacy around me and wondered if I would go mad. It was a relief when 'Saturday Night' signalled the end of the torture that was that night's gig. How did it only seem like five minutes since I was the happiest kid alive when I was singing that song?

By mid-August we were nearly done in the States: Des Moines, Iowa; Milwaukee, Wisconsin; Louisville, Kentucky; Columbus, Ohio.

We were in Ohio when the news came through that Elvis was dead. Our fans didn't seem to care, some didn't even know who he was, and that made me feel insignificant and angry.

Things perked up a bit on 22 August when we found ourselves in Toronto, at the Canadian National Exhibition Stadium, in front of 18,000 people. The promoters and organisers had us walk across a field to get to our limos after the show. Two days later we were back in the States at Bay City, Michigan, itself – to be presented with the keys to the city. It was a great honour, considering that our own home town continued to refuse to acknowledge our success in any way.

The last gig was two shows in Charlotte, North Carolina, at an amusement park called Carowinds. We were so glad it was the last show, even the venue's nice white stage in the middle of a kids' playground couldnae dampen our spirits. We had a long break after that tour and it was fantastic to be away from each other.

We were sadly reunited for another tour of Japan in the middle of September. The Rollermania was more intense and more fraught than ever before. You could feel a thickness in the air as soon as you got off the plane. I think it must have been something to do with curfews and suppressed emotions.

As usual there'd been plenty of albums put out to try and meet the demand for the Rollers. *It's A Game* had come out a few months before the tour and was the same everywhere else apart from it had the song 'When I Say I Love You (The Pie)' on it. Then there was another couple of bootlegs, one of which was called *The Great Lost Rollers Album*, which was made up mostly of B-sides and included a recording of an interview we'd done in Atlantic City. That was funny because if the Americans couldnae understand us, I didn't hold out much hope for the Japanese.

The highlight of the tour was a few gigs at Tokyo's biggest concert hall – the Budokan – a massive venue which can seat about 14,000 people. By the time we got there, I was feeling a bit jumpy. Read on and you'll see what I mean by jumpy.

The soothing effects of the holiday had worn off and I was more than a little bit tense. I think it was the sheer scale of the Budokan that prompted my erratic behaviour. I'd always found the bigger crowds sort of intoxicating and this one was like having one over the eight. I found myself singing away on auto-pilot, wondering about these 14,000-odd kids who weren't allowed out after dark and who were now all sitting there politely clapping along with the music. I decided in a split second that things needed shaking up a bit. I moved as far back from the front of the stage as I could, turned, and took a suicidal running jump right off the stage. It was a high stage and I managed to project myself, arms and legs clawing through the air, quite a few rows out into the audience.

In that same split second, the fans who'd worked out that I was going to land on them stretched out their arms either to protect themselves or catch me. Then all hell let loose. Paddy the Plank nearly had a heart attack and launched himself into the crowd, along with hundreds of little stick-wielding policemen. They didn't share the same motive – while the police wanted to contain the uproar I'd created and settle the crowd, all of whom, were now trying to get a bit of me, Paddy was actually trying to push me further into the crowd, hoping – and I quote – that I'd get myself fucking killed. Mr Plank now recounts the story with amusement and nostalgia, though he hated me at the time: 'The whole fucking Budokan was trying to get a hold of him. It was fucking mental.'

Eventually normality was restored and Paddy had to spend longer than usual with the police the next day. They were not his favourite people because they'd waded in with batons and quite a bit of force the night before and Paddy had been on the receiving end of a good few clouts. He was tired and at a loss to explain what had possessed the lead singer to behave in such an outrageous manner, remarking to the chief of police that 'this fucking group is driving me mad'. His unedited comment made the headlines the following day.

The rest of the year was comparatively calm. More singles were released ('Don't Let The Music Die' in Japan; Harvey Shield's 'The Way I Feel Tonight' in the US) and greatest hits albums came out in both territories. The US *Greatest Hits* went gold, as had all the other albums before it. We did loads more high-profile TV shows like *The Chuck Barris Rah Rah Show, Don Kirschner's Rock Concert* and, being America, it was one talk show after another – Mike Douglas, Merv Griffin and Dinah Shore were the most memorable. Towards the end of the year, we were asked to host *The Midnight Special* again, on which we got rave reviews for a kick-ass version of 'Money Honey'and our first performance of 'When I Say I Love You'. There were a few gigs here and there, including an important one at the Boston Garden where we headlined with Andy Gibb, the youngest Bee Gee.

Nineteen seventy-seven had been the year of the brothers. Andy Gibb had hit the big time, as had Shaun Cassidy, David's younger half-brother. Elsewhere in the world, a certain Hari McKeown had got himself signed up by Polydor and released a song called 'You're My Baby' in Japan and the UK, under the name of Jamie Wilde. Tam went ballistic when he found out about it. He went on and on about how Hari was using me and my fame for his own ends and how this was proved by the fact that there was a picture of Hari and me together on the cover of his Japanese single. Now it was my turn to be brainwashed. I came to believe that Hari had committed a heinous crime. I'm told that Tam served an injunction on Polydor preventing them from using my image to sell their product. For a long time Hari blamed me for that and, although we've had it all out many times since, I think he still does. What makes it all the more gut-wrenching is knowing what I know now about what Hari went through and how important that chance was for him.

The new year, 1978, didn't start any better than the last had ended. Just as we were starting to get some real credibility in the States, an article written by Per Lunne, who had been Tam's assistant for a wee while, appeared in a Danish gay magazine appropriately called *Coq*. It said that the Rollers preferred sleeping with each other to sleeping with girls. Not surprisingly, the allegation found its way into most of the international press, and in a desperate attempt to disassociate myself, I talked to the *News Of The World*. They headlined the feature 'I feel like I've made love to a million women' and opened the first paragraph with me saying that when it came to sex, I'd tried everything. By the time you reached the end of the article, you were left in no doubt about my sexual preferences. There was a lot of stuff in there that I didn't say, and a lot of stuff I did say just sort of came out in my desperation to prove I was a man of the world. The problem was that most people had no idea about the *Coq* article and I came across as an over-confident radge.

When we got back from a tour of Germany, we tried to have sensible discussions about our next album, to be called *Strangers In The Wind*. I'd recently teamed up with a guy called Scobie Ryder and we'd written a few songs that I thought could go on there, but I scuppered my chances really by suggesting that Scobie and I should get the royalties from them. It was a tongue-in-cheek comment but Eric went off on one because up till then, all Faulkner/Wood royalties had been split between the whole band. At the same time, I was more than a little bit worried about some of the other songs Eric was putting forward, like 'Stoned Houses', which eventually went on the first Rollers album without me. It seemed to me that the direction he wanted to take the band in was all about drugs and depravity.

In April we set off to Mountain Studios in Montreux, Switzerland. Queen, the Stones, BB King and Marvin Gaye had all worked there. Better still, it was a fire at the very same studios that had inspired Deep Purple's 'Smoke On The Water', the song I used to thrash out with Threshold in my mum and dad's back garden all those (five) years before. I got a kick out of that but realised it was nothing like the kick I got when I first set foot in Mayfair Studios to sing 'Shang-A-Lang'. I needed a stronger fix.

A welcome escape from the continuous rows about 'direction' and the horrible atmosphere was provided by the girls from a nearby finishing school who hung out at the same bar as we did in the evenings. Imagine my surprise when, having been taken home by one of them, I find myself on the doorstep of the fantastic cuckoo-clock house at Corsier-sur-Vevey – where David Bowie was living. My date turned out to be not one of the girls from the school, but Zowie Bowie's nanny! Being with her in my hero's house was kind of weird. But not as weird as having to sing a song written by another Roller for his girlfriend who had a thing about making love with me in the band's van, while listening to a yodelling shepherd passing by outside.

We'd asked Alan Longmuir to come and help us out with the *Strangers* sessions. He decided to rejoin the band, as he had grown tired of civvy street and needed his adrenaline, too. He'd attempted a solo career with a song called 'I'm Confessing' released in Germany, but ended up deciding he'd be better off back with his old Roller chums. Al had always been a calming influence but, by this time, things were so bad between us that even he couldnae make a difference.

I was being increasingly shut out and the irony was that the others felt that I was being turned against them by my new pal, Scobie. In fact, it was a chat with Rod Stewart quite a bit later that eventually gave me the confidence to take steps towards going it alone. Scobie was just a new focus for the paranoia that had been carefully cultivated since the very beginning. Scobie didn't want me out of the Rollers, he just saw that I was imprisoned creatively and encouraged me to write more songs. To the others, that was interpreted as a serious threat to their own existence.

With things between us at an all-time low, we finished the album and went to Los Angeles.

While we'd been recording, we'd been approached by a couple of US TV producers called Sid and Marty Krofft with a proposal to make a series of 13 shows to go out on a Saturday morning. It sounds great, a peak-time show to air throughout America. But it wasn't so great. The show was aimed at little kids – even the pre-teens wouldnae have watched it – and they wanted the Rollers to appear alongside a bunch of puppets and other established 'Saturday Superstars' like Witchiepoo and H.R. Pufnstuf. I really didnae want to do it and I'd finally had enough of being coerced into doing things I didn't want to do. I wasn't allowed any input into the music; *they* said they wanted to change the direction and image of the band to appeal to a wider audience while at the same time they were contemplating signing up to do a TV series for five-year-olds. Even our ideas of a wider audience were poles apart. I was convinced this latest venture would destroy the Bay City Rollers for ever, but, as usual, no one wanted to listen.

The more I felt left out, the more I retaliated by winding them up. The best way to do that was to act superior and play on their insecurities. We argued, negotiated and deliberated, all with the assistance of our own very expensive personal lawyers. I said I wasn't going anywhere unless I had my own dressing-room with a big gold star on the door and more light bulbs round my mirror than they had, or something like that. On 9 June I wrote a letter to the rest of the band saying that I did not agree with their plans to change the band's direction and that they should all leave the band immediately. Outrageous? Now there's a debate!

By mid-June the Bay City Rollers were resident in Hollywood.

Tam and the band were graciously accommodated in the Kroffts' mansion. I didn't want to stay there so I got a suite at the Chateau Marmont on Sunset Boulevard. A few weeks later, I moved to Stevie Wonder's Regency Hotel Apartments. Wherever we went, we were surrounded by opulence and big money, and I was able to get an endless supply of free coke – and I was going to make the most of it. If I had to be stuck somewhere I didn't want to be, doing something I didn't want to do, I'd damn well compensate for it somehow.

That whole Hollywood party scene was like a whirlwind that sucked you in. It was the perfect antidote for the poison that was spreading through the band and that would finally kill it. Those few months were at the same time some of the best and worst of my life. Invitations to this party and that premiere filled the mailbox every day, and the hardest decisions I had to make were which to accept and which to decline. It helped detract from the real issues of the day, as did the pre-cut lines of coke that were passed around like peanuts at other parties when a certain rock legend took over a restaurant on Sunset for the night.

The premiere party for *Grease* was another one of the highlights. My date for that occasion was Jodie Foster, as documented in the press the day after, and we did go out a few more times. I also dated Britt Ekland, as documented in the press some years later in more detail than was necessary, when I was desperate for cash and could only get it by selling my story to the press. It's one of my biggest regrets because I really cared about Britt. We managed to keep the relationship surprisingly private, which is probably why most people think it was just a matter of a couple of dates, but in the end we wanted different things.

Jake Duncan used to come partying with me. He says he always preferred to hang out with me because that's where the fun and the action was. He didn't want to watch telly or get involved in parties at the Krofft house. One time, we were supposed to be up and out by nine for our elocution lessons (it was part of the stupid contract that we should speak better). Jake remembers that we were so busy 'lording it up' that we completely forgot about getting me to my speech therapy for that day, and so we incurred the wrath of the Rollers yet again.

At the beginning of July, the others finally deigned to reply to my letter written a month before. Predictably, they hadn't taken my suggestion seriously and felt they were being dictated to. That's when I realised how clever Eric actually was – he'd never dictated anything, he just put his views across consistently and persistently until invariably you truly believed that what he wanted was the right thing. In their letter, they counter-suggested that I should be the one to leave the band, because I wouldnae go along with their majority decisions. They also stopped paying my expenses. I went off on a bender and couldnae face replying, so they wrote again a few days later saying they assumed I wanted to leave. We all met up the following day and I found the courage to clearly state that, yes, I wanted to leave, and with immediate effect. For all my fake bravado, I felt sad, scared and sorry.

One day on the Krofft show set, near the end of filming the series, someone started flinging custard pies around and one landed in my face. A photo of it ended up on the front cover of some teen mag accompanied by a story about how impossible I was to work with. That was just some PR person's way of explaining why I'd walked off the set and not returned. They elaborated the story by saying it was one of the Rollers who'd thrown the offending pie and that he'd done it to 'break the tension'. The fact that I'd lost it with Marty Krofft over some embarrassing sketch he wanted us to do was not mentioned. I was up against the studio

shang-a-lang
shang-a-lang

wall and he'd pulled a gun on me, screaming something like: 'If you ever think of leaving this show, I'll fucking kill you.' Of course, I know he didn't mean it and it was just an idle threat made out of exasperation. I've lost count of how many times I've been asked since about the time *I* pulled a gun on someone in America.

I left and went back to England that night, leaving the others to rehearse for the upcoming tour of Japan on their own.

I enjoyed writing to Tam, having a go at him for being an ineffective manager and severing all links with him.

Goodbye to all the friends I never had.

On 7 September, which was a Friday, a preview of *The Bay City Rollers Meet The Saturday Superstars* went out. It was the most sickening thing I'd ever had to sit through and by the time it got to the closing scene with us all in gold lamé suits singing some godawful '50s medley, I wanted to cry. The next day saw the first episode aired on NBC. There was Les, dressed up as a Hollywood film director and sporting a stick-on moustache. And they had all been convinced this show was the best move for the Rollers.

After a few episodes, with ratings a fraction of what had been expected, the show was cut from an hour to half an hour, the puppets were taken out and it was renamed *The Bay City Rollers Show*. Too late. We'd lost any credibility we'd started to build on shows like *The Midnight Special* and with *It's A Game*, and no one would touch us with a barge pole. NBC axed the new-format show swiftly.

'I told you so.'

'Fucking know-it-all fucking arrogant shite!'

The *Strangers* album failed to chart in the US or Britain.

Ironically, the Faulkner/Wood compositions that made it onto that album were the strongest they'd written, but I feared for some of the fans who really did believe that Eric and Woody could become the next John and Paul, having picked up on the paraphrasing of some of the 'Yesterday' lyrics that appeared in 'Another Rainy Day In New York City'.

The other numbers on *Strangers* like 'Where Will I Be Now' and

shang-a-lang

the two Iain Sutherland tracks ('Every Tear I Cry' and 'The Pie'), were good songs made great by Harry Maslin's highly skilled production and David Richards' engineering. Woody was finally allowed to sing on 'Love Brought Me Such A Magical Thing'. It was our best work to date, but the kids who watched the Krofft show wanted nursery rhymes and the kids who bought *It's A Game* and the other albums didn't want an album by a kids' TV show band in their increasingly sophisticated collections. Looking at the photos on the inner sleeve, you can see how weary we were. Our eyes are older than our faces. I've seen exactly the same look recently in the publicity shots of the two Tatu girls.

After *Strangers*, with the exception of Rollers' albums I didn't feature on and the much later *Breakout*, the only further albums were compilations – nearly 40 of them. Not surprisingly, 50 per cent of those originated in Japan. We went back there for our third tour later that month. I hadn't wanted to go, but contractually I was in the shite if I didn't. At that point I didn't know I was in the shite anyway, so I might as well have not gone. In the end I decided to go, to network, and stay as far away from the others as I could. Luckily they were of the same mind, or so I'd thought.

I had my own security guys and Tam hired some Welsh guy to watch me. Word had got out that my departure from the Rollers was about to happen, and the banners in the audience which said things like 'Don't leave, Leslie' and 'Please come back' made me feel loved when I needed it most.

Making the most of the gadgetry on hand in Japan, I bought a load of bugs and snuck them into the others' rooms, my sixth sense telling me that there were probably long legal battles ahead. The recordings I have of the things they were saying about me are gut-wrenching. First, there was Tam asking whichever Rollers were in the room with him what I was up to and telling them all to make sure they kept an eye on me at all times. Then they were plotting to start playing songs in the right key and then change key as I started singing to fuck me up. Another idea put forward was getting the light show changed so that I didn't have a spotlight. It made me want to cry. I knew they'd never really liked me but the sheer hatred that I was now up against was torture.

In Shizuoka, things came to a head. With those threats still burning in my mind, I started invading Eric's spotlight which stopped him getting his fix of attention. While he was doing his solo, I jumped around, up and down off PAs, in and out of the audience, drawing the attention back to me. This, together with more of the pleading banners in the audience, sent them over the edge. Woody got narked and we had a fight in the middle of the stage. I went off and refused to come back on. The gig was cut short and the next day I was allowed to go home.

The end.

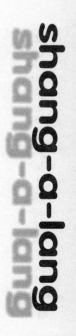

All Washed Up

This would seem like a good place to tell the story of the Bay City Rollers after I left them.

In October, a report was delivered by accountants Prager and Fenton that was the result of an investigation we'd commissioned at the beginning of the year. It looked at more than four years worth of books and records at Goldberg Ravden, and also at records held at the offices of Satin, Tenenbaum, Eichler & Zimmerman in New York. Some royalties had not been paid into the accounts set up to receive them. Prager and Fenton queried the amounts the New York firm appeared to be charging and Mr Tenenbaum was asked to give details 'as to the basis for all charges for officers' salaries and accounting and auditing fees', and to advise who got the $34,362 'business management fee' deducted from the proceeds of the '77 tour. He hadn't replied by the time the report was presented. The outcome was that we were all left with a major tax bill. In 1980, Prager and Fenton's Martin Goldberg (no relation to Stephen at Goldberg Ravden) said in his affidavit that Goldberg Ravden had put together 'a tax avoidance scheme [that was] extremely complex and extremely expensive'. They had received £132,411.14 for accounting services rendered. Neither Goldberg nor his former employee, John Fogarty, have responded to opportunities to comment while I've been writing this book.

The Bay City Rollers sued Goldberg Ravden. I think that's the point where we effectively kissed goodbye to any chance of ever getting on top of our finances, having cut off all avenues of communication with the only people who knew the ins and outs of it.

The litigation went on for years, channelling a whole lot more money into lawyers' pockets and keeping Eric occupied. It was a good job really, because there wasn't much else happening for the band.

Duncan Faure, the singer in a South African band called Rabbitt, was brought in to replace me. They headed off to tour Germany without Tam, who objected on moral and political grounds to having a white South African in the band. One night in Hamburg, Alan and Woody called Tam up and sacked him. Apparently they'd just watched a documentary about sharks and were inspired to act.

An album called *Elevator* was released in the summer of 1979. By now, they'd dropped the Bay City from the band's name and were just the Rollers. Their next album, *Voxx*, was released in Germany and Japan. The last album – I forget the name of it – only drummed up a few club dates by way of a promo tour.

Loyal Jake, the road manager since the very beginning, stuck with the band through their decline, but the long relationship ended when they did him up like a kipper. While they were all in South Africa, he was asked to go and fetch some marijuana from the hotel and got apprehended on the way out. Someone had told the police the band had dope. The band shat themselves. They all had their passports taken away, but soon got their own back by promising to stay until the case was heard. They were out of there that night, leaving Jake behind to face the music. When he got back, Jake sued for wrongful dismissal. Only Derek bothered to show up in court, and offered no contest. There was a happy ending for Jake – he was awarded £1,800, which was a lot in the early '80s, and thanked his lucky stars he was rid of the Rollers, just like I had.

Based back in London, I began trying to get my affairs in order. I spent my first week as a solo artist in numerous accountants' and lawyers' offices, trying to find out where all my money was. Slowly the horrible truth became clear – I didn't have any. All the band members' money was tied up in that complex web of company accounts. Next I found out that I was liable for a $24,000 American Express bill which had been spent mainly on band-related expenses and then the news came through about the tax we owed. The worst part was finding out that my house at Torphichen wasn't really mine at all, and having to turf out my mum and dad and my brother who'd been living there. I moved out of my smart London flat into a tiny £19-a-week bedsit.

Eventually I managed to get £35,000 out of the band but that went on settling outstanding tax payments due on earnings and legal fees. Luckily there were a lot of record companies eager to sign me. I signed a single-sheet contract setting me up with a £100,000 five-album deal with Eastworld, a division of Toshiba EMI in Japan, almost immediately, and against that piece of paper I was able to borrow £50,000 from Coutts. That night, I went out celebrating with Mr Nakamura from my new publishing company at the House of Osami Restaurant in Soho. It was there that I first laid eyes on the most beautiful Japanese lady I had ever seen. Her name was Keiko, but when she was little she'd been the inspiration for a famous Japanese kids' TV character called Peko, which was the name she chose to go by. If there is such a thing as love at first sight, that was it. Things were looking good.

Scobie and I booked ourselves into the Kinks' Konk Studios and got straight to work on the songs that would make up my first solo album. It was an incredible feeling to be able to do stuff the way I wanted to and not have to argue with anyone or give in to someone else's way of thinking for the first time since Threshold.

Following the Scottish tradition of being careful with money, especially as I wasn't sure what other nasty surprises might be lurking round the corner, I was grateful to find the likes of Teresa, Abbie and Claire – the hard-core girls (not in the porn sense) – waiting outside when I arrived at the studios one day. We were needing backing vocals on one of the tracks and as far as I was concerned, they'd do. It took hours to get it right because they were laughing too much to be able to sing a note. It was gone midnight when we finished and I took them all for a drive down the King's Road. We had 'King's Road Chelsea', one of the album tracks, blaring out as we drove up and down. None of those girls expected anything from me and none of them judged me, and we had some fun as a result. I know they appreciated times like that, because there weren't many artists around who'd mingle with fans the same way.

I had a meeting with dear old Clive Davis at the Dorchester Hotel and played him the tapes a few days later. Never very appreciative of pop, to put it mildly, he declared that he wouldnae be signing me as a solo artist. I started having serious discussions with other record companies outside of Japan who were thrilled that Arista were letting me go. There were some very attractive deals in the offing, but the best was with Chrysalis, who had Blondie and loads of other hot acts. While I was going through the final details of the deal at Chrysalis, literally on the verge of signing, a telex came through from Arista saying they would sue Chrysalis or any other record company that signed me. It turned out that, thanks to that contract negotiated by Marty Machat, I was tied to Arista – not only as a band member, but *also* as a potential solo recording artist. I think I can be forgiven for becoming very bitter at that point.

My lawyer at the time, who was also the lawyer for a record company called Warwick, came up with a way round the Arista contract. It was a major risk but something that had to be done if I was to salvage any chance of a successful solo career outside of Japan. I'd have to indemnify any record company I dealt with against any Arista action. I had to do the same with Eastworld.

I signed with Warwick Records. Their catalogue consisted mainly of things like *Twenty Golden Flute Greats*, the kind of thing our mums might buy, and quite uniquely used only TV advertising to sell their records. I really resented that I had no other option than to sign with an outfit like Warwick when I was so close to Chrysalis. I managed to stay positive by focusing on the 60 per cent I would earn, which was a much higher yield than one of the top record companies would have paid. To give them their due, it was all systems go at Warwick. I don't think they could believe their luck when they ended up with an ex-Roller alongside their pipe and harp albums, so they flung money at promoting the album, doing lots more than their usual straightforward TV ad campaigns. In Woolworths windows, you could see a life-size cardboard cut-out of me emerging from the sea as per the album cover. The 1XBCR painted on the tail of the plane wreck in the background didn't make it clear who I was, and I'd undergone such a transformation that no one recognised me in the windows. Bereft of tartan, at last,

I was kitted out in a black one-shouldered Lycra catsuit and had long hair. It didn't matter, though, because that and all the other promo stuff that Warwick created would be pulled together with a mega-intensive TV ad campaign that was about to go out. Then sales of *All Washed Up*, the first solo album by Leslie McKeown and his self-deprecatingly named band, Ego Trip, would go through the roof.

That's when the workers at ITV decided to strike. It wasn't just a few hours a night, it was a complete shutdown from August through to October. The ads never went out, no one knew about the album and people took no notice of the bloke in the catsuit in shop windows. The shops returned the unsold albums to Warwick. The fickle finger of fate had pointed at me and said 'Die!'.

Warwick pressed on and released the single 'Shall I Do It' from the album. Without a high-profile album behind it, and not much PR, it flopped. I agreed to be the prize in *Fab 208* magazine's 'Dream Come True' competition and to do an in-depth interview with a newspaper that for once fairly accurately reported what I said. I was less happy with the outcome of the *Fab 208* deal. The prize was for me to have lunch with a nice little girl from Manchester called Christine. After lunch, I wanted to take Christine, who was in a wheelchair, and her mum around London as they'd never been before, but they were put back on a train. My new androgynous look seemed to attract more attention than the single. The *Daily Mirror* talked about my bodysuits, ballet tights and leotards at some length before eventually getting round to mentioning the music. Nothing much changed there, then. They even ran the article on the women's fashion page instead of the music page. I also remember doing a radio interview with a rookie reporter called Dale Winton, in the days way before he became permanently tanned and very famous. I ran into Dale again a few months back coming out of the gents in a restaurant. He was just the same but much more confident. He'd probably say I was just the same but much *less* confident!

It was decided that we'd put out another song we'd recorded but that wasn't on the album, 'Replaced By A Microchip', under the pseudonym of Mighty Micro. It was written, not by McKeown/Ryder, but Mean Hymn. BCR aficionado Hannes A. Jonsson wrote on his website:

> In the tradition of . . . 'Video Killed The Radio Star' and
> other similar records of the day, this one should have fared
> a lot better had it not leaked out who the Mighty Micro
> really was and people's preconceived and snobbish attitudes
> towards an ex-Bay City Roller [hadn't] consequently,
> inevitably, kicked in.

If it wasn't for Peko, I'd probably have ended up drinking or
drugging myself to death at that point. We'd really hit it off after
that first meeting, not only because she was drop-dead gorgeous
and sexy but also because she'd never cared for the Bay City Rollers.
We moved in together quickly and it must have been hard for her
to have to weave her way through the hard-core girls to get to our
front door every day, but she used to stop and chat with them all,
in pidgin English, and everyone loved her. We couldnae really
behave like other young lovers, though, because there was no
privacy anywhere. Our solution to the problem was to cross-dress
and go out in each other's clothes.

We moved into a better place when I got some money through
from Japan for delivering the songs for the album. My first priority
was to get my parents somewhere to live, and I found them a
beautiful house high on the cliffs in Cornwall, overlooking St Ives.
I was looking forward to some income from Germany as well,
because a company called Metronome had put out 'Shall I Do It'
and it had gone straight into the Top 10. Strangely coincidental was
the fact that Eric and Tam chose the exact same week to talk to the
Sunday People about how debauched life as a Roller had been. Tam
fessed up to having been 'the worst of the lot' where drugs were
concerned and that he'd been seeing a Harley Street shrink to help
him get off them. Eric talked about how he'd devoured a whole
box of cornflakes while tripping on LSD, and had to be locked in
his room so that he couldnae try and fly out the window. It was all
sensationalist bullshit undertaken, I would guess, with the aim of
making the Rollers seem like a proper rock 'n' roll band. It
depressed me that Faulkner and Paton were still there, controlling
and contriving, and making us all even more of a laughing stock
than the Krofft show had.

I was pleased to have the opportunity to get out of England and
go to Germany to perform the new single on a couple of music

programmes. It got me away from the reporters begging for my own sordid stories. A group of the fans who hung around outside my flat decided to go with me. With a bit of success under my wide, ornately decorated belt at last, I was in better humour and happy to have their company. When we got to the airport, I felt sorry for one of the girls who'd gone along to see us off but didn't have enough money for a ticket, so I bought one for her. Yet again, it looks like I was played like a fiddle because that person still to this day gets herself to gigs and events with other people's money and by pleading poverty. Real poverty is something you get when you take your German record company execs to a very exclusive club and pay for everything without knowing the cost of it. A lot of the royalties from 'Shall I Do It', and more, got blown in one night in Hamburg – my fault, not the record company's!

Another key event from that visit to Germany was running into my old friends the Rollers in the TV studios – it must have been just before Tam was sacked. It was a *Bravo* (*TOTP* equivalent) special, and the Rollers were there to promote *Elevator*, I guess. The show's producers, who included my friend Bubi Heilemann, had also asked me to appear, without the others knowing about it. When the Rollers had done their song, the show's host shouted out 'Surprise! And tonight we also have the missing Bay City Roller . . . LES McKEOWN!' Needless to say, Tam and the remains of his band weren't very happy and I cannae remember who it was who threw the first punch.

They must have all been very insecure and bitter – even more so when *All Washed Up* went to the top of the album charts in Japan and earned me my first solo gold disc. Soon I was back at the enormous Budokan with the Ego Trip band, but minus the turmoil and the need to throw myself into the audience. I was on a massive high again and it felt like all the crap had been worth it to arrive at this. Now the Japanese loved me even more because my girlfriend was one of their own, and they probably thought they'd be in with more of a chance when we split up. 'Shall I Do It' was swiftly followed by the next single from the album, 'Long Distance Love', and the decade ended on a high note, all things considered. My mantra from that era – if you cannae join them, beat them – had worked.

It was obvious where I should concentrate my efforts at the beginning of the '80s. Things were going great in Japan and I was more than happy to spend as much time as possible there, as was Peko. Scobie and I quickly started work on the follow-up album, *The Face Of Love*, the first of three solo albums to be released in Japan that year, which was followed by the *100% Live* album and then *The Greatest*, a combination of the first two. There was another Ego Trip tour, loads of TV, and the Budokan sold out again. I was also honoured to be asked to perform my single 'Tender Love' at the Budokan the following year, 1981, this time for the tenth anniversary of the Tokyo Music Festival. Stevie Wonder topped the bill, and it was a bit of a comedown to do a dinner show the next night at the Prince Hotel and share the bill with The Nolans! Before the year was out, I was awarded the prestigious 'Mr Valentine' award for the third year in a row by the readers of *Rock Show* magazine (in 1982, I dropped to No. 3 and was replaced in the top spot by David Sylvian, helped by his band's name . . . Japan).

The next single was 'Sylvie My Love', which was mine and Scobie's words set to an old Japanese '60s hit, as was the B-side. Next came the double-A-side 'Sayonara'/'Dedicate This Record' from *The Face Of Love*. With everything going so well in Japan, Scobie and I took off for Los Angeles in search of a US record deal and some good dope. We found one of those.

Having stayed at the Magic Hotel to start with, we then found ourselves a place to rent in the Echo Park district of LA, where all the cool, aspiring musos lived. We did a great interview with staunch BCR supporter and top DJ Rodney Bingenheimer at the famous KROQ radio station, and had a lot of fun. It was like a sunny home from home; there was always a bunch of LA fans on the doorstep but, without dissing the London girls, these ones were honed, tanned and rich.

With no US record deal forthcoming, Scobie and I agreed we'd given it our best shot and decided not to waste any more time in America. We called it a day and went home, each going our separate ways. Apart from a short visit later that year to Disneyland to do some filming on the way to Hawaii for a 'holiday' with some competition-winning fans, that was the last time I went to America for a long time.

Nineteen eighty-one started well with the release of my fifth solo album, *Sweet Pain*, and another hit single, 'Tender Love'.

Then the Eastworld people called me in to their offices to tell me that *Sweet Pain* wasn't doing as well as the other albums. They wanted to amend our contract in line with the projected income from the remaining two albums to be made, which might well achieve levels of sales similar to *Sweet Pain*'s predecessors. Since parting with Scobie, I'd hired myself a manager called Olav Viper.

Olav thought Eastworld's proposition was unfair and convinced me I would be well rid of them. He got me a deal with Trio Kenwood for an album of covers. *Heart Control*, released in 1982, featured songs like Martha Reeves' 'Heatwave', the Eagles' 'Heartache Tonight' and Randy Vanwarmer's 'Just When I Needed You Most'. I wasn't sure it was the right thing to do but it was a pleasure to duet with Tessa Niles, who was later snapped up by Robbie Williams. The album didn't do well, Viper got 50 per cent of the profits, which he wouldnae have got if I'd stuck with Eastworld, leaving me, once again, short on funds and wondering how I got into something against my better judgement and that all-important sixth sense of mine. I came to the conclusion that it was because I didn't have a lot of confidence, and I spent most my time pretending I did.

By the time I got a phone call from Eric Faulkner, I was feeling vulnerable and pretty desperate.

Breakout, Breakdown

Peko and I had moved back to Scotland. I was thinking about what I might do next, career-wise.

'So I was thinking we should get the original five back together,' Eric said, or words to that effect, while implying that in terms of musical direction we should grow the true Bay City Rollers style as I saw it. The litigation with Goldberg Ravden was still going on and as we were all short of cash, I agreed. Stupid mistake number three hundred and something.

It wasn't bad to start with. There was no talk of anything negative from the past. We rehearsed the old numbers and set off for a gig in Bangkok in August. Well, there were worse places you could play. The Rollers, who had now regained the Bay City that Eric had dropped earlier, were never going to have problems getting gigs in Asia.

From Bangkok we travelled to Japan for an event on the fourth of September billed as 'Once More! Saturday Night With The Bay City Rollers' at the Budokan. In fact it was twice more, because there were two performances, one at three and one at seven, to meet demand. It was also filmed for television broadcast later. The old Rollers (average age about 28) still pulled them in.

Peko and I decided we'd like to make a baby, so having practised lots of times, we got married in March the following year to do it all right. Her dad, who was a Buddhist monk, performed the very private ceremony at the Iwaya Temple in Toyotomi-cho, Himeji. I had to completely shave my head and Peko was breathtaking in full traditional dress. I felt centred and complete. This year we have been married for 20 years and I'm glad I found someone who would love me for life and not move on as the limelight faded, like certain serial star shaggers I could mention.

Not everything was so rosy on the family front. My brother Brian and his wife in Edinburgh had been expressing concern for some time that with me being away a lot again, it wasn't a good idea for Mum and Dad to stay down in Cornwall, in case one of them took ill. To avoid wasting more paper than I have to with this story, I'll keep it short by saying I agreed in principle, and the house my mum and dad loved was sold, freeing up a load of equity. Brian used the cash not only to buy them a new flat, but to buy a snooker hall with his mate, where the idea was that I'd be a partner in the business and get my money back in no time. I wasn't a partner and I didn't get my money back in no time; I think it took over a year, and the year in question was one in which I really needed it. I cannae begin to explain how it felt to discover after having been so royally let down by the music industry, that it had happened again – but this time it was my own flesh and blood. Worse was that, he'd taken advantage of my mum and dad, who could've been living in a small castle in Scotland for what he'd sold the Cornwall house for.

Earlier that year, 1983, we'd managed to entice Ian Mitchell and Pat McGlynn back into the Rollers, so for the first time there were seven Rollers. Buoyed up by our renewed success in Japan and the free availability of cocaine once again, together with the fact that as yet we hadn't come to blows, we recorded a single – a cover of Bucks Fizz's 'Piece Of The Action', which was released in Japan in July (and no, it wasn't me who suggested that song). We did our fifth Japanese tour and Arista Japan brought out a double live album, *Bay City Rollers . . . And Forever.*

In September, we played our first British show in seven years in Leeds, to an audience who were there predominantly to see the likes of The Cult and Killing Joke. The punks weren't renowned for their love of the Rollers and they spent most of the set gobbing at us and chucking bottles onto the stage. We were going down a storm. I went radge, threw a few bottles back and got arrested.

Nothing new there, then. That bloody McKeown. The Lyceum gig in London was pretty much the same, but at least the punks at the front were girls and they'd loved us when they were kids.

A strange thing happened in November. Eric, putting his PR hat on, did a series of three articles in the *Daily Record*, once again telling the story of the Rollers and talking about our relaunch. I don't know how he did it, but he managed to get the journalist to share the copyright on the article with him. That's got to be rare, but the true significance of that single act wouldnae become clear for another eight years . . .

In April 1984, Peko gave birth to our son, Jube Richard, at the Edinburgh Royal Infirmary. He was born by Caesarean section. Twenty years ago dads didn't have the option to be there for C-section deliveries, and I have to be honest and say in all selfishness that I'm glad about that. I could not have stood by and watched my wife cut open and I'm sure most men feel the same about their wives. It didn't detract from the joyfulness of his birth.

Inspired, Pat and I started writing songs, and we all started work on a new album. There were none of the usual rows about whose songs would go on it, because we were pretty chilled most of the time. Pat and I ended up with a whopping six numbers on *Breakout*. The recording sessions in Edinburgh didn't go well, though. I didn't like the production, so one night, aided and abetted by my good friend Charlie, I went back to the studio and wiped the tapes! Derek quit, and Alan and the others didn't really have a lot to do with the album after that. Pat and I finished it off with session musicians at Matrix in London.

The old tensions were mounting again, sometimes diminished and sometimes exacerbated by the various substances around. We managed to hold everything together a bit longer and toured Ireland at the beginning of '85. Finally, *Breakout* was released in Japan and then Australia, although just like the old days, there were a few differences between the two versions. We toured the album in both territories with a guy called George Spencer on drums, just ahead of the release of a single called 'When You Find Out'. Also on the road were Eric's new bird Kass, Pat's girlfriend Janine, Peko and my 16-month-old son.

One night, Pat, Charlie and I got well out of it again and decided we were pissed off with Eric for organising the rider – the part of the tour contract that specifies what we'll need to drink. There was only beer on the bus and not a drop of Jack Daniels. We got into the bus's storage area and systematically knifed every can of beer in there. It was a right laugh, but I can see now that our behaviour wasn't exactly conducive to a happy band existence. Eric threw in the towel, taking Kass and, allegedly, 16,000 Aussie dollars of tour cash with him, and quit before the end of the tour. He went back to England and started liquidating all the BCR-related companies, partly to free up funds to carry on paying Prager and Fenton, but also freeing up the copyrights to his and Woody's songs.

By the time Eric left, the bus driver and road crew had also quit because of my attitude, it was later stated. I *did* have an attitude, but for good reason. Some of the crew were continually going on about the Aborigines, jesting about how many they could shoot and that sort of shite. Groups of native Australians used to hang around outside gig venues and some members of our crew would take it upon themselves to tell them to fuck off and that they couldnae go in. That did our rep the world of good. I told them that if they carried on like that, I wasn't going to be nice to them any more, or something like that. They did start letting them in then, but they were kept sectioned off on their own at the back. Australian apartheid. I had major rows with these guys about their racism, while the others all just stood there. The Aussies hated that I was siding with 'the Abos', so they quit.

The last true Bay City Rollers tour of Japan took place in 1986, by which time the line-up was me, Woody, Ian, Pat and a drum machine – arguably the best line-up to date! The last gig was in Osaka in April. It was exactly ten years since we'd first toured in Japan.

By the time we got back to England, I had to admit I had a coke problem. I could bore you for ages with stories about coming to terms with addiction but there's probably not much to differentiate my experiences from other people's you've already read or heard about. It's enough to say that, with the support of my wife and the presence of a beautiful boy in my life, the realisation of what I stood to lose if I carried on down that road was enough to turn things around. We bought a house in Faversham, Kent, and took control of the situation.

Eric Faulkner put together a band called The Eric Faulkner Initiative or Co-Operative or something, but gave up when promoters insisted on billing him as a former Bay City Roller. I've also experienced how frustrating that can be. In 1987, he went out as The New Rollers with Kass, and when Woody later joined them, the band was once again renamed the Bay City Rollers. In early 1990, Alan too was enticed back. The band toured pubs, clubs and universities and recorded a single, which I believe was only available through their fan club.

Simultaneously, I'd got a job as production manager for a German TV show called *Formel Eins* (Formula One), which involved going to stars' homes for a chat. The weekly feature was aptly called 'Stars At Home' and one such visit took me to the house of a writer/producer called Dieter Bohlen – the German equivalent of Stock, Aitken and Waterman. He said he could make things happen for me and came up with five songs that seemed promising. In 1988, my 12-inches came out in Germany and Japan (by this time hardly anyone released standard-length singles – you had to have an extended length and a couple of other mixes before you could even think about putting something out). The first song, 'She's A Lady', was pure Euro-pop and went straight into Germany's Top 40. It stayed in the charts for 16 weeks. It came out on the Hansa label, which was a great little company run by really nice people; there was a lovely family feel about it. The formulaic 'Love Is Just A Breath Away' came next, followed by an album called *It's A Game* (no connection) in early 1989. The title track and the fourth Bohlen number, 'Love Hurts And Love Heals', charted in April and July of that year. The last one was called 'Nobody Makes Me Crazy'. I should have been really happy with the success I was having but by now I'd come to realise that in my life, whenever anything is going well, a great deal of shite is sure to be about to fall from a great height . . .

All five singles and the album came out on a newfangled medium – the compact disc. Around the same time the first Bay City Rollers CD, *Starke Zeiten*, was released in Germany by Arista, who then released the first Japanese CD compilation of Rollers hits, *Memorial*, followed by an eight-CD box set of all the albums except *Ricochet* or *Breakout*, which had come out on different labels. They claimed they could not pay us our royalties because they

shang-a-lang

191

didn't know where to send the money. I didn't want them sending anything to Eric and the others and he didn't want anything sent to me, so we only had ourselves to blame at that stage.

On to the Nightmare '90s, then.

They started well enough – I was attracting attention from songwriters, record companies and promoters back at home. Danny McIntosh and John Griggs had written a song called 'Ball And Chain', which Johnny's wife submitted to the Eurovision Song Contest without them knowing about it. When it got into the last twenty, they needed to find a singer for the song and asked me if I'd do it if it reached the last eight. It was a great song and I was happy to oblige, performing the song on *Wogan*. In the end, it came fourth out of the eight, losing out to the far more Eurovision-friendly 'Give A Little Love Back To The World' by poodle-permed Kelly.

I recorded another five or six songs of Danny and John's which I could have probably done something with, but after the *Wogan* show I was inundated with calls from promoters who wanted to put me back on the road, singing Rollers songs. It was a question of economics taking precedence over creative integrity.

Early in 1991, I was asked to appear on *Jim'll Fix It*– wasn't he just great? On this occasion, Jim wanted to fix it for a lady called Sharon to meet me, so off I went to do the deed and present the medallion. As soon as Eric got wind of it, he got on to the BBC to enquire whether or not I would be performing with a band and if so, they would have to make it clear that the band was not the Bay City Rollers. The BBC politely reassured him that the performance in question would be made by Les McKeown and that there would be no attempt by anybody to pass themselves off as a Bay City Roller (they'd have had to have gone to a mental home to find anyone willing to do that, for God's sake!).

I started looking around for a new backing band. Meanwhile, I was also approached by Adam Baker, son of the actor Stanley Baker, with an idea for a theatrical act aimed at club audiences that would play on my history but move me forward at the same time. The Tartan Army, as the act was called, did well. We recorded a brilliant dance version of 'Bye Bye Baby', 'Feels Like Making Love' and a couple of other numbers. We invested in promo videos and got loads of gigs after London club mogul Sean McLusky fell in love with the act. 'The first time I saw Les McKeown he was coming out of a coffin, wearing Ray-Bans and holding a Holsten Pils and a Marlboro, to the applause of a thousand students on Ecstasy,' he says. Financial rewards for product placement can be sent care of my publisher!

Keen to keep all my irons in the fire, I also accepted a couple of retro gigs in Germany after Rainer Hass, a big promoter, asked me to put together a band that would convey the original sound of the Rollers. I also took a booking to do a glam rock gig at the Town and Country Club in Camden for 7 September. It was very short notice and I didn't yet have my new band together, so Danny McIntosh and a bunch of mates kindly agreed to help me out.

Meanwhile, someone had found out from the lady that ran an 'appreciation society' for me that we were booked at the Town and Country. Next, some Eric fans were on the phone to the venue asking if the Bay City Rollers were playing. The poor telephonist probably took the easiest option in confirming that they were, for which she was rewarded with streams of venomous abuse for being part of the set-up which had booked me. It's sad that at least two of those three lackeys still come backstage after gigs today, feign friendship and help themselves to free drinks, probably thinking I have no idea who they are.

A week before the gig, I received a letter from Eric's solicitors. After a while, I managed to take in what it meant. Eric, interestingly now Falconer and not Faulkner, had set up a company called Bay City Rollers Ltd in 1989, appointed himself and Kass as sole directors and then registered the name as a trademark in the UK and US. Applications were pending in Japan and Australia. The letter was telling me that I was infringing their copyright by using the name Bay City Rollers (which I wasn't doing – I was using Les McKeown's Bay City Rollers), that I was not allowed to sing any songs owned by their company (as these were only Faulkner/Wood songs that bit didn't matter) and that I must not 'pass myself off' as a Bay City Roller. Stunned, I was unable to respond at first. My good friend Jack Daniels took a good thrashing. I met with their solicitors and was told that a High Court interlocutory injunction was to be served which actually made it illegal for me to use the Bay City Rollers name.

shang-a-lang

I wasn't in the best frame of mind for my first big UK gig for years. I realised when I rocked up at the stage door without a backstage pass and couldnae get in that I'd been away a fair wee while. Once inside and ready to go on, a reporter asked me about the tartan I was wearing. I explained it was only mock tartan because the way my luck was going, it wouldnae have been surprising if some clan came out and slapped an injunction on me for wearing the real thing.

The gig was great and I got rebooked for another one a few weeks later, as plain old Les McKeown. Meanwhile, Eric quickly signed up Alan and Woody as directors of Bay City Rollers Ltd. I decided to take The Tartan Army to the next gig and we put together a cool rap intro to tell the younger members of the audience a bit about my history. The raved-up 'Bye Bye Baby' and 'Ye Cannie Touch This', a spoof of MC Hammer's number, went into the set along with some revamped Rollers songs not copyrighted by Faulkner. I didn't know what would happen after that, because promoters and agents said they couldnae get me any more work if they weren't allowed to make any reference to the Rollers.

Affidavits were sworn and the contents of those would make for a whole book in its own right; it was unbelievable. My two alone, in response to theirs, covered 185 pages and contained nearly 300 points, all of which were necessary and relevant. For example, they hadn't even got the year I joined the band right, so that had to be corrected for a start. And then they'd neglected to make any mention of the fact that I was back in the band between '82 and '86. I could go on.

The crux of the matter was who *should* have the right to use the name: Eric said only his Bay City Rollers, as represented by the newly expanded corporate entity, should use it. I argued that all of us should be able to. Their affidavits claimed that I was damaging the reputation that went with the name 'Bay City Rollers', a reputation they alone had been striving for several years to build up. To me, that clearly demonstrated that the core of Eric's resentment was that I'd just waltzed into the Rollers at the last minute and hit the big time. It seemed he couldnae deal with the fact that once again, while he'd been trawling the pubs and clubs, I was the one that had then come back and gone straight on at the

Town and Country. He said I was trying to 'trade on the market' they created. He felt I was confusing and disappointing the public by using their name. He thought the people who went to see me, and found no other original Rollers in the band, were four times more disappointed than those who went to see his band, who only found one Roller missing.

I did agree with them when they suggested that I didn't need to use the name, as they grudgingly had to admit that I had achieved substantial success on my own. That much was true, but it was a matter of principle. I wasnae going to be told by Eric Faulkner what I could and couldnae do now, any more than I was back on the night of that first gig when he told me to ditch my bird.

One of the most pathetic things about the whole case was the constant reference to the reputation linked with the name. This was coming from someone who'd allowed Skol to use his picture in a nationwide poster campaign with the strap line 'Buy me one and we'll cancel our comeback', and someone who'd thought so much of the name that he'd chopped and changed it from Rollers to The New Rollers and back again countless times, and even dropped it completely when trying to get some credibility. He argued that it wasn't the historical reputation but the *new* one he was protecting. I'm *sorry*?

At the same time, the plaintiffs stated that the band's success was the result of the efforts of all five members of the group. Phil Coulter begged to differ, and responded that 'certainly Les McKeown's musical contribution to the group's success was far greater than that of Eric Faulkner'. John Hudson, the recording engineer at Mayfair Studios, confirmed that the usual studio procedure would be for Phil Coulter to play me a melody, for me to record the lead vocal, then for the others to come in for a few hours to do the backing vocals. He went on to say that usually those backing vocals were not of sufficient quality and that Phil and I would have to do them ourselves. A number of other heavyweight affidavits confirmed that I was perceived as the 'front man' of the group; a fact that the rest of them, including Tam Paton, just couldnae accept.

The matter finally went before a judge in February 1992, by which time I'd lost thousands in cancelled bookings. The judge squashed the injunction and ruled that I was allowed to continue to use the Bay City Rollers name provided I added something like 'ex', 'former', "70s', 'Real' or 'Legendary' before it to make it clear that it was only the 'historical' association with the name I was to draw on and not the new one. The outcome reflected the stupidity of the whole case. Anyone can see that 'Les McKeown's Legendary Bay City Rollers' implies more original Rollers than the straightforward 'Les McKeown's Bay City Rollers' ever did.

Intent on making his mark till the end, Eric said whatever went before 'Bay City Rollers' had to be 'printed in letters of at least equal size and in the same colour and design as those of the remaining words'. Apparently the litigation cost him all of the money he'd been paid by Skol and more. It was probably all worthwhile, though, because he'd been able to state in the first numbered point of his affidavit: 'I am the lead singer and guitarist of the rock and roll group known as the Bay City Rollers.'

Soon after the two Town and Country gigs, I found myself booked to play in a grotty holiday camp. The people there put up with the cold and discomfort because the acts booked for the event, one of the first theme weekends which have become so popular today, included Alvin Stardust, Mud, the Rubettes, Mungo Jerry and Brian Connolly's Sweet (there's an Andy Scott's Sweet, too). By then, I had the beginnings of a new band on board – Terry Munday on lead guitar; Russell Keefe on keyboards. After the gig we sat in the bar chatting with a few birds so pissed on Diamond Whites one of them didn't realise she was unconsciously rubbing Russell's leg and not her own. Terry invited the other one to go and help him find his guitar backstage but she wasnae *that* pissed. It was good to be back on the road in England.

Eric and his Rollers recorded a double-A-side, 'Flower of Scotland' and 'Bye Bye Baby'. Their promo included a 'Where Are They Now?' feature in *Best* or *Bella,* in which Eric said I was an unemployed van driver. He then called on the services, once again, of his mate Adrian to create a parody of my *Jim'll Fix It* spot for Channel 4's *The Word.* The band appeared on this guy's doorstep, supposedly out of the blue, and sang 'Bye Bye Baby' in his kitchen (having passed through a shrine and talked about how Les McKeown was never mentioned because it was 'taboo'). What great TV!

Early the next year, I received a phone call from a friend, who told me she'd found a new Bay City Rollers CD in the Virgin Megastore. It had been released by Eric's lot and featured seven re-recorded Rollers songs and six new ones. Not that they wanted to trade on past success. But that wasn't the best bit: they'd used a picture of the band with me in it on the cover.

197

Trauma and a Truce

My new band was going from strength to strength. Early in 1992, I'd got Ian Mitchell back on board, and also Terry Chimes, The Clash's drummer. The market for retro gigs all over Europe was growing – we had gigs in Germany with attendances ranging from 5,000 to 15,000. It was a nice little earner.

For the first time in years, I started writing songs again, with Russ and Terry. By 1993 we had enough good stuff to put out an album in Japan, which was called *Love Letter*. It did pretty well so we released a *Greatest Hits* album in the UK, too, both featuring some of the new material. Ray Dorset (Mungo Jerry) produced it and it did OK.

Later that year, I did my first gig in my home town since 1976, at the Cavendish. Straight after that, we left for a two-week tour of Japan and then we were back at the Cavendish for their Hogmanay celebrations.

What we really wanted to do was go to America, and in 1994 I found a new manager who put together a tour which took us to New York, Atlanta, and other mainly Canadian cities at the beginning of 1995. On the way over, I got upgraded to first class where my every need was attended to by a lovely steward who insisted on plying me with Courvoisier. When I tried to stand up to get off the plane, I was literally legless, and had to be taken from the plane to the terminal in a wheelchair. It wasn't exactly

shang-a-lang shang-a-lang

comparable with the first time I'd arrived in New York nearly 20 years before.

Luckily I was fully recovered in time for the first sold-out gig at a club in Manhattan. We played 'Open Your Heart' (written with Terry) and 'Killing The Blues' (a duet with Russ) for the first time and they were well received alongside the Rollers hits. It was more of the same in Atlanta and throughout Canada; everywhere was sold out and I had a great time meeting and chatting with fans of old after the shows. Ian, who'd since returned to America with his new wife, was still in the line-up for that tour but seemed to spend most of it sitting on an amp in an alcohol-induced trance. He ended up missing the last three gigs through being hospitalised on account of an alcohol-inflicted illness. Back in Scotland, the Roller he'd replaced all those years before, Alan Longmuir, was in hospital on a life-support machine following a heart attack.

When we returned to Europe and another string of gigs in Germany, we were joined by Si Mulvey on bass and everyone was happy again – until Terry Munday left because his Japanese fiancée was being terrorised by other fans. In came Ross Ladner, who was the complete opposite of the consistently serious Terry and bounced around on stage, dreadlocks flying, like a wild animal. The line-up, which had also featured an ace drummer called Kev Magill since 1995, was great.

Arista came up with the idea of bringing out a high-profile 20th-anniversary megamix single and another compilation album. There were a lot of arguments about style and content and the only good to come out of it all was that all the original Rollers were refocused. The single never happened and the album was downgraded from a high-profile release to another budget title.

Then, the *Daily Record* reported that there was £2 million sitting somewhere in a US bank account but that continual feuding within the band prevented us getting our hands on it. It was a variation of what Arista had said before about not knowing where to send the money. I responded that I would be willing to work with the other Rollers to get what was ours, hoping that the article would initiate some kind of response from the other camp, but it didn't.

I wasn't all that bothered because I had a tight little band together and it was like the second coming of Rollermania. At

Jackie O's in Kirkcaldy that year, the audience went mental and what little security there was went into a blind panic. They couldnae get the women off the stage and we couldnae get ourselves off. It was the same wherever we played and I was lapping it up.

Having sold out our US tour earlier that year, my manager started planning a return visit to Canada. It was originally scheduled for July, but postponed till autumn. I should have known how it would turn out when people starting posting on the Internet about their disgust with the band for mucking them around. I discovered later that most of those complaints were coming from a small group of Eric's fans, some of whom remained loyal even though they were told those who used BCR in their e-mail addresses or nicknames were doing so illegally. The Internet was just starting to become accessible to the masses at that time, especially in North America, but all it seemed to do was provide a real-time forum for rival groups of fans to fight each other, just like they used to on the letters pages of teen mags in the '70s. This Canada tour had a bad vibe about it before we even set off.

The tour consisted of 16 gigs over 18 days. At the first, in Toronto, some bird grabbed my mike and wouldnae return it, which made me feel like a prat trying to get it back and pissed off the rest of the crowd. Whereas we'd flown everywhere on the previous trip, this time we had to sleep and drive cross-country, crammed into a Winnebago. Peko and Jube had come along with us and they were fed up with the discomfort, so all in all it was a shite experience. The manager said we should be grateful to have the work and was immediately dispensed with. Everyone was glad when it was all over.

The positive aspects of the Internet started to become apparent. When the bitching that surrounded the Canada tour died down, a host of Bay City Rollers websites sprang up, with fans of old clambering not to get on stage but to get online. Letters started arriving that began with 'I couldnae believe it when I logged on and typed in Les McKeown . . . '. A couple of years earlier, the girls I'd met at that first '70s weekender had set up an information service called RollerManiaks, and thanks to the net, membership shot up. Suddenly you could do anything online – find old penpals, find out about local fan 'gatherings' (of which there were many) or buy and sell all manner of merchandise from tacky cardboard lampshades *circa* 1975 to a genuine Roller jacket. But still most of the bulletin boards and chatrooms seemed to exist only to stir up controversy, which tells you something about the state of humanity today – or at least the state of Rollerland in 1996.

At the end of the previous year, I'd received an e-mail from Andrew Scott, a promoter with offices on Santa Monica Boulevard, LA. He was really enthusiastic, having been a fan, and asked what I thought about him putting a tour together for us. I explained that at the onset of any discussions with possible venues, the club owners and marketing people would have to understand the importance of qualifying the name Bay City Rollers with 'Les McKeown's 70s . . .'. Andrew took everything on board and set to work.

As soon as word got out that we planned to return to the US, all hell broke loose. Eric started sabotaging the plans, presumably because, a month or so before, he'd got word to me that he wanted me to stay out of the US clubs and I hadn't, principally because of an ongoing dispute with him. As venues were announced, details found their way back to Eric, who would then ring the club and offer his Rollers at a lower price. Some of the venues, having been warned that this sort of thing might happen, said no thanks – they'd prefer to have the lead singer's Rollers. This resulted in threats of legal action if the Bay City Rollers were advertised, at which point a lot of them threw their hands in the air and pulled out, saying it wasn't worth the hassle. Other venues kept the bookings but didn't promote us for fear of getting sued. That resulted in another load of slagging later, with fans blaming me personally for the fact that we'd been in their town and they'd not known about it till after the event. In other instances, booked gigs were cancelled because the lack of promotion meant they didn't sell enough tickets. In the chatrooms, the consensus was that gigs were cancelled because 'Les can't be bothered' and 'Les doesn't care about the fans'. Andrew and the RollerManiaks office were being bombarded with questions night and day: 'How can he do this?', 'What's going ON?', 'Why is he letting us down?'. It was all too much.

The Internet uproar died down when it got around that Ian and Pat would be on the tour with us. Andrew and I had asked them if they'd like to be part of it in the early stages. I welcomed the idea of a chance to patch things up with Ian after the fiasco of the Canadian tour, and having Pat along would mean we too would have three Rollers in the line-up. But it wasn't to be. Under relentless pressure, more and more venues buckled. Andrew called me up to tell me he'd been doing the costings, and with seven band members on board and far fewer gigs than we'd hoped for, we'd be touring at a loss. I was gutted; there was no way I could drop members of my usual band in favour of Ian and Pat, so I had to break the news to them that they wouldnae be able to come along after all. Pat was disappointed but understood why and wished me luck. I then called Ian to tell him that I'd had to let Pat down and why, but that I could still afford to include him on the second leg of the tour as he was already in the States and there was no air fare to factor in for him.

Meanwhile, two Michigan lassies were in the process of organising a fan gathering in Bay City which was to take place that August. They approached Andrew to see if there was any chance we could be there. I loved the concept, but it was now very unlikely that the tour would extend past the end of July because there just wasn't the number of gigs we'd hoped for. Andrew told the girls that, if it was at all possible, Les and the guys would be thrilled to join them in Bay City. Almost immediately, word was out that I'd be performing at the event. Andrew found out that the hotel where it was to take place didn't have the facilities to accommodate a live band. The news that we wouldnae therefore be going to Rollerfest – but not the reason – travelled as quickly as the inaccurate news that we were.

By the end of May, I was on the verge of insanity and something had to give. Not having any way of contacting Eric directly, and needing to get the frustration and anger out somehow, I wrote him a letter which went out with the RollerManiaks newsletter. It also clarified a few points about recent events that some fans seemed to think they knew all about when in fact they knew nothing. I pointed out that all Eric needed to do was answer my questions so that we could all unite. The ball was left in his court and everybody knew it.

The tour finally kicked off on 3 June, and there was never a dull moment. I spent as much time laughing as I'd spent being miserable over the previous weeks. It must have been the release of all the tension.

Wee Kevin's face when he was asked to prove he was over 18 in Victoria, BC, was a classic. He thought one of the rest of us was winding him up when it happened again a week later in Eugene, Oregon. In Seattle, where we were booked for a three-night stint, we debated whether we should stick around when we arrived at the Ballard Firehouse for the sound check and found a guy on the floor, delirious and apparently in pain, while everyone else just ignored him. We spent the third week in California and then it was on to Atlanta, although we nearly didn't make it because Kev and I missed the flight and ended up driving 14 hours, mainly across desert, to get there. After California being in Georgia and South Carolina was like being in another world. First, we found ourselves caught up in a gay pride march on Atlanta's Peachtree Street, and one night after a gig, we went out to investigate the nightlife and found ourselves in a strip joint on a tumbleweed-strewn dusty highway. As soon as we realised every guy in the place had a gun, we were out of there. In Charleston, South Carolina, we had to stay in a horrible hotel full of drug dealers and I couldnae get to sleep for fear of my windows being shot in. Another night, after our gig in Myrtle Beach, we were all in the car, Andrew driving like a maniac. The others were more than a bit nervous when we got lost in the dead of night, and I called out to a group of Mr. T lookalikes hanging out on a street corner to ask for directions. They didn't understand Scottish and their expressions convinced Kev we were going to be shot, but then they just told us we all shouldn't be driving like that, boy, or we'd get locked up. My Scottish accent let me down again after another gig when we couldnae get back to the hotel because the only route to it, over a long bridge, was closed because of an accident. I got tired of waiting at one end for the cops to tell me when we might be able to cross, so I got out and started walking over, shouting out as I went. Within seconds one of the cops was crouching down with his gun trained on me. I stood there like a rabbit in headlights for a while, with thoughts of friendly fire and overzealous policemen running through my head. I remembered I was in America and therefore much safer than I was at my house in Hackney, chilled, and got back into the car to wait. I was having good times with this band like I'd had all those years before with Threshold, and like I'd never had with the Rollers.

It wasnae long after I got back that I had a phone call from a guy called Mark St John, contacting me on Eric Faulkner's behalf. Mark explained that he was a friend of Eric's and a lawyer who had been successful in getting back royalties for other bands. In September, I met the pony-tailed, black-legginged Mark, and Eric, in London and we had a sensible discussion about our chances of recovering the money owed to us. The essence of the meeting was that we both had to put our differences aside and unite to fight. That agreed, Mark went off and started pulling files and documents and old contracts together and making a case. Again, there's enough material here to write another separate book, but I'll try to summarise.

Things really kicked off when, early in 1997, it was reported in a Scottish newspaper – thanks to Mark, I presume – that the Rollers were reuniting. A wee while later, Nobby Clark suddenly cropped up in the *Sunday Mail*, saying how he never got any money for getting Rollers songs to No. 1 all over the world. Among other things, it was reported that he'd 'rather give money to charity than McKeown'. Later, there was another article reporting that Pat was after his share of £34 million held in bank accounts around the world. Apparently he was saying he'd helped make the band famous in 1975 (he joined and left the following year), and that it was his songwriting and guitar skills that had kick-started the band's success (which occurred in 1974) – nice to see the press as accurate as ever. One thing was clear – we could expect anybody and everybody with a Roller connection to be jumping on the bandwagon from now on. Even within the reacquainted 'core five' there were issues on how any money should be split, mainly relating to the Alan/Ian/Pat era.

That aside, everything was progressing well. The plan was that Arista would release the reunited Bay City Rollers first album and pay us an amount of money in line with the royalties they had been allegedly unable to pay while the band members were at odds with each other. Eric, Woody and I all put forward possible tracks for the album and Mark talked vaguely about a kind of glam 'pink

shang-a-lang
shang-a-lang

satin' concept he and Eric had been playing around with. The reunion concept gathered speed and there was even talk of a UK tour. Mark set about increasing awareness of our sorry story and soon two major documentaries for BBC and VH1 were under way.

Then a big fat cat landed squarely in the middle of the pigeons. In the autumn of 1998, Derek Longmuir was charged, according to the *Scotsman*, with having committed sexual offences against an underage youth. When Derek first appeared in court, he made no plea or declaration and was released on bail. He eventually pleaded guilty to having various photos and videos in his possession (slightly at variance to what the *Scotsman* had reported he was charged with) because they were found in his flat, but the Sheriff 'fully accepted' that the stuff actually belonged to an American 'friend' who'd since returned to the US. The case dragged on for the best part of two years and cast a black cloud over our plans. Derek had no option but to withdraw from recording and tour plans because of the sensationalist reporting surrounding his arrest. His post-Roller career as a nurse at the Edinburgh Royal Infirmary was almost destroyed.

Gigs at the Manchester Apollo, Leeds Town and Country, Bristol's Colston Hall, Glasgow's Barrowlands and two nights at the Forum in London, among others, were scheduled for December 1999. With more time needed to rehearse, they were postponed till the following February. The BBC and VH1 documentaries had aired the previous year and raised our profile big time. At the same time, 'Bye Bye Baby' was being used as the theme music for the comedy series *The Grimleys*, and Catherine Johnson's play *Shang-A-Lang* was doing the rounds in theatres around the country. Caroline Sullivan's book *Bye Bye Baby* was published, Courtney Love bought the film rights and there was talk of Ewan McGregor playing me and Leonardo di Caprio playing Woody. It seemed everything was coming together.

Late in 1999, we all met up in the studios to record some new songs. Woody and I had been told the sessions would begin with a discussion about what those songs would be, but when we got there Mark and Eric said in the absence of anything else we'd only be recording Eric's material. We were told it wasn't feasible to pick and choose a selection of them because they were a 'concept' – a 'body of work' (just like the albums 'serious' bands in the '70s used to bring out). I found the imagery associated with that body of work, which talked about bitches and sugar daddies, completely wrong. This repulsion was strengthened by Mark's assertion that, in terms of marketing, we should be going for the 'pink pound' (gay market) and he'd already written some prose around the subject with references to vomit and nasty stains.

The St John/Faulkner co-operative was asking me to be a party to my own creative disembowelment. They were trying to force themselves upon us when they thought we'd no escape, but Woody and I weren't having any of it, and there was a major blow-up which ended with Woody and me walking out and slamming the door. As Woody wrote to Mark in response to a letter accusing the two of us of wrecking everything, we felt 'used, bullied and treated with absolutely no respect'. Déjà vu.

The fact that a happy conclusion was becoming increasingly unlikely was brought home to me at the millennium gig. The reformed Rollers were returning to their home town to play at the Princes Street celebrations. I couldnae believe it when Eric emerged from the dressing-room draped in a Saltire with his face painted blue. I could believe it even less when he started switching keys just as I was about to start singing just like he had 21 years before in Japan. What a way to start the new millennium.

The gigs that were supposed to happen in February 2000 were cancelled partly on account of Alan's continued ill health and partly because of the bad publicity surrounding Derek.

I was tired, depressed and broke. For nearly four years we'd tried to work together and for two of those I'd not done any gigs because Mark St John had advised me it would be detrimental to do so. I'd accepted that, losing thousands from rejected gig bookings and the comfortable lifestyle I'd finally got for myself. I started doing a spot of DJing here and there to raise some cash and soon got myself a couple of residences, which cheered me up a bit, and there was still a glimmer of hope that something could be salvaged out of the reunion wreckage.

Apparently, Eric had master tapes of a recording made at the Budokan in 1977 and was prepared to donate those tapes to the cause so that a new live album could be released, which would hopefully generate enough funds to step up the fight with Arista. In June, it was announced that a small US label would release *Rollerworld*, a live album made from those tapes, and then the fun really began.

There were rows about nearly every aspect of the packaging of the product. Mark's draft sleeve notes contained some factual and grammatical errors, the worst part being that he was still harping on about 'a massive teen-gay following'. He went on to talk more about the 'built-in trust of authority and "professionals" that the British class system instills [sic] into the young almost at birth' and other inconsequentialities.

I was more than a little concerned about how those sleeve notes would reflect on the band as a whole, but the others were apathetic. I approached a number of respected journalists whose prose would certainly lend the album more kudos than Mark's, but it was when I suggested that Caroline Sullivan might be approached that the shite really hit the fan. Woody, who'd previously been a staunch ally, was horrified that I could make such a cruel and unfeeling suggestion. For those of you for whom that doesn't make any sense, Woody was the unnamed Roller Caroline was close to in her youth.

It was a horrible time. I did a gig at Butlins while in the depths of depression and with a voice which was pretty much on its last legs because of a week-old chest infection. Other gigs I'd booked throughout the spring and summer got cancelled as the nation buckled under mountains of charred and burning sheep and cattle carcasses. It fascinated me that we'd all been willing to take everything Mark St John said as gospel, but as it had been with Tam it was often only me who questioned anything. I deduced that this was all to do with basic personality traits – the others needed someone in authority with either real or perceived strength to guide, or control, them. While I too had the same basic need, it was tempered with a tendency to question total authority.

The biggest question related to our original agreement in which it was stated that Mark would take a 20 per cent commission on anything we earned. There was a rider to that agreement regarding what was called the interpleader monies – a small interim payment to be made while the parties discussed the case and settlement. Eric and I had agreed with Mark that his commission with relation to that money would be ten per cent because of the straightforward nature of the job in question. When the money was eventually received, Mark claimed the rider was not a legal document and took 20 per cent, later defending it by saying that it had taken longer than anticipated to get it and that, ultimately, there was more money there than we'd thought there'd be when the agreement was first made.

I was really uncomfortable about it all and frustrated that the others seemed to be accepting what they were told, just like before, although a lot of that was down to lethargy rather than a lack of desire to protect themselves. It all got pretty nasty and Mark St John resigned as manager of the Bay City Rollers telling me, and the others, that it had all fallen apart because I hadnae provided some documentation I'd said I would. I'd explained I couldnae provide that file because of the costs involved in retrieving it from my lawyer's archives, as soon as I'd found out there were costs involved. When I'd put across my viewpoint, St John started telling the others how difficult I was being. Once more I was the one causing the disruption; I was the pariah. I was out on my own again.

Maybe I should have just buttoned it and let it all go.

Epilogue

Friends at Last?

We've none of us given up on one day getting what's rightfully ours, but it looks like Eric has disappeared off the face of the earth so that makes it hard to progress.

My dad died last autumn after a heart attack. When he went into hospital, I was really touched that Derek took the time to talk to the various doctors and specialists and translate everything they'd told me in medicalese into plain English. He was a true friend at a time when nothing was really making much sense. Then Woody and his wife Denise came along to the funeral to pay their respects to my father. We hadn't spoken since the Budokan CD fiasco and it meant a lot. I've also had a few beers with Alan and they were all genuinely concerned and supportive at a time when I really needed it. It doesn't seem so long now since we'd all flown to London to do 'Shang-A-Lang' on *Top Of The Pops* the day after the Longmuir brothers' beloved mum died.

Apart from a stressy phone call from Eric shortly after Tam Paton was arrested earlier this year, which was only to find out what the press were saying about him, no one's heard a word from him. I'm fairly confident this book will draw him out, though. There's even a remote possibility we can continue to work with Mark St John, providing he takes on board the nature of the collective Roller beast.

I sometimes imagine Eric sitting in his hideout, eagerly awaiting this book so that he can find something else to sue me for. But that's negative, so instead I fantasise that he's reached the conclusion we've wasted too much time and energy on this war, and that it's time to make the most of what we've got and what we've achieved, rather than worrying about what we haven't got or haven't achieved. I hope the fact that his old arch rival has been the one to tell the Rollers story doesn't stir up an unmanageable amount of resentment. I'll take this opportunity to say I'm sorry that I joined the Rollers too late and missed out on the slogging around the country. I'm sorry that lead singers generally get more attention than other band members. But none of these things are my fault. I feel that if Eric can sort out his own issues and prejudices and stop blaming me for things that he feels haven't gone right with his life, everything will be fine. We are inextricably bound by our past and we could be so strong together, but progress – not revenge – has to be the priority. Some good must come out of everything we've all been through. Let it be that the Bay City Rollers showed the music world that artists win through in the end.

There's a lot of good stuff going on right now, which really makes me feel the tide is about to turn. Roller-bashing is dying out. More and more people are now accepting the Rollers are an important part of pop history and aren't scared to say so. Real men are the ones who can now say actually, yeah, they did make good pop songs, despite the fact they hated us when they were 14! Maybe someone in Edinburgh will even take note of their most important writer's view that the Bay City Rollers should be as celebrated in Edinburgh as The Beatles are in Liverpool!

Our fans from the '70s continue to come together on the Internet. The number of hits on www.lesmckeown.com and the attendance figures at 'Rave' – a cool, classy event where we all get together and party – keep going up and up. Thanks to the selfless efforts of mates like Gail and Lori, fanland is finally not such a bad place to be.

I've never been one to hide from fans and I enjoy meeting them at gigs. I still get a kick out of being recognised on the street – by people who are pleased to see me – but on one occasion recently it was *not* being recognised that gave everyone around a good laugh, and it's this kind of thing that makes me glad I was in the BCR.

Peko and I had gone to a club to see Kev in his other band. We got thrown out for getting caught doing the things that people in love do in the toilets. Someone asked the manager if he knew he'd just thrown out Les McKeown, the Bay City Roller. Disbelievingly, he asked the other club-goers milling around if they thought that's who I was, and when it was confirmed, we were thrown straight back in! The point is, it's all just a laugh, and I don't take myself too seriously. How could I, when I've spent more than half my life always turning round whenever someone's shouted out 'WANKER!'.

It's things like that which have led to the defence mechanism I developed years back against being insulted, whether it's personally or professionally, for the sin of having been a Bay City Roller. The defence mechanism is to feign confidence. When I'm approaching a situation where I don't know how I'll be received, I'll act the '70s superstar. In the past, there were occasions, specifically in some newspaper interviews, where it might have seemed I carried the confidence thing too far, saying things like: 'There's a market gap for a sexy hero and I'm the man to fill it!' Then, my tongue was so firmly in my cheek when I came out with stuff like that, but somehow that never came across. In the '70s, no one cared to analyse things like they do now. Today, Robbie can sing a song called 'The World's Most Handsome Man' – some people will say he's an egotistical tosser, but others will argue it shows charming self-deprecation, and that really he's lonely and insecure. PR's far more sophisticated now and Robbie's got it across that, in spite of everything, he really is vulnerable and deserving of our sympathy. It wasn't like that in my day. Look who was doing *my* PR!

Last year, 2002, was the worst of my life. I lost a nephew first, then my dad, and lastly my mum – on Christmas Eve. Hopefully this one will be better and I'll try not to panic about what might happen to wreck it. Tam's arrest in connection with claims of sexual abuse of young boys, following articles about him leaving all his money to animal charities and having won £500,000 in back royalties, got 2003 off to a flying start. The allegations of sexual abuse were dropped and Tam was cleared, but he was also arrested by the Lothian and Borders Police in connection with drugs found in his house. He appeared in court and was bailed. In late March he was arrested again and a Lothian and Borders spokeswoman said: 'As a result of an operation, officers recovered a quantity of drugs in the Gogar area of Edinburgh. We can confirm that three people were stopped in a vehicle leaving the house and a quantity of crack cocaine and cash was recovered. Thereafter, a house in the area was also searched and a quantity of cannabis and further cash was recovered.' The *Edinburgh Evening News* reported that 'crack cocaine worth over £7000, 1.5kg of Cannabis resin and thousands of pounds' had been recovered. Again, Paton was bailed. Tam Paton's involvement in these charges is now a matter for the court to decide.

I still write music, but it comes naturally from jamming with mates and not from shutting myself away in an attic looking for another top tune. There was a TV series recently in which Leo Sayer was portrayed as a sad figure of a former chart star, desperate to achieve another hit single (I say 'portrayed' because I know better than most how the media manipulate things to suit their needs).

There is more to life.

Today, I spend time only with friends who have no ulterior motive in associating with me, who don't judge me and who are willing to make allowances for the fact that I've had a pretty abnormal life, charmed though it might have been. For me, that means a lot, because friendships like that have been few and far between so far, and I think I might know why.

I do feel that in the same way that Michael Jackson lost his childhood, I lost those years when other young lads are going off to the match on a Saturday, going clubbing and drinking, doing Ibiza in the summer and generally bonding with mates they'll have for life – and missing out on that can be detrimental to your future life, too. I missed the bit where you learn to interact and communicate with other people because at that crucial time everyone was bending over backwards to please me and I didn't need to reciprocate.

After my dad died, I took Mum back to Northern Ireland, to the graveyard where her little brother and the nan I never knew are buried. We arranged headstones for them, because my mum had always felt bad that they'd not had one. That made me feel more worthwhile than any gold disc or millions of pounds ever could.

Appendix 1

Band Line-ups

*'I used to be/know/shag a Bay City Roller (or his brother)' –
the most commonly made claim in Edinburgh! Use this
handy guide to verify claims.*

This list includes band members from 1968 until the Rollers finally disbanded in 1986. It does not include the numerous members of Eric Faulkner's Rollers, New Rollers or Bay City Rollers from 1989 onwards. It does include members of Les McKeown's Legendary Bay City Rollers (1991–present) and differentiates these from the 'original' Rollers with bold type. Unfortunately, space restrictions dictate that brothers of Bay City Rollers (see above) cannot be included on this occasion.

LEAD VOCALS
Nobby CLARK   1968–73
Leslie McKEOWN   1973–8
                        1982–6
                        1991–present
Duncan FAURE   1979–81

GUITAR (Bass, Lead and/or Rhythm, and Combinations Thereof)
Alan LONGMUIR   1968–1976
                        1978–1985

Ian MITCHELL	1976
	1983–6
	1992–4
Pat McGLYNN	1976–7
	1983–6

Dave PETTIGREW	1968-1969
Keith NORMAN	1969
Billy LYALL	1969–71
Archie MARR	1971–2
Eric FAULKNER	1972–85

Greg ELLISON	1968–9
Dave PATON	1969–70
Neil HENDERSON	1970–72
John DEVINE	1972–74
Stuart 'Woody' WOOD	1974–86
Mike ELLISON	1968
Eric MANCLARK	1970–1

Terry MUNDAY	**1991–5**
Ross LADNER	**1995–7**
Pete LANGMAN	**1996**
Ian IREDALE	**1997**
Darius KHWAJA	**2002**
Mike KOCH	**2002–present**

Gary MEAD	**1994**
John BERRY	**1995**
Si MULVEY	**1996–present**

DRUMS
Derek LONGMUIR	1968–84
George SPENCER	1985
Terry CHIMES	**1991–3**
Kev MAGILL	**1993–present**

KEYBOARDS
| **Russell KEEFE** | **1991–present** |

Appendix 2

Timeline

1955
12 November   Les McKeown is born in Edinburgh.

1972   Les McKeown becomes lead vocalist with Threshold.

1973
November   Les McKeown leaves Threshold and joins the Bay City Rollers.

1974
January   First appearance on *Top Of The Pops* with 'Remember'.
Stuart 'Woody' Wood joins the Rollers and the line-up that will colour the world tartan is in place.

February   'Remember' enters the UK charts and reaches No. 6.

April   'Shang-A-Lang' enters the UK charts and reaches No. 2.

July   'Summerlove Sensation' enters the UK charts and reaches No. 3.

September   The first album, *Rollin'*, is released and goes straight to No. 1 – the first debut album to do so. It stays in the chart for 62 weeks.

October   'All Of Me Loves All Of You' enters the UK charts and reaches No. 4.

October/November First national UK tour.

1975
January   The official *Bay City Rollers Magazine* is launched.

February   The Rollers receive a Carl Alan Award (Brits forerunner) for

	Most Popular Group of 1974, presented by HRH Princess Anne.
March	'Bye Bye Baby' enters the UK charts and gives the Rollers their first No. 1 single.
April	The TV series *Shang-A-Lang* airs for the first time. The second album, *Once Upon A Star*, is released which also goes to No. 1, staying in the charts for 37 weeks.
April/June	Second national UK tour.
May	Sid Bernstein becomes the Rollers' US manager. Les is involved in a fatal car crash.
July	'Give A Little Love' enters the UK charts and reaches No. 1. The Radio One Fun Day at Mallory Park demonstrates the scale of Rollermania.
September	'Saturday Night' is released in the US. The Bay City Rollers appear on US TV for the first time.
November	'Money Honey' enters the UK charts and reaches No. 3. First Australia tour. A fan is shot outside Les's house.
December	The third album, *Wouldn't You Like It?*, enters the UK charts and reaches No. 3.
1976 January	'Saturday Night' reaches No. 1 in the US Billboard charts.
April	Founder member Alan Longmuir is replaced by Ian Mitchell. 'Love Me Like I Love You' enters the UK charts and reaches No. 4. Eric Faulkner takes an overdose at Tam Paton's house.
April/May	European tour.
June	First US concert in Atlantic City.
August/September	First North American tour.
September	'I Only Want To Be With You' enters the UK charts and reaches No. 4. The fourth album, *Dedication*, enters the UK charts and reaches No. 4. Third UK tour.
November	Ian Mitchell is replaced by Pat McGlynn.
November/ December	Australia and New Zealand tour, followed by first tour of Japan.

1977
May   'It's A Game' enters the UK charts and reaches No. 16.

May/June   US tour.

July   US tour.
                    'You Made Me Believe In Magic' enters the UK charts and
                    reaches No. 34 (it is the last BCR single to chart in the UK).

August   The fifth album, *It's A Game*, enters the UK charts and
                    reaches No. 16. It is the last BCR album to chart in the UK.

September   Second tour of Japan.

1978
January   European tour.

April   Alan Longmuir rejoins the Rollers while recording their
                    sixth album.

June   The sixth album, *Strangers In The Wind*, is released but fails
                    to chart in Britain or the US.
                    The Bay City Rollers move to Hollywood.

September   Third tour of Japan.
                    The Bay City Rollers Meets The Saturday Superstars airs for the
                    first time in the US.

November   Les McKeown leaves the Bay City Rollers.

1979   First solo album, *All Washed Up*, released in the UK and Japan.
                    The single 'Shall I Do It?' reaches the Top Ten in Germany.

1980   Three solo albums in Japan – *The Face Of Love, 100% Live*
                    and *The Greatest*.

1981   Fifth solo album – *Sweet Pain*.

1982   Sixth solo album – *Heart Control*.
                    Eric and Les reform the Bay City Rollers with Alan, Derek
                    and Woody.
                    Fourth tour of Japan.

1983   Pat McGlynn and Ian Mitchell rejoin the Rollers.
                    Les marries Peko.
                    A cover of Bucks Fizz's 'Piece Of The Action' is released.
                    Bay City Rollers Live In Japan released (Japan only).
                    UK tour.

1984   Jube Richard McKeown is born.
                    Derek retires.

1985   The album, *Breakout*, is released in Japan followed by the
                    sixth tour there, continuing in Australia.

Eric quits, followed by Alan.

1986	Seventh and final tour of Japan with remaining members Les, Woody, Ian and Pat.
1988	Solo single 'She's A Lady' charts in Germany, followed by 'Love Is Just A Breath Away'.
1989	Solo album *It's A Game*, and the title track, chart in Germany, followed by the single 'Love Hurts And Love Heals'.
1990	'Ball And Chain' reaches finals in 'A Song For Europe'.
1991	Les appears at London's Town & Country Club with the Tartan Army, and at a '70s weekend in Norfolk with his new band. Eric Faulkner gets a High Court injunction to stop Les using the Bay City Rollers name.
1992	Ian Mitchell joins Les's new band. The High Court rules that Les can continue to use the Bay City Rollers name if he includes an historical reference. The albums *Love Letter* (Japan) and *Greatest Hits* (UK) are released in Japan by Les McKeown's 70s Bay City Rollers. The band tours Germany and Japan.
1993–6	Numerous tours and appearances throughout the UK and Europe, Canada and the US.
1997	Mark St John attempts to build bridges in order to try and obtain royalties.
1999	Two BCR documentaries made for the BBC and VH1. A reunion tour is planned and the Rollers perform together at Edinburgh's Millennium celebrations.
2000	Reunion tour cancelled. Les McKeown's Legendary Bay City Rollers finally resume touring.
2001	The live album Rollerworld is released in the US and Japan. Les begins researching his autobiography.

shang-a-lang
shang-a-lang

Appendix 3

Websites

Official Les McKeown website
www.lesmckeown.com

BEST FAN SITES
Strangers In The Wind
http://members.shaw.ca/therollers/rollers.htm
Gerd Büsken's Bay City Rollers Homepage
http://users.aol.com/buesken/bcr/bcr.htm
Bay City Rollers Discography Page
www.lcv.ne.jp/~ryhokaya/bcr-home
Ziggy's Les McKeown Music Tribute
http://lesmactribute.tripod.com/LRMIntro.html
Lesaholics
http://lesaholic.tripod.com/index.html

BEST INTERACTIVE SITES
Les McKeown Message Board
www.voy.com/15325/
Les McKeown Discussion List
http://groups.yahoo.com/group/lesmckeown
Les McKeown Chat
www.lesmckeown.com/chat.htm

BEST MISCELLANEOUS BAY CITY ROLLERS STUFF
Kathy F's Eric Faulkner site
   www.ericfaulkner.com
Official Alan Longmuir site
   www.inescreations.com/alan.htm
Official Derek Longmuir site
   www.geocities.com/bcrzoe/baycityrollersderek.html
Official Ian Mitchell site
   www.ianmitchell.com
Official Stuart Wood site
   www.stuartwood.net/public-_html
Official Duncan Faure site
   www.duncanfauremusic.com
Bay City Rollers Swap Board
   www.voy.com/76122/

BEST '70S ROCK AND POP PHOTO ARCHIVE
www.rockfoto.de

BEST KARAOKE HARDWARE AND SOFTWARE SITE
www.karaoke.de

BEST LONDON NIGHTLIFE SITE
www.myshoreditch.co.uk/shoreditch&hoxton/bars&music.htm
(Specifically On The Rocks)

BEST '70S NOSTALGIA SITES
www.loadofold.com/boots/index.html
www.idv8.com/feelgroovy/

BEST EDINBURGH WRITER'S SITE
www.irvinewelsh.net

BEST FOOTWEAR SITE
www.acupuncturefootwear.com

Appendix 4

Tartan Memories

During my raging hormonal, pimple-filled, awkward teen years, the Bay City Rollers were there. They made all of their fans feel loved, no matter what they looked like or where they were from. At a time in my life when the last thing I wanted to do was stand out, the Rollers ultimately helped to bring me out of my shell. It was OK to be different; it was OK to be me.

Cassie V., Brisbane, Australia

I can remember camping out in the living-room anytime the Rollers appeared on the Midnight Special. My twin sister Lisa and I would set up our sleeping bags and alarm clock so that we wouldn't miss the show. I also remember seeing them perform on the Mike Douglas Show. It took place at a beach and I cried as they sang 'Dedication'. Since it was the days before VCRs I tried to take pictures of them when they were on TV. Needless to say they didn't come out very well.

Laura B., Plymouth, Massachusetts, USA

At the age of 13 I had a nice boyfriend. The only problem I had with him was that he couldn't live with Les. He always criticised Les and that made me angry with him.

Petra S., Sorgenloch, Germany

As a child from the ages eight to ten years old I was sexually abused by my eldest brother. When my mother moved me from Australia to NZ at the age of ten I thought my life was over. After about a year I started to come out of my shell, I had made some new friends and I was starting to learn to trust people again. One of my friends showed me a picture of the Bay City Rollers and I was hooked.

Things started to go wrong at home. My stepfather started sexually harassing me; it went on for years. I would put my Bay City Roller music on and play it loud for hours on end. After all these years, those memories of my life still haunt me and guess what I do to cope – I put my walkman on with my Bay City Roller music and I go for very long power walks.

I would like to thank the Bay City Rollers for being there for me (even though they didn't know they were). You have saved my life more times than I wish to remember.

Anonymous

My name is Colin and I am ten years old. I watch your videos with my mom, and I really like the one of 'Summerlove Sensation' where you are swinging on the rope. I want to swing on that rope too. But I would probably fall off and break my leg. Or maybe that dog would bite my butt while I was swinging.

Colin F.A., Zillah, WA, USA

It's so neat that we can chat with Les on computer. It's so great that I got a lot of friends with whom I share in the same feeling. I don't want to lose sight of Les again. Though all I can do within my power may be small, I'm going to continue supporting Les.

Yurie Y., Mabara, Japan

I will never forget the day I became a Roller fan. I was 13 at the time and watching *Lift Off* with my cousin, Val, when you came on singing 'Remember'. I was knocked out by Leslie with his sexy brown eyes and cheeky face, my cousin fell for Eric's sparkling blue eyes and spiky hair. We rushed out and bought the single and life was never to be the same again.

Angela A., Lewes, England

During my teen years you brought me my first experiences of music, your songs filled me with happy thoughts, dreams of love and fun. I fell in love for the first time, with a boy I would never meet, a boy who would never know me, yet my love for Leslie Richard McKeown was as real as any love could be.

Shaz F., Sydney, Australia

We never gave them any peace, we hounded them day and night just to get a glimpse of them. We never considered that they had a right to some privacy, to some time alone, out of the limelight. We saw them as our property, we were incredibly selfish – but in our defence, we were just kids. I would therefore like to take this opportunity to apologise on behalf of fans worldwide for constantly invading the privacy of the guys we adored at a time when they, too, were little more than kids themselves.

Anonymous

I met Les after 18 years last year! I think this long time is for loving them again and more than those days. Yes, I've been falling in love with him for the second time. He is a very big part of my life. I love all of him from the bottom of my heart, his excellent-looking, best voice in the world and the really lovely calactor [sic]. Les, I love you so!!

Itsuko E., Ibaraki, Japan

The Bay City Rollers helped me through the biggest turning point in my entire life. When I was 16, my mother was diagnosed with an incurable brain tumour. I remember those hard times and I felt like the BCR were there for me, in a way. Listening to their music and looking at their pictures brought me a little joy when there was nothing but sadness all around me.

Lucy B., New York City, USA

shang-a-lang

shang-a-lang
shang-a-lang